The Science of Equestrian

The Science of Equestrian Sports is a comprehensive study of the theory and practice of the rider in equine sport. While most scholarship to date has focused on the horse in competition, this is the first book to collate current data relating specifically to riders. It provides valuable insight into improving sporting performance and maintaining the safety of both the horse and the rider.

Drawing on the latest scientific research and covering a wide range of equestrian disciplines from horseracing to eventing, the book systematically explores core subjects such as:

- biomechanics and kinematics
- physiology of the rider
- sport psychology in equestrian sport
- coaching equestrian sport
- preventing injury
- the nature of horse–rider relationships.

This holistic and scientific examination of the role of the rider is essential reading for sport science students with an interest in equestrian sports and equitation. Furthermore, it will be an invaluable resource for instructors, coaches, sport psychologists or physiologists working with equestrian athletes.

Inga A. Wolframm PhD is a Senior Lecturer at the University of Applied Sciences Van Hall Larenstein, the Netherlands, an accredited sport psychologist and a Council Member of the International Society for Equitation Science (ISES). Her research interests focus on psychological, physiological and social processes in the rider, including horse–rider interactions.

The Science of Equestrian Sports

Theory, practice and performance of the equestrian rider

Inga A. Wolframm

LONDON AND NEW YORK

First published 2014
by Routledge
2 Park Square, Milton Park, Abingdon, Oxfordshire OX14 4RN

Simultaneously published in the USA and Canada
by Routledge
711 Third Avenue, New York, NY 10017

First issued in paperback 2014

Routledge is an imprint of the Taylor & Francis Group, an informa business

British Library Cataloguing in Publication Data
A catalogue record for this book is available from the British Library

Library of Congress Cataloging in Publication Data
Wolframm, Inga.
The science of equestrian sports / Inga Wolframm.
pages cm
ISBN 978-0-415-63725-1 (hardback) — ISBN 978-0-203-08471-7 (ebk)
1. Horsemen and horsewomen—Psychology. 2. Horse sports—Psychological
aspects. 3. Horsemanship. I. Title.
SF284.4.W65 2014
798.2—dc23
2013005197

ISBN 978-0-415-63725-1 (hbk)
ISBN 978-1-138-86039-1 (pbk)
ISBN 978-0-203-08471-7 (ebk)

Typeset in Times New Roman
by FiSH Books Ltd, Enfield

To Jeroen

Contents

Figure and tables

Figure

Tables

Foreword

Twenty years ago, the literature on horse riding was limited to texts written entirely by highly skilled horsemen and women. There is little doubt that the equestrian skills of such experts was beyond dispute; however, the explanation of why horses do what they do and how they learn to become great riding horses has undergone considerable change since the recent advent of equitation science.

In the same vein, what is going on in the rider's body and mind has also been thoroughly described by expert horse folk. Did they get it wrong or did they get it right? *The Science of Equestrian Sports: Theory, Practice and Performance of the Equestrian Rider* takes a new approach and is a thorough compilation of the latest research in rider physiology and psychology. It is now no longer necessary to simply swallow the various theories of rider biomechanics and mentality or to believe the various lay interpretations of what makes a good coach. This is a landmark text for all riders, if they are truly committed to do the best for their horses rather than simply to pay lip service to the notion of excellence in training and riding.

Not every practitioner who teaches their own version of rider biomechanics or sports psychology will necessarily agree with the contents of this book but every one of them should read it and juxtapose their own knowledge alongside it, on the basis of the plethora of robust research that lies at the heart of this book.

Every horse deserves a rider who has read this book! And what is more, the time will come in the future when the majority of riders, especially competitive riders, will all seek evidence-based knowledge to improve equestrian performance, and that time is just around the corner.

Dr Andrew McLean
Director Australian Equine Behavior Centre and
Equitation Science International
President of the International Society for Equitation Science

Acknowledgements

Writing this book has been an incredible journey; stimulating and motivating every step of the way. What started out as an idea at a scientific conference almost two years ago has now grown into a finished product that I hope readers will enjoy and appreciate. But no man is an island and neither is this woman! None of this would have been possible had it not been for the help and support of my family, friends, colleagues and students. Thank you all!

More specifically, I would like to offer my sincere and heartfelt gratitude to my fantastic editors, Joshua Wells and Simon Whitmore; my erudite colleagues, Eric van Breda, Ruud Meulenbroek, Sandra van Iwaarden and Alexandra de Rotte; my trusted friends, Jo Barron, Sophie Smeenk and Daphne Bottenberg; my enthusiastic students on the Bachelor program Equine Leisure and Sports at Van Hall Larenstein (year 2010/2011), in particular Lisa Rubruk, Silke de Bruijn and Anne Hoogenboom; my supportive mother, Ingrid Wolframm; and, last but definitely not least, my ever-patient husband Jeroen Hendrikse.

Introduction

No hour of life is wasted that is spent in the saddle.

Winston S. Churchill

Churchill's comment is a sentiment with which most riders would probably agree and one that succinctly summarizes much of the passion involved when riding and dealing with horses. In all likelihood, it was Churchill's passion for horses that ensured the return of thousands of war horses to the shores of Britain at the end of World War I. At the time, Churchill was the Secretary of State and had received word that the rescue attempt of what were generally considered the unsung heroes of the war was failing. Several memos later, from a man who was not known for mincing his words, the horses were returned to Britain at a rate of nine thousand per week. The recovery of tens of thousands of horses from a terrible fate on mainland Europe undoubtedly struck a chord with horse- and animal-lovers back in those days just as much as it would today. In fact, in 2011, film director Steven Spielberg took up the theme of war horses and heroes to great effect in his box-office hit *War Horse*. The film tells the story of young Albert, who forms a strong friendship with the Thoroughbred colt 'Joey' only to see him being sold off to the army and shipped to the continent. After years of hardship in battle and against all odds, horse and previous owner are reunited in the end, fuelling the notion that the bond between humans and horses is both awe-inspiring and wondrous.

The horse: a catalyst for change

There can be no doubt that horses have captured the imagination of entire nations for millennia. Indeed, the equine species may well be considered one of the most prominent forces to have driven civilizations forward. Without horses, the human race would be unlikely to have achieved as much as it has, admittedly both in the negative as in the positive sense. As we are continuously being reminded, the world has become a much smaller place and, in part, because of the horse. On horseback, humans were able to travel faster and further, taking with them goods to trade, their languages and cultures but frequently also the need for conquest. As a result, empires were won and lost on the backs of horses.

It is true that one of the greatest military feats of Hannibal, son of Hamilcar Barca, is the crossing of the Alps in 218BC with 37 elephants in tow – but he certainly also had an army of horses at his disposal!

In view of these and other historical facts, it is not surprising that the earliest recorded anecdotal accounts of horse–rider interaction date back to 1350BC, a time when horses were already being trained for a primary use in warfare (McMiken 1990). In all likelihood, the impact of horses on the cultural and economic development of ancient civilizations was more direct and tangible than it is now. However, even in the modernized world of today, horses are thought to contribute considerably to the national economic growth of, primarily, Western countries, seeing that an entire industry has been built around equestrian leisure and sporting activities. At the very top of this industry are the equestrian sports performed competitively at an international level. In fact, a number of countries, most notably Germany, the Netherlands, Great Britain, the USA, Australia, New Zealand, Denmark, France, Sweden and, more recently, Saudi Arabia, consider the disciplines of dressage, showjumping and eventing as important opportunities to add to their medal tally at the Olympic Games. In turn, this means considerable investment from governmental or private funding to further support and encourage progression in the sport. Especially in the field of breeding, the progress that has been made over the past 50 years or so is nothing short of astounding.

The emergence of 'equitation science'…

Nevertheless, most, if not all, horses will only ever be as good as the riders who train them. Yet, in many equestrian circles, excellent horse riding and training skills are often portrayed as something akin to magic and not easily attainable by 'just anyone'. These types of misrepresentations, of course, do very little to ensure that all riders, no matter what level they are at, train their horses in a manner that embraces all aspects relating to equine welfare, health, safety and performance. Put differently, as long as the rationale that lies at the root of different equine training practices and principles remains opaque, very little progress is likely to be made on improving the relationships between equine welfare, rider safety and horse–rider performance.

As riders, trainers and owners of horses, we retain the ethical responsibility to ensure that the way in which we keep, manage and train them does not undermine their physical and mental wellbeing but remains in line with their intrinsic needs. Recent advances in equitation science as the 'objective, evidence-based understanding of the welfare of horses during training and competition' (ISES 2013) have shown that the correct application of learning theory can go a very long way towards achieving the desired responses in horses at any level (e.g. McGreevy and McLean 2010a; McLean and McGreevy 2010). Yet, while we are several steps closer to unravelling how horses should be trained, there is still much work to be done to ensure that riders of all levels are able and willing to implement the relevant aspects of horse training. Only the very best in terms of training and management is likely to produce horses that enjoy a good standard of welfare, are healthy, safe to ride and perform to a reasonable standard. Clearly, the responsibility for such training and management will always lie directly with riders, trainers and owners of horses.

...And 'equestrian science'

There can also be no doubt that, to be able to ride, train and manage horses in an appropriate manner, riders, trainers and owners must acquire sufficient knowledge regarding their own skills and ability when on the back of or around horses. Such knowledge must be based on solid, empirical evidence to foster the kind of true understanding of all aspects of rider functioning that is fundamental to any horse–rider relationship. Only riders who are optimally prepared, both physically and mentally, will be able to perform to the best of their ability. Even more importantly, perhaps, they stand a much better chance of containing the elements of danger inherent in equestrian sports. While equine-related activities can never be completely safe, appropriate knowledge and application of all the different aspects relating to rider performance are likely to go a long way towards preventing accidents and injury.

But even aside from the sporting context, horses and humans have been found to interact meaningfully in a number of different settings. Some considerable empirical evidence tends to support the positive effect of equine therapeutic or semi-therapeutic interactions with humans suffering from a wide variety of mental and/or physical impairments. However, at present, there still remains considerable reliance on anecdotal accounts of how horses affect humans in a broader sense. To develop a true understanding of the different demands, dangers and opportunities that riders face while interacting with horses, the scientific, evidence-based method of investigation is not only necessary but essential.

This book therefore aims to draw together current research findings relating to different aspects of the equestrian rider, trainer and owner, ranging from motor control, sport physiology and psychology to injury occurrence and prevention, coaching and horse–human relationships. To provide a broad understanding of the 'human partner' in the horse–rider dyad, it also takes into account existing knowledge of related scientific disciplines, such as sport science, psychology and sociology. In addition to providing students of equine science and equitation with a work of reference that is evidence based, the link with current practice in the equine sector will be established and maintained throughout.

Finally, these are exciting times for those interested in the field of equitation and equestrian science. New methods and methodologies for measuring, quantifying and defining what riders do and do not do when interacting with horses provide ample opportunity for objective, unbiased, scientific investigation. Readers of this book – students of equitation science in the broadest sense of the word – are therefore encouraged to look upon the world of equestrian sports with an open mind and a questioning attitude, allowing us to take another step towards a better future with our horses.

1　Motor control of the rider

On moving and being moved

Introduction: the value of seeing and believing

In 1882, the British photographer Eadweard Muybridge caused a sensation with his series of still photographs showing the 'horse in motion'. To prove that, when galloping, a horse would indeed become airborne, he employed the then highly innovative method of installing a series of fifty cameras along the course of a racetrack. The shutter mechanism of each of the cameras was connected via a trip wire laid across the track. The moment the horse thundered past, each camera took a picture, resulting in a sequence of photographs that depicted in detail the movement sequence of a full gallop stride (Figure 1.1). Muybridge's series of photographs is often quoted today as the foundation of cinematography and it proved a revelation in terms of understanding and appreciating animal locomotion.[1]

Figure 1.1　The horse in motion by Eadweard Muybridge; the horse is 'Sallie Gardner' owned by Leland Stanford, running at a 1:40 gait over the Palo Alto track on 19 June 1878

Over the twentieth century, interest in biomechanics, locomotion and kinematics, and their link to performance in equestrian sports, continued to deepen. In fact, once the perception of the horse as an animal primarily used for agriculture, transport and warfare started to change towards it being a partner with which to pursue sports and leisure activities, the specifics of equine movement became increasingly more important – especially to the more competitive rider. Spectacular movement often seems to be valued above and beyond any other factors relevant to performance. However, notwithstanding some of the more ethical and welfare-related issues (on which we will touch throughout this book), the emphasis on equine movement is, at least in part, perfectly understandable. There can be little doubt that the biomechanical ability of horses is, together with their temperament and character, paramount in performance. The way that horses move in the disciplines of dressage, driving, reining and the first phase of eventing or how they clear a fence in the jumping-related disciplines will at least in part determine whether they will rise through the ranks of the competitive levels or primarily remain a 'leisure' horse. It is therefore not surprising that considerable research effort has been spent on investigating equine biomechanics, kinematics and locomotion.[2]

But what about the rider? To many in the equine industry, the way in which the rider moves often comes as a mere afterthought. It is the horse's natural ability that is considered the vital prerequisite for eventual top performances. Nevertheless, as important as equine natural ability may be, it is the correct shaping and training of horses, their gaits, reactions to rider commands and, ultimately, their self-carriage which will determine their future as either leisure or performance horses. But correct and effective equine training is only possible if riders and trainers move their own bodies in such a way as to elicit and maintain precisely the kind of responses they desire from their horses.

Arguably then, the way that humans move when interacting with horses is, in fact, one of the most important and fundamental elements to both horse and rider performance and safety. Yet even though the skill and ability of many of the world's top equestrian performers is undisputed, one of the most difficult elements is the exact and consistent analysis of the relevant principles of biomechanics that enable these riders to move their own bodies with such far-reaching effects. Luckily, the recent increase in the use of technology to measure and monitor different aspects relating to horse and rider allows for a more detailed and critical examination of how the functional system of the rider can be at its most effective on the back of a horse.

Empirical findings in the field of rider and horse–rider motor control are likely to go some way towards identifying functional parameters of rider movement and may subsequently help humans interacting with horses to develop more effective, safe ways of moving while on and around horses. This chapter aims to examine in more detail the broader principles relating to what constitutes human motor control, biomechanics, kinematics and kinetics and how they might be applied to the general context of equestrian sports. Furthermore, existing empirical knowledge on how riders do and ideally should move will be discussed in the light of more practical contexts and examples. Lastly, our current knowledge of rider influence on equine movement will be examined more closely, with a view to highlighting the variables most prevalent in promoting optimal safety and performance components.

Biomechanics, kinematics, kinetics, human motor control: principles of movement analysis

What does studying the various principles of human – and rider – movement actually entail? As is the case in virtually all scientific disciplines, understanding starts with terminology. Movement of all objects, whether animate or inanimate, is subject to the same mechanical laws. However, when applied to humans or animals, these laws need to be applied more carefully, as a living body is composed of a number of articulate segments, all working together in complex unison. *Bio*mechanics is therefore concerned with the principles of mechanics that govern the movement and structure of living organisms. Two complementary methods assist in the study of organisms in motion: kinematics and kinetics. Kinematics is concerned with changes in position of a particular body segment through time and consequently expresses relevant movement parameters, such as time, displacement, velocity and acceleration through linear and angular variables (Barrey 2008). Kinetics, on the other hand, helps to determine the cause of motion through forces applied to a body, the energy that is released or the mass that is distributed and work that is expended. Traditionally, research efforts in the field of equitation science have focused primarily on using kinematic means of investigation to explain and describe movement (e.g. Byström *et al.* 2009; Lovett *et al.* 2004; Peham *et al.* 2004; Schils *et al.* 1993), in all likelihood because parameters such as displacement or velocity are easier to measure than, for example, energy released or forces applied (Barrey 2008). However, an increase in the use of more sophisticated measuring equipment in recent years has also allowed for the study of kinetic variables as indicators of horse–rider interaction (e.g. Belock *et al.* 2012; de Cocq *et al.* 2009a; Peham *et al.* 2010).

Lastly, the umbrella term 'human motor control' focuses on how people are able to control (i.e. initiate, stabilize or alter) any kind of movement, ranging from speech or handwriting, through to high-performance athletic pursuits. To improve the performance and safety of horse–rider dyads, the field of human motor control holds considerable promise. Even though empirical evidence remains relatively sparse, efforts to date have included determining the impact of rider movement on equine gaits (e.g. Peham *et al.* 1998, 2001, 2004; Schöllhorn *et al.* 2006), on jumping parameters (e.g. Lewczuk *et al.* 2006) or establishing differences in movement patterns between advanced and novice riders (e.g. Lagarde *et al.* 2005).

The structured analysis of motor control

But, to tackle existing questions relating to rider movement and motor control in a structured and consistent manner, it is important to understand what, precisely, is being studied. The British neuroscientist and psychologist, David Marr, came up with what is commonly known as Marr's tri-level hypothesis (Marr 1982). He initially developed his theory to understand human vision as a complex information processing system at three distinct levels of analysis. However, movement or motor control may be considered an essentially similar information processing system as vision and Marr's theory is therefore thought to apply in equal terms (Rosenbaum 2010).

Marr identified the first level of analysis as the *computational* level, which includes an often mathematical description of the different functions that a system has to achieve. Applied to the context of horse riding, the computational level of, say, a rider jumping an obstacle, might be expressed through a number of diagrams depicting the exact angles between a rider's torso and upper leg or between lower and upper arm, while adopting the two-point position over the fence. In essence then, this computational level is primarily concerned with the theoretical foundations of an action or movement. The second level of Marr's (1982) analysis is called the *algorithmic* or *procedural* level and describes how a specific movement is executed in real time. From an equestrian point of view, this would include how far riders fold their upper body and rotate their shoulders forward to follow the shape of the bascule of their horses over the fence. Lastly, the *implementation* level determines which biological systems are activated to facilitate the execution of the movement. To equestrians, this would include, for example, the activation of the larger muscles rectus abdominis (the stomach muscles) and the latissimus dorsi (the back muscles), as well as the deeper oblique muscles, to stabilize the upper body; the shoulder muscles, such as the pectoralis major, and the deltoid muscle to allow for the movement of the shoulder joints to accommodate the forward movement of the upper arms; and the thigh muscles (e.g. quadriceps and hamstrings) to enable extension and flexion of the knee during take off and landing.

Essentially then, Marr's three levels of analysis allow for an analysis and understanding of movement from a theoretical, behavioral and applied level. Any future research activities investigating rider biomechanics and motor control should clearly aim to differentiate between these three levels to allow for the appropriate interpretation of results and integration into practical settings.

Learning how to move: principles of motor learning

To what extent does knowing how to study human movement patterns help in achieving actual performance? Is it merely a matter of observing what more experienced riders do and replicating the kind of movements they make? Anyone who has ever attempted to master a new skill, whether in or out of the saddle, knows that the acquisition of new motor skills can be rather complex. In fact, learning new motor skills often requires a combination of processes, ranging from what is referred to as perceptual-motor integration through to various forms of motor learning. Yet before we discuss salient theories of motor learning, a couple of additional definitions relating to motor skills seem in order. Firstly, motor skills may be defined according to the level of precision of movements and are thought to be situated on a continuum ranging from 'gross' to 'fine' motor skills (Stallings 1973). Gross motor skills involve large muscle movements which are generally not very precise. Fundamental movement sequences, such as walking, running or jumping, are considered examples of gross motor skills. Fine motor skills, on the other hand, are intricate, precise movements involving smaller muscle groups and often include high levels of coordinative effort. Clearly, especially at the more advanced level, horse riding relies heavily on fine motor control. While some gross motor skills are involved in stabilizing the rider, the fundamental elements of communication with the horse occur primarily through the execution of fine motor skills. Secondly, motor skills may also be categorized according to their interaction with the environment, also referred to as the 'open–closed' skill continuum (Knapp 1967). Closed skills generally take place in stable, predictable environments and motor performance sequences remain largely unchanged and are likely to have a clear beginning and end. Open skills, on the other hand, are very much dependent on and executed to cope with ever-changing environmental demands (Schmidt 1975). By their very nature, horse sports are primarily open skilled, as the horse, regardless of its level of training, remains essentially unpredictable. In many ways, this makes mastering equestrian sports particularly challenging, as the conditions that determine the execution of the skills are ever-changing.

The action–perception link: perceiving is doing!

The current literature on perception in human motor control and motor learning is vast and so this book does not permit a detailed examination but rather only allows for an overview of some of the most important topics.[3] To begin with, one of the most prevalent issues is that, to perform certain movements gracefully and effortlessly, humans (and indeed animals) are dependent on sensory feedback;[4] for example, from the object(s) with which they are engaging or from the environment that surrounds them (e.g. Paillard 1982). In fact, motor control can be viewed as the link between sensory input and movement output (Wolpert *et al.* 2001). Most riders are likely to recognize the impact of sensory feedback on their own motor performance; for instance, they will be able to judge the gait they are riding in (e.g. walk as opposed to canter) on the basis of how they feel their horses move underneath them and will decide on what to do next depending on whether they wish to stay in that particular gait or execute an upwards or downwards transition. When training horses, riders are at all times dependent on the sensory feedback they receive from their horses, as the content of such feedback will determine the next aids, i.e. specific movements of their seat, legs and hands.

Closed and open feedback loops

Closed-loop theory, as proposed by Adams (1971), postulates that motor learning occurs through the continuous refinement of what he calls perceptual-motor feedback loops. Initially, when someone is still learning a task, movements are clumsy and stilted. With each repetition, the sensory feedback that is received develops a number of perceptual reference points, which guide successful performances of movement patterns. Adams (1971) refers to these reference points as 'perceptual traces' and argues that motor learning includes the development of such perceptual traces, which gradually lead to more successful performance outcomes. However, this also means that, during initial motor learning, people are dependent on receiving sensory feedback to confirm initial movements, before performing the next set of movements. In terms of motor performance, this can be a rather tedious process as the fastest reaction time to external stimuli is measured at a relatively slow 200 milliseconds (Schmidt 1988). This explains why learning how to perform, for example, the relatively complex set of aids for canter, can be so disconcerting for many riders. Initially, they will attempt to move their limbs independently of one another, 'waiting' as it were for perceptual affirmation that they have placed first their outside leg then their inside leg in the correct position, then soften their inner rein to allow the horse to initiate the first canter stride forward. Frequently, however, the horse will have already responded to the increase in leg pressure and will have started to trot faster. Beginner riders are literally thrown off balance, resulting in their bouncing up and down in the saddle and being unable to complete the canter aid. Finally, the horse might start to canter just to restore its own balance.

We know, of course, that, with practice, most riders will eventually master the transition to canter without even having to think about or wait for confirmatory perceptual feedback. From a motor learning perspective, this can be explained by the concept of 'motor programmes'; that is, 'pre-packaged sequences of actions' (Anderson 2000: 326). Motor programmes consist of open-loop segments of behavior that do not require sensory feedback after every isolated movement but instead rely on a fixed sequence of motor behaviors (Schmidt 1988). Incidentally, research has shown that once instructions to execute a certain open-loop sequence of motor behaviors have been sent to the muscles, they cannot be stopped. Studies by Salthouse (1985, 1986) have shown that, even after having been instructed to stop, skilled typists keep typing the last few characters of a word. The existence of such open-loop motor programmes help in explaining why experts in any given task are able to execute certain sequences of motor behavior much faster than the relatively slow reaction time of 200 milliseconds, in response to a certain stimulus. In a riding-related context, this means that, as riders progress from novice to experienced, systems of motor learning will also move from closed-loop to open-loop. Rather than the painstakingly slow and uncomfortable sequence of aids for canter, riders are now able to initiate the 'aid for canter open-loop motor program'. However, while experienced riders might have appropriated a number of motor packages relating to how to execute certain aids, equestrian sports are defined as open skill. This means that riders continuously have to adapt their motor behavior to the reaction of their horses and the environment the horse–rider dyad performs in.

As such, perceptual feedback remains an essential prerequisite to successful rider motor control and performance. There can be little doubt that more experienced riders are more adept at recognizing relevant perceptual feedback from their horse, which allows them to initiate the application of more effective sequences of motor behavior, i.e. aids. The more experienced that riders become, the more easily they are able to recognize and identify the relevant sensory signals they receive from their horses and adopt the most appropriate motor response. The recent advancement of technological equipment to study principles of rider biomechanics, such as recording equipment (Lovett *et al.* 2004; Schils *et al.* 1993), pressure pads to measure saddle (e.g. Belock *et al.* 2012; de Cocq *et al.* 2006; Frühwirth *et al.* 2004), and leg pressure (de Cocq *et al.* 2010), or rein tension gauges (Heleski *et al.* 2009; Warren-Smith *et al.* 2007) can thus go some way towards improving our understanding and subsequent performance of rider motor behavior because of the objective provision of sensory feedback. Relevant current research findings will be discussed later on in this chapter.

The stages of motor learning: step by step towards automaticity

While the distinction between closed- and open-loop motor behavior helps to understand some of the intricacies of the association between perception and movement (and also why novice riders might find it hard to get their horses to canter), the question of the developmental process of relevant motor programmes requires further explanation. Researchers now agree that motor learning occurs in separate stages (e.g. Fitts 1964; Keele 1968; Halsband 2006) with new motor programmes being created through the step-by-step fusion of smaller, newly learned units of motor behavior. The initial or cognitive stage of motor learning is characterized by what is essentially a process of trial and error and describes how perceived sensory cues are linked with correct motor commands (Halsband and Lange 2006). Individuals learning a new skill will have to attend to the various perceptual sensations, followed by the decision on and selection of relevant motor behavior patterns – providing some indication as to why stages of early practice are often painstakingly slow. During the inter-mediate, associative stage of motor learning, the linkages between perceptual feedback and correct motor behaviors are stored as sensorimotor maps in working memory and can be accessed to achieve the desired motor output (Deiber *et al.* 1997). Seeing that the relevant maps need to be accessed from working memory and demand considerable attentional resources, motor performance remains relatively slow and stilted (Atkeson 1989). After a period of practice, sensorimotor maps become more established and are stored in long-term memory. Perceptual cues trigger the correct sequence of specific motor perform-ances, which are performed at higher speeds and no longer rely on continuous sensory feedback. In the advanced, autonomous stage, performance has become automatic, even if individuals do not pay any attention to what they are doing (Halsband and Lange 2006). Performing in such a state of automaticity can feel effortless and really rather pleasant. Riders might even go as far as saying that their horses are reading their minds – when, in fact, they are only responding to automated sequences of motor programmes.

Incidentally, the various stages of motor learning involve different cerebral areas as well. Unfortunately, space restrictions limit us to outlining only some of the most poignant findings. Research has shown, for example, that the prefrontal cortex seems to be particularly active during early stages of learning (Shadmehr and Holocomb 1997). Considering that the prefrontal cortex also plays a major role in decision making and selection of movements (Deiber *et al.* 1997; Jueptner *et al.* 1997), these findings come as no real surprise. There also seem to be indications that the right premotor cortex, also responsible for spatial processing, shows high activity during early motor learning, while the left frontal cortex seems to be more heavily involved in the storage of acquired skill and the association between sensory cues and motor commands (Halsband and Lange 2006). While interesting in themselves, these findings also demonstrate that motor learning is a complex process that cannot be rushed or hurried along. Time and sufficient practice is necessary to develop the appropriate associations between perceptual cues and motor performance.

Beyond such general claims, however, little is known about how riding-specific motor skills actually develop over time. In one of the only studies on the topic of equestrian kinematics and motor learning, Kang *et al.* (2010) showed that, after a 24-week training period, riders with no prior riding experience were able to adopt and maintain postures in walk that resembled those of advanced riders, yet showed no improvement in their positions in trot. These findings suggest that even learning the motor skills necessary to stay on the horse in the correct manner requires time and practice. Future equestrian-related research clearly needs to investigate motor learning in riders in more detail, preferably in view of Marr's (1982) tri-level hypothesis, contemplating it from the computational, procedural and implementation levels.

Visual perception: the importance of seeing clearly

There can be little doubt by now that perceptual cues are of the utmost importance during motor performance and motor learning. But even though the visual system does perhaps not come to mind immediately when thinking about human motor control, it nevertheless contributes considerably to success or failure in most sports settings. Visual restrictions of the peripheral visual field have been shown to hinder movement control (Graybiel *et al.* 1955) as peripheral vision is thought to be particularly important for velocity coding and direction selectivity (Paillard 1982). In one of the only studies to date investigating the importance of visual information in equestrian sports, Laurent *et al.* (1989) initially hypothesized that occlusion of the peripheral field in showjumping riders would lead to an impairment of the riders' ability to accurately judge the speed and stride length of their horses, impairing their performance to jump a fence accurately. Two of the elementary tasks of showjumping riders are, firstly, to judge the correct take-off point to a fence and, secondly, to regulate the horse's gait so as to present it at precisely that take-off point. Restrictions of the peripheral visual field might result in poor performance, owing to the impairment of the rider's ability to gauge the horse's stride length because of the lack of visual information relating to the judging of velocity. Perhaps not an altogether surprising to riders, study results showed no impairment in riders' ability to judge the correct take-off point. The authors subsequently argue that rider's regulation of gait depends primarily on proprioceptive cues. Furthermore, seeing that the subjects in the study were all experienced, national-level showjumping riders performing on experienced horses, much of the motor behavior necessary to present the horses correctly at the fence is highly likely to have become automated on the riders' part, while the experienced horses were likely to have adjusted their own strides as well. Nevertheless, this early study makes an important start on the question of how visual information and optical cues might influence ridden motor performance.

Gaze behavior in horse sports: watching where you are going

Another rapidly growing field of research in sports is investigating gaze behavior;[5] that is, the manner in which athletes look at and focus on sport-specific targets and/or environments. In fact, gaze behavior has been shown to be a function of expertise: more skilled performers tend to look at the elements important to successful performance sooner and with more accuracy than their novice counterparts (Land and Tatler 2009). A study by Hall *et al.* (2009) used a photograph of a showjumping fence and a subsequent selection of four smaller photographs all depicting different sections of several showjumping fences. All of the fences in the four photographs were of the same colour and design scheme as the original fence, yet only one of them actually originated from the original fence. Participants with varying degrees of experience in equestrian sports were asked to identify the smaller photograph that matched the original. Results showed that participants' real-life showjumping experience correlated positively with the recall of salient information of showjumping fences: more experienced riders were able to identify the correct smaller photograph more successfully than participants without showjumping experience. The study by Hall *et al.* (2009) seemed to support earlier findings by Moran *et al.* (2002), who asserted that expert riders assimilated more visual information relating to fences than their novice counterparts. A second experiment by Laurent *et al.* (1989) tried to determine showjumpers' gaze behavior in relation to three different fences, namely an upright, an oxer and a triple bar. Results showed that the visual scanning patterns did not change for any of the three fences. During the approach phase, riders directed their gaze steadily towards the upper part of the fence, regardless of the motion of the horse. The authors argued that riders were able to keep their heads stable, because they were able to absorb the horses' movement through their hips, knees and ankles – a notion that has been supported by other researchers conducting studies on rider kinematics (Kang *et al.* 2010; Lagarde *et al.* 2005). The experiment only used two experienced riders. This, on the one hand, prevented any comparisons between riders of different skill but, on the other, makes any generalization of results virtually impossible. Nevertheless, Laurent *et al.*'s study presents a valid starting point for further investigations into gaze behavior in equestrian sports.

Thought-provoking research by Witt and Proffitt (2008) describes the phenomenon of the visual perception–motor performance paradigm. 'Action-specific influences on perception' seem to indicate that the appearance of task-relevant objects alters depending on the success of performance. Witt and Dorsch (2009) have shown that, on successful days, football players perceive goal posts to be farther apart than they actually are. Similarly, when performing well, softball players considered their ball (Witt and Proffitt 2008) and golf players the holes on the course (Witt *et al.* 2008) to be bigger. According to Witt *et al.* (2008) the way in which an individual perceives the environment is not solely determined by optical information but also by the individual's perception of their own ability to perform in it. Cañal-Bruland and van der Kamp (2009) argue that these types of changes in perception might be functional and serve to facilitate performance related to that specific target. In view of these findings in other sports, it might be theorized that these types of action-specific influences on perception might also be of relevance to equestrian riders. Showjumping or eventing riders, for example, might perceive fences as being lower, following successful completion of a course as opposed to unsuccessful performance, while polo or polocross players might consider the ball to be bigger following a successful match. Future studies might wish to investigate these or similar hypotheses in more detail.

A kinematic analysis of the rider: 'posturing' and 'jostling for position' on the moving horse

The Spanish Riding School of Vienna[6] is not only world-renowned for its impressive displays of classical equitation on their predominantly white Lipizzaner stallions but also for its exceedingly high standards of equestrian skills and commitment. It takes 8–12 years to achieve the status of fully qualified 'Rider', with only a select few ever reaching the coveted position of 'Chief Rider'. What makes the Spanish Riding School so very exceptional is not merely their unwavering commitment to the traditional principles of equitation but also their conscientious and painstaking training of the rider: newly recruited cadets or *élèves* ('students' in French) spend their first years exclusively on the lunge (and mostly without stirrups, too). They are being educated on the principles of a strong, independent and correct seat, considered fundamental to any further equestrian training. Indeed, most individuals actively involved in horse sports will, in all likelihood, agree with such sentiments. However, and perhaps to the detriment of future riding performance, only very few riders will go to the same lengths of spending a year or more on the lunge, working on a correct position and seat!

But what, exactly, are the characteristics of the correct rider position? The millennia-old history of equestrian sport has brought forth at least an anecdotal consensus of how riders should sit on their horses. A correct, effective seat is 'upright, balanced, elastic, solid and interactive – it follows the horse's movement' (Zetterqvist Blokhuis *et al.* 2008). The shoulder, hip and heel should be in alignment, with the forearm and the reins forming a straight, uninterrupted line to the horse's mouth (Meyners 2004). While these characteristics sound relatively straightforward, their real-life application can be difficult at best. Issues such as rider 'handedness' (Kuhnke *et al.* 2010), asymmetry (Symes and Ellis 2010) and rider morphology potentially affect riders' ability to achieve and maintain an ideal position at all times. Yet riders whose centre of balance align with that of their horses are not only more likely to elicit optimal performance from their four-legged partner (Steinbrecht 1884), they are also more likely to substantially reduce the risk of injury: a more stable, balanced seat will at least on some occasions help to prevent the most common cause of rider injury: falling from the horse (e.g. Ekberg *et al.* 2011; Loder 2008). A balanced, effective seat is also likely to assist in the prevention of equine musculoskeletal injury (Zimmerman *et al.* 2011) and consequently will also help to safeguard the health and welfare of the horse.

Considering the importance generally attributed to correct rider positioning, it is surprising that relatively little attention has been paid to the empirical documentation of rider position so far. As Terada *et al.* (2006) aptly state 'In the absence of comprehensive data describing equestrian technique, teaching of equestrian skills is based more on tradition than on science.' (p. 179).

But before discussing the research studies that do exist and focusing on elements of rider biomechanics, a short description of the most common equine gaits (walk, trot and canter) seems in order. Interested readers are encouraged to study appropriate texts to further deepen their understanding of equine kinematics (e.g. Clayton 2004). The walk is a symmetrical gait and consists of a four-beat sequence with no suspension phase. Each hind limb is followed by the forelimb on the same side and each forelimb is followed by the diagonally opposite hind limb. The symmetrical trot is a two-beat gait, whereby diagonal pairs of front and hind limbs move together and contralateral pairs are 180 degrees out of phase (Dalin and Jeffcott 1994). Each stride cycle consists of two stride-stance phases and two suspension phases. During the rising (or posting) trot, the rider lifts his trunk out of the saddle for the duration of one phase and sits down again in the saddle for the following phase. In sitting trot, the rider remains seated in the saddle throughout the entire stride cycle. At the canter, the limb movements of one side do not exactly repeat those on the other side, making it an asymmetrical gait. The horse may initiate the canter by either the right or left hind limb, followed by the joint footfall of the other hind limb and opposite forelimb and, finally, the remaining forelimb. The stride cycle ends with the suspension phase, throughout which the horse is airborne. Even though empirical evidence is sparse, initial studies have shown that the different biomechanical properties of equine gaits also impact on rider kinematics, the details of which will be expanded on in the following section.

Kinematic variables as a function of rider expertise and equine gait

In a fairly comprehensive study in the field of rider biomechanics, Schils *et al.* (1993), using high-speed video recordings, aimed to compare kinematic variables between novice, intermediate and advanced riders at the walk, sitting trot in mid-stance and mid-swing phase and in the rising trot in rise and sit phase. The authors determined relative angles between the upper arm and the torso ('shoulder'), the torso and the upper leg ('hip') and the upper and lower leg ('knee') and absolute angles (the angle between an imaginary horizontal line drawn through the relevant joint and the relevant part of the limb or torso) for the upper arm, the trunk, the thigh and the lower leg. Results clearly showed experience to be a function of rider posture. In all three gaits, the hip angle was shown to be greater in advanced riders than in novice riders, with some significant differences to be found between novice and intermediate riders, confirming anecdotal assumptions that more experienced riders sit closer to the vertical. Indeed, additional studies by Terada *et al.* (2006) and Kang *et al.* (2010) provide further evidence that trunk angulation may be considered a valid indicator for rider skill.

While Schils *et al.* (1993) found no significant differences for the knee angle, related absolute angles of the thigh and the lower leg indicated that advanced riders carried their lower leg further underneath their body than their novice counterparts. The findings of Kang *et al.* (2010) also showed that, while advanced riders maintained dorsiflexion in their ankle joints in trot, beginner riders retained plantar flexion even after a 24-week training programme. Clearly then, one of the key elements of advanced rider positioning is the ability to absorb the motion patterns caused by an increase in ground reaction forces at higher equine speeds through flexible ankle joints positioned in line with riders' centre of mass. These findings support previous results by Lagarde *et al.* (2005), who investigated differences between one male professional and one female hobby rider. In their study, the heel of the expert rider came up much later than the toe, whereas in the hobby rider heel and toe moved more closely together, suggesting increased ankle flexion of the professional rider to absorb the motion of the horse.

Investigations of the relative shoulder angle and absolute upper arm and trunk angles indicated that advanced riders carry their arms slightly ahead of their trunks, while novice riders carry their arms close to their bodies (Schils *et al.* 1993). Lagarde *et al.*'s (2005) comparison between professional and hobby riders revealed that, in the expert rider, the joints of the shoulder to the wrist oscillated together, while those of the hobby rider seemed to experience a delay that travelled from the shoulder to the wrist, with oscillations increasing in intensity. It is not difficult to imagine the effect such instability of the rider's arms and hands might have on the horse, in particular its mouth. Future research should aim to validate Lagarde *et al.*'s findings using a greater sample size.

Incidentally, the previous section has focused heavily on findings by Schils *et al.* (1993), as one of the earliest and most comprehensive studies on the subject. It should be noted, however, that 61% of their participants primarily rode in an English style, while the remaining 39% participated in Western activities. While differences in riding style or discipline may not be significant, research efforts should nevertheless be undertaken to further improve our understanding of functional rider biomechanics and kinematics across all types of riding activities.

Variations of rider kinematics within gaits

A study by Lovett *et al.* (2004), which in many ways might be considered a follow-up to the work by Schils *et al.* (1993), focused on investigating variations in rider position throughout the stride cycle at walk, rising trot and canter. At the walk, significant differences were found only in rider trunk angles. The impact of the horse's hind leg with the ground resulted in a trunk position slightly behind the vertical, while forelimb impact caused the riders' trunk to move in front of the vertical. Lovett *et al.* argue that the hip joints might best be considered a fulcrum around which the rider's trunks pivots, as they absorb the four-beat rhythm of the walk. At the rising trot, the rider's position of the trunk was shown to be in front of the vertical throughout the stride cycle, mirroring findings by Schils *et al.* (1993), which showed the tendency of all riders to lean forward more in the rising trot, compared with walk or sitting trot. However, as riders rose out of the saddle, their trunks were significantly closer to the vertical than when they returned to the sitting position half a stride later. Leg position also changed throughout the stride cycle, with the lower leg positioned more caudally once riders started to lower themselves back into the saddle and more vertically as riders began to rise again. The authors speculate that the most likely reason for such a shift in leg position is mechanical efficiency. In their study on saddle and rider kinematics on high-level dressage horses trotting on a treadmill, Byström *et al.* (2009) found similar variations in positional shift throughout the trot stride. They argued that vertical and horizontal slowing and acceleration of the horse caused changes in rider position, presumably to absorb resultant forces. It seems clear, however, that additional research is necessary to determine the exact effects of equine stride kinetics on rider kinematics.

From an applied perspective, the effect the continuous, albeit slight, repositioning of the leg throughout the stride cycle might have on the horse needs to be investigated more closely. Seeing that horses learn via principles of operant conditioning (McGreevy and McLean 2007; McLean and McGreevy 2010), leg pressure to their sides usually results in an increase in stride velocity or length or both. Involuntary changes in leg position and associated shifts in pressure might therefore lead to two possible effects: either the horse reacts with the same kind of response as it would to the 'normal' leg, thus continuously 'running away from the leg' or it might gradually become desensitized or 'dead' to the leg. Either response is, of course, less than ideal and riders should strive to attain as quiet a lower leg as possible. In any event, the findings on variability of rider posture throughout the stride cycle of the trot seem to point towards differences, if not difficulties, in coordination and balance, with future research needing to indicate at which point of the stride cycle changes in rider position occur (Lovett *et al.* 2004). In canter, on the other hand, riders' legs changed position only slightly. Much like in walk, the greatest range of movement was seen in the position of riders' trunks, depending on the impact of different limbs, but differences were not significant. Considering the increased ground reaction forces in canter, it is likely that stabilizing muscular activity is greater to maintain trunk position. Such notions are further supported by research identifying increased heart rates and oxygen uptakes, indicative of greater metabolic demands in canter (e.g. Devienne and Guezennec 2000; Westerling 1983). Elements relating to the physiology of equestrian sports will be discussed in Chapter 2.

The power of the rider: influencing equine movement

By their very nature, equestrian sports are dependent on the inherent biomechanical interaction between horse and rider and most, if not all, riders strive for the kind of physical coordination whereby horse and rider seem to be moving in complete synchrony with one another as if operating 'as one' (Brandt 2004; Meyers *et al.* 1997). In fact, one of the most desirable qualities of riders is the ability to guide their horses through a dressage test, showjumping round or any other equestrian challenge in a manner that appears effortless and harmonious. Especially in more recent years, elite riders at the very top are required to show that they are able to produce performances that are void of coercion or force. The term 'happy athlete' has been used as a synonym for dressage horses that are 'calm, supple, loose and flexible, but also confident, attentive and keen' (FEI 2011: 10). Albeit somewhat difficult to determine with absolute certainty whether horses can, in fact, be 'happy', the intention behind such terminology is laudable and aims to encourage riders to pay greater attention to how they ride their horses, as well as how their horses respond to being ridden. Olympic-level judge and president of the dressage ground jury of the 2012 London Olympic Games, Stephen Clarke, recently paid testimony to what is currently expected from dressage riders. Having been asked to comment on the dressage jury's final scores, which placed the British combination of Charlotte Dujardin and Valegro ahead of the Dutch Adeline Cornelissen and Parzival at the end of the Olympic freestyle, Clarke responded: 'They ended up very close together', he said. 'Maybe one had a little bit more power and the other one had a little bit more harmony and self-carriage. Lots of people will have different opinions but our decision was for the harmony' (Edmonds 2012). Yet, despite the long traditions of equestrian sports of trying to professionalize training situations and to optimize the relationship between horse and rider, the term 'harmony' or how riders might elicit 'harmonious' performances from their horses remains difficult to quantify. Perhaps even more importantly, many issues relating to lameness or back problems in horses may be due to poor riding (Greve and Dyson 2012; Peham *et al.* 2004).

Stability of equine movement: a function of rider expertise?

Animal locomotion patterns are thought to be partly controlled by a network of neurons in the central nervous system capable of rhythmic output, also referred to as the 'central pattern generator' (Collins and Richmond 1994). Animals that move in regular rhythms and at consistent speeds and frequencies – as horses do – have been found to exhibit 'steady-state-frequencies' (Bergerud 1975; Hurmuzlu and Basdogan 1994), which are particularly energy efficient. While a certain amount of variability in movement patterns is important to enable an animal (or indeed a human or any other kind of dynamical system) to deal with changes in a complex dynamic environment – a concept that is referred to as dynamic systems theory (Williams *et al.* 1999) – too much movement variability is likely to lead to the horse showing uneven gaits and increases the likelihood of stumbling or falling. A question that might even be considered to be at the heart of equestrian sports is what happens to innate movement patterns when humans (i.e. riders) climb on top of a horse. Do they invariably disturb or even prohibit the horse from ever achieving steady-state frequencies or might they be able to support the horse by effectively reducing unnecessary variability of movement patterns, thereby achieving steady-state frequencies more quickly and efficiently?

In what may be considered trailblazing studies on the topic of investigating rider effect on movement patterns of horses, Peham *et al.* (1998, 2001) showed that a professional rider was in fact able to get much closer to maintaining steady-state movement frequency on several horses compared with a hobby rider. Interestingly, the hobby rider was shown to 'waste' kinetic energy during riding, by (presumably unconscious) frequent acceleration and deceleration of movement. Most of us are likely to recognize the picture that is being painted here: on the one hand, there is the novice rider, who often wobbles rather unsteadily in the saddle, while the experienced, semi-professional or professional rider hardly seems to move a single muscle while flawlessly executing the most difficult of movements. Not surprisingly, associated instability of movement ends up disturbing the steady-state frequency of the horse. These findings by Peham *et al.* (1998, 2001) provided the first indications that movement stability in the ridden horse may at least in part be considered a function of rider expertise – results that were further supported by studies of Lagarde *et al.* (2005) and Schöllhorn *et al.* (2006). Their work seemed to suggest that expert riders were better able to coordinate their own motor behavior with that of the horse and to elicit more consistent, stable movement patterns in the horse. More specifically, Lagarde *et al.* (2005) captured the relative phase differences of a professional and a hobby rider performing on the same horse, meaning the extent to which horse and rider are 'in' or 'out' of phase with each other's movement patterns. The skilled, professional rider was seemingly significantly better at adapting his movements to those of the horse than the less-skilled hobby rider. The authors argue that effective horse–rider communication occurs in part through an exchange of haptic information via various contacts points, such as the saddle, reins, stirrups and where the seat of the rider meets the trunk of the horse. Skilled riders are likely to be better at anticipating and reacting to relevant information on the motion parameters made available by the horse via these haptic contact points. Schöllhorn *et al.* (2006), applied a statistical method named hierarchical cluster analysis to compare equine movement patterns without a rider, under a professional and a hobby rider. The authors found evidence once again that an expert rider seems to be able to control equine movement variables more effectively than a less experienced rider.

Basing their conclusions on the results of a study comparing movement patterns of non-ridden versus ridden horses on a treadmill, Peham *et al.* (2004) even went as far as to suggest that equine kinematics improved under a professional rider, under the proviso that a well-fitting saddle was used. The authors argued that. rather than destabilizing a horse, an experienced, skilled rider might even be able to induce a stabilizing effect by being able to react and counteract against externally disruptive influences.

Even in a showjumping context, tentative evidence to that effect was noted: in a study investigating the repeatability of jumping parameters in 141 young stallions with or without a rider (resulting in 4,323 jumping efforts), Lewczuk *et al.* (2006) found indications that repeatability for jumping parameters, such as bascule points over the fence, take-off and landing points, and angle of the head, was higher with the rider than without, providing tentative evidence that a competent rider might induce a stabilizing effect on equine performance. From an applied point of view, repeatability and stabilization of performance is, of course, highly desirable, as increased predictability of equine effort facilitates performances in the competitive arena while also potentially increasing aspects of rider safety. However, a study by Powers and Kavanagh (2005) investigating the effect of rider experience on jumping kinematics in ten seasoned showjumping horses, was unable to detect any significant differences between riders. The key differences between the studies by Lewczuk *et al.* (2006) and Powers and Kavanagh (2005), however, are discrepancies in statistical power because of the numbers of participating horses and the horses' level of showjumping experience. It is highly likely that experienced showjumping horses, as used in Powers' and Kavanagh's study, appropriate a certain style of jumping over time, which may not significantly change, even under a different rider. The young stallions used in the study by Lewczuk *et al.* might be much more susceptible to the effect of a rider, as their movement patterns over a fence would, in all likelihood, not have been fully formed. Nevertheless, a word or two of caution seems to be in order at this point. First of all, additional studies investigating the stabilizing effects of riders with different levels of skill and experience on equine performance are necessary. Furthermore, Greve and Dyson (2012), in an extensive review of aspects relating to the rider, saddle and horse interaction, comment that skilled riders' ability to continuously make subtle adjustments to how the horse moves might even be masking underlying issues related to lameness or pain, which only becomes apparent once the horse is ridden by a less-skilled individual. There can be no question that the considerable expertise by professional or highly experienced riders to modify and improve a horse's way of going should only be used as a means of heightening a horse's health by strengthening the horse's musculoskeletal system.

A matter of comfort: sitting or rising

A question that is likely to play on many riders' minds as soon as they have reached a level of expertise that allows them to train their horses, more or less independently, is which rider position is best to improve the suppleness and range of motion of a horse's back and, as a direct result, the quality of movement. From an anecdotal point of view, many trainers might, for example, swear by the practice of warming up their horses in the 'two-point position', whereby the rider effectively stands in the stirrups, with the torso bent forward. The 'two points' therefore refer to the contact points of the two legs with the sides of the horse. Some trainers might also insist on regular episodes of rising trot, to allow the horse to 'stretch', that is to flex its back upward to meet the rider's seat. The 'three-point position', whereby the rider adds the contact point of his seat to the two contact points of the legs, is, at least in trot, reserved for more strenuous dressage training.

Modern research techniques allow for the provision of more definite answers regarding the advantages and disadvantages of the different types of riding positions. In 2009, de Cocq *et al.* (2009b) used an infrared-based camera system to record kinematic variables of back movement during an unloaded condition (without rider), as well as during rising and sitting trot. Results showed that the overall range of movement of the equine back was greater in rising than in sitting trot, with horses also holding their heads lower during rising trot. In sitting trot, horses' backs showed greater extension than flexion compared with the unloaded condition while, in rising trot, the maximal flexion was comparable to that in the unloaded condition, with maximal extension comparable to that in sitting trot. Results thus seem to support anecdotal claims that working horses in rising trot tends to supple their backs, thereby encouraging looseness of movement.

A follow-up study by de Cocq *et al.* (2010) measured forces on horses' backs in rising or sitting trot. While no significant differences in average vertical forces between rising and sitting trot were found, vertical force peaks in rising trot were lower than in sitting trot. These results were supportive of similar findings by Peham *et al.* (2008, 2010), who also identified the rising trot as less strenuous for horses compared with sitting trot, due to lower maximal pressures. Furthermore, Peham *et al.* (2010) also included comparisons of the two-point position and were able to demonstrate that of the three positions (two-point position, rising and sitting trot), the two-point seat provided the lowest load on to the horse's back, followed, as already indicated above, by rising and subsequently sitting trot. The authors also identified rider stability to be greatest in the two-point position, followed again by rising trot and lastly sitting trot, lending support to claims from the industry that 'lightening' the seat decreases the stresses on the horse's back. Readers should bear in mind, however, that the rider who participated in the study was a professional rider, training at grand prix level. It is likely that he was able to absorb the horse's movement during trot through increased ankle flexion, which has been found to be indicative of rider skill (e.g. Kang *et al.* 2010; Lagarde *et al.* 2005) while also activating rectus abdominis (stomach) muscles and the latissimus dorsi (the back muscles), as well as the deeper oblique muscles in order to stabilize his upper body. Future research needs to determine whether the same effects are evident in riders with less experience and what the effects are of the two-point compared with the three-point position in canter.

While these existing studies on the influence of the rider on equine biomechanics undoubtedly provide an excellent starting point for future research, some of their limitations regarding the applicability of the results must be borne in mind. To date, most studies focus primarily on the equine gait of trot (e.g. Lagarde *et al.* 2005; Peham *et al.* 2004, 2001, 1998; Schöllhorn *et al.* 2006), with little research concentrating on investigating rider effects on the equine gaits of walk, canter, gallop or indeed tölt or pace, let alone in the more complex movement patterns required at the top level of the sport. Future research is clearly required to provide an even greater understanding of how kinematic and kinetic movement variables of the mounted rider affect movement patterns of the horse.

It should also be noted that, in addition to the studies previously discussed, which primarily investigate elements of rider kinematics, more recent research also uses aspects of rider kinetics to calculate the forces exerted on the horse by the rider (e.g. Peham *et al.* 2010). Much of this work uses an electronic saddle or other type of pressure pad, which measure the distribution of forces applied to the horse's back or sides via an array of sensors (e.g. de Cocq *et al.* 2009a; de Cocq *et al.* 2006; Jeffcott *et al.* 1999).

In addition to investigating how riders might shift their weight during a stride cycle, while executing different movements or to detect rider asymmetries, the use of such technology can also help to determine the amount and variability of forces applied by the rider. This, in turn, might provide clues to the potential causes for equine back pain, associated lameness and ridden behavioral problems. In a study investigating leg pressures of riders during two lateral movements and riding straight ahead, de Cocq *et al.* (2010) found high variation in both force magnitudes and peak frequencies, indicating that the way in which different riders apply aids can differ considerably, potentially causing problems when horses change owners or are being ridden by several people. Unfortunately, space restrictions of the current volume dictate that no detailed discussion of the varying effects of different saddles or other type of equipment on movement kinematics on horses can be provided here. In the first instance, readers are encouraged to consult the recent review article by Greve and Dyson (2012) on the topic of saddle fit on equine kinematics, pain and lameness.

Communication lines: reins, riders and other problems with asymmetry

One of the first things that a beginner rider is being taught is that the two reins form a direct communication line to the horse's mouth and, as is particularly the case for bitless bridles, other sensitive parts of the horse's head. What is more, anecdotal experience and empirical research findings agree that the position of the horse's head has a direct effect on equine kinematics (Rhodin *et al.* 2005; Gómez Álvarez *et al.* 2006). The impact of the way in which riders hold their reins when riding is therefore not to be underestimated. Instructors, traditional and modern riding manuals (e.g. Steinbrecht 1884; Meyners 2004), as well as indicative empirical evidence (Lagarde *et al.* 2005), all agree that one of the most important components of good riding is a calm and steady hand and arm. Many aspects relating to the training and riding of horses depend on the appropriate application of principles of negative reinforcement (e.g. McCall 1989, 1990), which refers to the removal of an aversive stimulus immediately after the desired response has been shown (e.g. McGreevy 2007; Waran *et al.* 2002) In a riding-related context, the correct use of negative reinforcement stipulates that aversive cues such as rein (or leg) pressure should be released immediately once the horse has responded appropriately. Inadvertent pulling or jarring of the horse's mouth might lead to irresponsive or even dangerous horses.[7] Yet keeping a constant, soft contact to a horse's mouth is quite often easier said (or written) than done!

The emergence of modern technology enables us once again to measure aspects relating to the forces that riders apply when trying to establish a contact with their horses' mouths. More specifically, as expounded by Warren-Smith *et al.* (2007), researchers and practising riders alike are better served to think of rein pressure as 'rein tension', to be measured in N (newton) rather than grams or kilo-grams. As most riders apply pressure to the reins by effectively pulling (even if it is only marginally) posteriorly and the horse, by being encouraged to 'take a contact', will pull anteriorly, the resulting force should be regarded as tension. Previous studies have recorded varying degrees of rein tensions, ranging between 6 N and 75 N (Clayton *et al.* 2005; Preuschoft *et al.* 1995, 1999). Rein tensions have also been shown to differ between different gaits, with increased tempi resulting in higher tension (e.g. Clayton *et al.* 2005; Kuhnke *et al.* 2010). When comparing tension employed during long-reining as opposed to riding, Warren-Smith *et al.* (2007) found higher mean tension levels for long-reining (10.7 ± 1.0 N) than during riding (7.4 ± 0.7 N) and the use of significantly less tension during riding for halting and turning left, as well as on the right rein when going straight. In view of the fact that the relatively greater length of the long reins only accounted for 1.5 N, the authors highlight the need for caution when using long reins, especially when horses are in the initial stages of training and are being taught to respond to only the lightest of aids. If long reins are used for reasons relating to horse–rider safety, the authors suggest other methods, such as habitu-ation training or similar. Perhaps not altogether surprisingly, in the ridden condition of Warren-Smith *et al.*'s (2007) study, rein tension during halt was significantly higher than while going straight and on the inside rein when turning. Differences in rein tension between left and right rein, however, tended to indi-cate that riders do not apply their aids equally with their left and right reins.

These findings were further supported by a study by Kuhnke *et al.* (2010), which investigated the interaction between rein tension, rider and horse laterality. Results showed that riders applied significantly more tension to the left rein of a horse with left laterality, presumably to compensate for the lack of contact on the horse's left side (what is commonly referred to as the horse's 'hollow side'). These symptoms of rider 'handedness' may be indicative of overall rider asym-metry and might even be at the source of a number of training issues. In one of the few studies investigating rider asymmetry, Symes and Ellis (2009) were able to demonstrate that, rather than moving symmetrically, riders show considerable unevenness throughout their bodies. The authors determined a greater range of displacement in the right compared with the left shoulder in all gaits bar the right canter, pointing towards inherent or acquired asymmetry of the rider. Considering that the aim of dressage training is to develop evenly muscled, balanced horses, current findings are somewhat disconcerting. Differences in tension on different reins, as well as asymmetries in rider position, are likely to lead to difficulties when developing straightness in the horse and/or counteracting equine asymmetries. Future studies should therefore aim to investigate interactive effects of horse–rider laterality and asymmetry more closely, in the hope of providing relevant training indicators to improve equine straightness, with associative positive effects on welfare and performance.

Lastly, Kuhnke *et al.*'s (2010) study highlighted another issue in equine training that deserves our attention: the authors measured intermittent tension on riders' outside rein, characterized by bouts of zero tension measured. From the perspective of learning theory and, in particular, the principles of negative reinforcement (e.g. McCall 1990), such inconsistencies might possibly end up reinforcing a horse's previously performed behavior – regardless of whether such behaviors were what the riders desired or not. The inability of riders to essentially control motor patterns of their limbs, as demonstrated by the findings of Kuhnke *et al.* (2010), is likely to have considerable, if not serious, consequences for equine training. Riders who release tension involuntary may well be reinforcing equine behavior that is unwanted or even dangerous. Current technologies measuring rider kinematics and kinetics clearly have an exceedingly important role to play in helping riders and coaches to recognize and improve motor control.

Concluding thoughts

It seems clear that the measurement and monitoring of the way in which riders influence the biomechanical dimensions of the quality of the horse–rider dyad have not, as yet, been fully explored. While existing studies undoubtedly provide an excellent starting point, more research is required on how rider kinematics and kinetics shape equine performance on the one hand and how rider motor control is affected by equine biomechanics on the other. Furthermore, only limited research exists to date that goes beyond the measurement of relatively isolated kinematic or kinetic variables of the rider or the horse. Future investigations should also focus on aspects of movement coordination between horse and rider across different gaits and varying levels of expertise.

Conducting movement analyses of the rider and horse–rider systems will almost certainly develop a more thorough understanding of the nature of harmonious horse–rider interaction. Kinematic and kinetic models of the way in which horse and rider coordinate their bodies are likely to provide an invaluable source of feedback to riders and their coaches, helping them to progress more quickly in their riding and training. Relevant training concepts that focus on improving relevant physical and physiological components, while also taking into account physical asymmetries, are therefore likely to go a long way towards optimizing motor control in riders. In the long run, a more thorough analysis and evaluation of rider motor control is likely to be beneficial even to aspects beyond rider performance, such as talent identification, motor learning and coaching, as well as rider safety and equine health and welfare.

Chapter highlights

1. Movement of all objects is subject to the same mechanical laws, which can be measured in several ways. *Bio*mechanics is concerned with the principles of mechanics that govern the movement and structure of living organisms. Kinematics describes changes in position of a particular body segment through time, while kinetics helps to determine the cause of motion, through different forces applied to or released from a body.

2. Marr's (1982) tri-level hypothesis consists of three levels of analysis that help in the analysis of different information processing systems, such as motor control. The computational level focuses on a frequently mathematical description of the different functions a system has to achieve. The procedural level describes how a specific movement is executed in real time and the implementation level determines which biological systems are activated to facilitate the execution of the movement.

3. Motor skills can be defined according to the level of precision of movements; that is, gross or fine motor skills, or according to their interaction with the environment; that is, open or closed motor skills. Equestrian sports are primarily characterized by the use of fine and open motor skills.

4. Motor control should be viewed as the link between sensory input and movement output. When training horses, riders are at all times dependent on the sensory feedback they receive from their horses, as the content of such feedback will determine the next set of aids.

5. According to closed-loop theory, motor learning includes the development of 'perceptual traces', which are personal reference points on the way to successful performance. Every time a movement is executed, perceptual feedback indicates how successful that particular performance was, allowing for gradual improvement of motor performance.

6. Open-loop segments are motor programmes that do not require sensory feedback after every isolated movement but instead rely on a fixed sequence of motor behaviors.

7. Motor learning occurs in separate stages. During the initial, cognitive stage, perceived sensory cues are linked with correct motor commands. The linkages between perceptual feedback and correct motor behaviors are stored as sensorimotor maps and can be accessed in working memory throughout the intermediate, associative stage. At the advanced, autonomous stage performance has become automatic and does not require thinking about.

8. The correct and effective training of horses is only possible if riders and equine trainers move their own bodies in such a way as to elicit and maintain precisely the kind of responses they desire from their horses. The way that

humans move when interacting with horses is one of the most important and fundamental elements to horse–rider performance and safety.

9. Empirical findings seem to support anecdotal evidence that experienced riders sit closer to the vertical, position their legs underneath their body and carry their upper arms slightly ahead of the trunk. Ankle joints in experienced riders tend to move elastically, helping to absorb the movement of the horse.

10. More experienced riders show more consistent movement patterns, with fewer variations within gait cycles, and are able to synchronize their own movement more closely with that of the horse. As a result, they might also be able to elicit more stable movement patterns in horses.

11. While little is known regarding the principles of motor learning in equestrian sports, increasing motor development of riders is likely to lead to improvements in posture, which are thought to be due to an increase of appropriate muscle tone on the one hand and relevant motor skills on the other.

12. While existing studies provide an excellent starting point, more research is required on how rider kinematics and kinetics influence equine performance on the one hand, and how rider motor control is affected by equine biomechanics on the other.

2 Performance physiology and rider fitness

Riders are athletes too!

Introduction: in the name of top sport

She is the Reem Acra FEI World Cup Dressage Champion for the years 2011 and 2012. In 2009, at the European Championships in Windsor, UK, she won individual gold medals in the Grand Prix Special and the Freestyle. In 2010, at the World Championship in Kentucky, USA, she experienced an unfortunate low point in her career when her horse bit himself on the underside of his tongue during the pair's Grand Prix test. The pair were disqualified from the rest of the competition because of blood on the horse's mouth. Only one year later, at the 2011 European Championships in Rotterdam, the Netherlands, she practiced the art of one-upmanship and won individual gold in the Special and Freestyle. A gold medal at the Olympic Games in London 2012 would have been the proverbial icing on the cake. But even the silver medal she managed to procure in the end was no mean feat considering the formidable competition, the likes of which no Olympics had ever seen before.

'She' is of course none other than the Dutch equestrian, Adelinde Cornelissen. A former English teacher turned dressage superstar, she completed the rise to the upper echelons of the dressage world on the back of the chestnut KWPN gelding, Parzival, who, by Adelinde's own account, was not the most straightforward horse in his youth. In addition to the obvious tenacity she showed by persevering when others would have given up long ago, she clearly possesses another vital trait that has helped her in the pursuit of excellence. Adelinde is absolutely and unfailingly dedicated, not simply to her horses (a trait that probably all top riders share) but also to getting herself in the best possible mental and physical shape she can be.

Adelinde Cornelissen has evidently embraced what it means to be a top rider – and in preparation for the London Olympics she turned herself into a top athlete too. Her fitness programme was composed and supervised by Tjalling van den Berg, one of the Netherlands' top gymnastic coaches. Under van den Berg's expert guidance – and let us not forget that the physical demands of gymnastics are gruelling, demanding a combination of strength, flexibility, power and coordination – Adelinde worked on just about every aspect of fitness imaginable. She was taught to control every muscle in her body separately, she improved her core stability and posture, coordination and reflexes through a combination of breath-ing exercises, boxing and rope skipping, balancing on a skipping ball and juggling. In addition to the 'mere' physical aspects of this strenuous training programme, which also included a nutritional dimension, her new-found fitness seems to have honed her concentration skills, her commitment and her ability to work towards her goal in a single-minded manner even further – elements from which riders, no matter what level they are at, can benefit. Incidentally, the fact that Adelinde chose to look for innovative solutions outside of her own sport is indicative of another quality of top athletes: being able to think 'outside of the box' rather than sticking to the tried-and-tested routines of those that have gone before her.

Fitness and riding – in the past, these two concepts did not always go together naturally. Non-riders frequently joke that in equestrian sports 'the horse does all the work'. Riders generally know better and will testify that trying to make an animal approximately ten times their own weight do what they wish it to do consti-tutes a physically highly demanding activity. However, as with a number of other sports, riding horses can be pursued at a leisurely pace or more vigorously, such as in competition. Both the demands on the human (and equine) body and subsequent effects on rider fitness over time are likely to differ considerably, both at different levels of riding and in different disciplines. Furthermore, equestrianism is one of the very few sports where men and women compete on equal terms, giving rise to the idea that some of the innate superior physical attributes of men (see below) provide little to no advantages (Whitaker *et al.* 2012; Westerling 1983).

Following a spate of high-profile deaths in the sport of eventing in the years of 1999 and, more recently, in 2007, the notion that rider fitness may be an impor-tant factor in improving both safety and performance has gained renewed strength. It can only be hoped that the high-profile example of Adelinde Cornelissen might inspire more riders to embrace their own fitness with the same enthusiasm. This chapter analyzes and evaluates existing empirical evidence regarding rider physiology, while at the same time providing a better understand-ing of the general physiological requirements of the different equestrian disciplines. Broader principles from the field of general sport science will help to place equestrian fitness into context, while also providing a better understanding of the direction rider training should take in future.

'Rider physiology' – what is it and how to define it

Before we get into the complex matters of measuring and analyzing physiologi-cal components of equestrian activities, it is useful to define in more detail the field of research with which we are going to concern ourselves throughout the rest of this chapter. Readers should note that, even though commonly in use in sport science circles, the term 'sport and exercise physiology' and by extension 'rider physiology' are in fact somewhat misleading. For starters, the area of study that is being described here does not merely concern itself with the different functions of the body's organs, systems and cells (i.e. its *physiology*) but also with the structure of its various body parts i.e. *anatomy*. The study of sport and exercise physiology (and thereby rider physiology) is therefore concerned with the structural elements of the body (anatomy), its relevant functions (physiology) and how these are altered in a sport and exercise context.

Furthermore, even though the terms 'sport' and 'exercise' physiology are often used, either in conjunction with one another or synonymously, there does exist a slight, yet important distinction between 'sport' and 'exercise' physiology. The study of *exercise* physiology concerns itself with the way in which the human body copes during strenuous activity (exercise) while *sport* physiology applies relevant principles of exercise physiology to improve sporting performance (Kenney *et al.* 2012). To that effect and in the context of this book, 'rider physiology' might be referred to as the study of how the principles of exercise physiology might apply to the performance of the rider while engaged in equestrian activities.

In practical terms, this means that every time riders get on their horses, their bodies will automatically respond with a series of complex actions that allow them to complete the required movements of riding (more or less) successfully. The bones, tendons, ligaments and muscles of the musculoskeletal systems all work together to ensure that riders manage to stay on their horses and do not topple off their backs (or at least most of the time). The cardiovascular system is charged with delivering fuel to muscles and other cells of the body, necessary to keep them working at optimal efficiency. Together with the respiratory system, the cardiovascular system also ensures that oxygen is delivered to the body's cells and that carbon dioxide (a by-product of energy production) is removed. The skin, also referred to as the integumentary system, is the organ responsible for preventing the body from overheating by allowing for heat exchange with the immediate environment. These different and complex activities are coordinated and controlled by the nervous and endocrine systems, which also regulate fluid balance and blood pressure (e.g. Kenney *et al.* 2012).

Furthermore, an additional important concept when studying the impact of physical activity on the (human) body is that of 'homeostasis' (Cannon 1929). The various systems of the body are all integrated to regulate and stabilize the internal environment to enable optimal health and functioning. Not surprisingly, exercise presents a considerable challenge to the body for maintaining homeostasis. Exercise physiologists therefore aim to determine the reaction of the body to essentially two different conditions: acute exercise (i.e. individual bouts of exercise) and chronic adaptations to training (i.e. the reactions of the body to repeated bouts of exercise over time). In the context of equestrian sports, measuring the physiological reactions of different riders during bouts of 'acute exercise' allows for an assessment of the strenuousness of different equestrian activities. Monitoring physiological changes in those riders over time assists in determining the long-term effects of riding. A thorough grasp of the short- and long-term effects of riding would subsequently also allow for any future conditioning and training programmes for riders to be based on empirical evidence, making them, in all likelihood, more effective at enhancing performance.

The stuff we are made of: energy requirements of the body

It will come as no surprise to anyone that the field of exercise physiology and associated areas is vast. The following sections will therefore only provide an initial outline of the principles most important to the understanding and evaluation of existing research in rider physiology.[1]

It is a – if not *the* – fact of life that the body uses energy, regardless of whether we are currently engaged in exercise or merely resting. In this context, the first law of thermodynamics is refreshingly straightforward and states that while energy can be converted from one form to another, it can never be destroyed or created out of nothing (Clausius 1850). Consequently, this means that the body first needs to take in energy – energy that, for virtually all life forms, comes in the shape of food. But the processes that turn the less than healthy – albeit tasty – staple diet of many competition riders, consisting primarily of French fries and burgers, into useable fuel for muscles are unfortunately anything but straightforward.

As most readers will undoubtedly know, the human (and animal) metabolism depends on three types of energy sources, namely carbohydrates, fats and proteins. These organic compounds, which are the building blocks of virtually any foodstuffs, are converted via chemical processes in the body into adenosine triphosphate (ATP), the energy substrate that fuels any form of muscular contractions (DiMenna and Jones 2009). In a resting state, the body depends in almost equal parts on the use of carbohydrates and fats to produce energy while, under normal circumstances, proteins primarily support the body's various chemical reactions. In contrast, during exercise, the use of carbohydrates is preferred but depends on both their availability and the metabolic system of the muscles to convert carbohydrates to glucose. This simple six-carbon form of sugar is then transported via the blood to all bodily tissues. At rest, glucose is stored as the more complex form of glycogen in muscles and liver, until it is needed again for active exercise. Especially during bouts of exercise lasting several hours, the liver breaks down its stores of glycogen into glucose, providing the body with additional energy resources to convert to ATP. Once initial carbohydrate reserves in the muscles become depleted, the body starts to rely more heavily on the oxidation of fats (lipolysis – see below) to supply muscles with energy. Fat as an energy source is largely used during less intensive but long lasting bouts of exercise (i.e. when the oxidative metabolic pathway is activated – see below). Still, fats take considerably longer to be broken down from their complex form of triglyceride to glycerol and free fatty acids. In addition, the energy release from free fatty acids does not occur fast enough to meet all of the energy demands of intensive exercise. Much like protein, fat also serves a number of structural functions to preserve the health of cell membranes and nerves. As an energy source, proteins play only a secondary role, as their most basic building blocks, amino acids, must first be converted to glucose. In a nutshell, even though substantially more energy is derived from one gram of fat (9.4 kcal/g) than from carbohydrates or protein (4.1 kcal/g each), carbohydrates form by far the most important energy resource

during exercise. On a side note, this is of course the primary reason why carbohydrates are the preferred source of energy for athletes (including riders) and
should make up the bulk of their diet.

Most importantly, however, the different cells of the body can only access and
use the energy available from the three substrates of carbohydrate, fat and protein,
if they have first been converted to ATP, the body's 'energy currency'. Cells therefore engage with one of three (or a combination of three) 'metabolic pathways':

- the ATP-PCr system;
- the glycolytic system;
- the oxidative system.

The ATP-PCr system

The ATP-PCr system is the simplest of the energy systems and does not require
oxygen for the production of ATP, even though oxygen is frequently available. In
addition to storing a small amount of ATP, cells also store phosphocreatine (PCr).
Once PCr is broken down, it helps to regenerate ATP to facilitate a constant
supply of ATP, particularly during rest. However, the production of ATP via the
breakdown of PCr is inhibited as soon as other sources of ATP become more readily available. This means that, as soon as exercise becomes more intensive and
more ATP is produced via the glycolytic and oxidative systems (see below), the
metabolic pathway of ATP-PCr will be halted. As a result, the metabolic pathway
of ATP-PCr is only able to generate sufficient ATP to last for the first few seconds
of exercise right at the onset of a workout.

The glycolytic system

The equally anaerobic glycolytic system (also called glycolysis) requires the
breakdown of glucose for the production of ATP. Glycolysis is very complex in
that it involves a number of enzymatic reactions which convert glycogen first to
pyruvic acid and then to lactic acid, leading to the release of three molecules of
ATP to one molecule of glycogen. If glucose were used instead of glycogen, there
would only be a net gain of two molecules of ATP, as one ATP molecule would
have been used for the initial conversion of glucose. Even though glycolysis does
not produce great amounts of energy, it operates without oxygen and is thus
particularly important in the early minutes of high-intensity exercise. However,
without the presence of oxygen, the by-product of glycolysis, pyruvic acid, is
immediately converted to lactic acid (and subsequently lactate), which in turn
accumulates in the muscles. Such acidification prevents further glycogen breakdown and, at its worst, inhibits muscle contraction. These processes explain why,
after very intensive bouts of exercise, for example a long, hard gallop, leg
muscles feel like they are 'burning' – the intense exertion of standing in the stirrups and continuously balancing the body has caused the build-up of lactate.

The oxidative system

While the ATP-PCr and glycolytic systems are vital in providing energy in, respectively, the first few seconds and minutes of exercise, another system is clearly needed to provide the body with the necessary energy to sustain exercise over a prolonged period of time. The oxidative system (oxidative phosphorylation) relies on the cellular ability to break down substrates with the aid of oxygen – a process also called cellular respiration. Because of its reliance on oxygen, this process is called 'aerobic'. The oxidative system takes a lot longer to be activated but has a much greater net gain of energy. In return, it places considerable demands on both the cardiovascular and respiratory systems for the continuous delivery of oxygen to active muscles. Energy substrates are either carbohydrates (which will be initially transformed during glycolysis) or fats. Incidentally, the process of glycolysis is the same, regardless of the presence of oxygen. However, whenever oxygen is present, pyruvic acid is converted into the substrate acetyl coenzyme A (acetyl CoA), which, in turn, will enter the 'Krebs cycle' to be fully oxidized. In combination with the additional chemical reactions of the 'electron transport chain', 32 molecules of ATP are produced for one molecule of glucose (33 molecules of ATP per one molecule of muscle glycogen), making oxidation by far the most efficient energy pathway. Incidentally, free fatty acids produced from fat via the process of lipolysis also enter the bloodstream and are transported to muscle fibres, where they will be converted to acetyl CoA. Interestingly, while fat is more energy-dense than carbohydrates, fat oxidation yields 5.6 ATP molecules per oxygen molecule used, while carbohydrates produce 6.3 ATP molecules.[2]

Quite clearly, this is an awful lot of theory that, at first glance, seems to have rather little to do with the sport of riding. However, understanding the different types of energy systems used during exercise in general and different equestrian disciplines in particular will allow riders to appreciate the specific physiological demands on their bodies to perform at optimum levels. One only needs to consider, for example, the differences between disciplines such as showjumping versus endurance in terms of duration and intensity of exertion to appreciate the value of the information presented here for the development of appropriate conditioning and training programmes.

Faster, higher, stronger: measuring intensity of exercise

While it is one thing to appreciate in theory how energy is converted in a human (or animal) body, it is entirely another to measure precisely how much energy someone is currently using and come up with an objective way of defining how exhausting a particular activity is. From an anecdotal point of view, riders know, of course, that, all things being equal, riding a horse in a walk on a long rein is much less exhausting than riding at a canter or even over a series of obstacles. Most of the time, they will feel themselves starting to breathe harder or their hearts to beat faster when training at higher intensities and can usually indicate fairly accurately how exhausting one particular riding session is compared with another. While these personal impressions can provide an excellent indication of someone's subjective 'rate of perceived exertion' (RPE; Borg 1982), more objective markers to determining exercise intensity are clearly needed as well.

Oxygen consumption: it's the air you breathe

The rate at which people burn energy is generally calculated using their whole-body oxygen consumption (VO_2). The underlying principle dates as far back as the 1870s, to a researcher named Adolph Fick. He developed the 'Fick principle', which stipulates that the oxygen consumption of live tissue is dependent on:

- how much blood is transported *to* the tissue; and
- how much oxygen is extracted *from* the blood *by* the tissue.

Oxygen consumption as the basis of energy consumed constitutes the difference of oxygen in the blood between arterial blood supplying the tissue and venous blood draining from it (Fritts and Cournand 1958). Oxygen consumption is therefore one of the most fundamental means of determining exercise intensity during acute bouts of activity, while also providing a marker of athlete (or rider) fitness over time. Early work by Hill and Lupton (1923) determined that VO_2 rises approximately exponentially with exercise intensity. Modern research techniques, such as breath-by-breath analysis, managed to show however that the behavior of VO_2 during moderate exercise can be divided into distinctive phases, with each phase characterized by steady-state levels of VO_2. Phase 1 occurs during the first 10–25 seconds of the onset of exercise, believed to be primarily related to an increase in cardiac output (Wasserman *et al.* 1974), changes in the composition of oxygen (Casaburi *et al.* 1989) and lung gas stores (Barstow and Mole 1987). During phase 2, oxygen consumption rises quickly and exponentially until steady-state levels are reached, usually within a couple of minutes of exercising. Phase 3 marks another, higher, level of steady-state VO_2, generally achieved within three minutes of constant work rate exercise (e.g. Davies *et al.* 1972). Depending on the type of exercise performed, it is possible that additional steady state VO_2 values are achieved. It is important to note here that exercise intensities are classified as moderate as long as they are below the lactic threshold (e.g. Casaburi *et al.* 1989), the threshold at which lactate starts to accumulate above the levels typically found at rest (more on lactate thresholds below).

Beyond this point of lactate acid accumulation (i.e. at higher intensities of exercise) oxygen consumption continues to increase at a steeper rate than that previously observed, which has been attributed to the recruitment of type-II muscle fibres that are less efficient at using oxygen to generate power (e.g. Barstow *et al.* 1996). Once oxygen consumption fails to change despite increases in exercise intensity, individuals are thought to have reached their maximum oxygen consumption, also called: VO_{2max}. VO_{2max} is widely thought to provide a

---

It's all in the fibre...

The body is composed of different types of muscle fibres, which are recruited for different types of activities. Type-I fibres generally have higher levels of aerobic endurance and are thus particularly efficient at producing ATP from oxidation of carbohydrates and fats. The category of type-II fibres, which includes IIa and IIx fibres, has poor oxidative qualities and performs much better in anaerobic conditions. Type-IIa fibres are used primarily during shorter, higher-intensity endurance events, while type-IIx fibres appear to be primarily used in highly explosive activities. However, the specific role of IIx fibres is, as yet, not fully understood. There exists virtually no research on the recruitment of muscle fibres in equestrians. It is likely however, that type-I fibres play a prominent role, with type-II fibres recruited during intensive, explosive activities such as jumping.

---

good indication for aerobic endurance and is useful to determine and compare levels of fitness between sedentary individuals and athletes participating in different disciplines.

Lactate threshold: the exercising equivalent of 'the point of no return'

Let us return briefly to the important concept of lactate threshold, as it may be considered to hold the key for exercising longer and harder, without succumbing to fatigue – an aspect particularly important in riding, as preliminary findings seem to suggest a relationship between lower levels of fitness and higher fall rates in jockeys (Hitchens *et al.* 2011). Readers might recall at this point that one of the by-products of glycolysis is pyruvic acid, which, in the absence of oxygen is converted into lactate. During oxidative phosphorylation (i.e. in the presence of oxygen), pyruvic acid enters the Krebs cycle and is converted into ATP. At increasing intensities of exercise, the lactate threshold reflects the interaction between the aerobic and anaerobic metabolic systems. The onset of lactate accumulation is likely to be caused by a combination of additional anaerobic energy systems (i.e. glycolysis) producing additional by-products of lactate and existing levels of pyruvate acid exceeding oxidative capacities (Cerretelli and Samaja 2003). The lactate threshold is therefore traditionally considered the dividing line between moderate, aerobic and high-intensity, anaerobic exercise and is usually expressed as the percentage of maximal oxygen uptake at which it occurred (% VO_{2max}; Kenney *et al.* 2012). Incidentally, athletes (and riders) who are able to exercise at higher intensities without accumulating lactate are generally at an advantage, as lactate contributes to muscular fatigue. In numerical terms, this means that riders with lactate thresholds of 80% of their VO_{2max} will be able to ride their horses at higher intensities and for longer than riders with excessive lactate

The battle of the sexes

In modern equestrian sports, male and female riders generally compete on equal terms, with exceptions in vaulting and racing. But while physiological differences are unlikely to cause any substantial advantages, male and female riders should nevertheless bear in mind how they differ, if for no other reason than to develop the most appropriate approach to fitness and conditioning. Men are on average bigger and stronger than women – no surprises there! Owing to hormonal differences, most notably greater testosterone levels in men (responsible for bone formation and increased muscle mass) and estrogen in women (influences fat deposition in the thighs and hips), men also have considerably higher percentages of fat-free mass than women; the average fat content of men reaches 15% of total body mass compared with 25% in women. Fat-free mass obviously means more muscle, partly explaining differences in strength – although, having said this, if strength is expressed per unit of muscle, research has been unable to detect sex differences in trained individuals (Schantz *et al.* 1983). In terms of muscle distribution, women have a higher percentage of muscle mass in their lower bodies. With regard to cardiovascular and respiratory function, many of the differences between men and women can be explained by their size, differences in blood haemoglobin and, perhaps somewhat regrettably, by differences in average levels of activity: maximum oxygen consumption of normally active but untrained 18–22-year-old students has been determined at 38–42 ml/kg/minute for women, while men achieved rates of 44–50 ml/kg/minute. Incidentally, regardless of sex, beyond the age of 25–30 years, maximum oxygen consumption of inactive individuals decreases by about 1% a year (Kenney *et al.* 2012). While maximal heart rates in males and females are generally the same, women on average have higher heart rates at absolute levels of submaximal exercise. Women are smaller and thus have smaller hearts, which simply need to pump faster to get sufficient blood to the muscles. In addition, lower blood haemoglobin levels mean somewhat less oxygen, requiring, again, more blood to make up the difference. In summary, some of the sex differences found between men and women may be because men frequently lead more active lifestyles, resulting in better levels of fitness. Still, the good news is that long-term benefits and adaptations to training are the same for both men and women!

accumulation at 60% of their VO_{2max}. Moderate- to high-intensity endurance training is known to positively affect levels of VO_{2max} and may need to be considered by riders in addition to equestrian activities. We will focus more on this topic throughout the following sections.

Heart rates during exercise: my heart will go on…

The preceding sections have outlined the importance of increased blood flow and associated oxygen delivery to muscles. The only manner in which the body is able to achieve greater levels of blood flow is, of course, to induce relevant changes to the cardiovascular system. While there are a number of additional components relevant to measuring cardiovascular capacity in the field of sport and exercise physiology (such as stroke volume, cardiac output, blood pressure and blood flow) we focus on the simplest yet most informative cardiovascular output signals, namely heart rate, oxygen consumption and their connection to exercise. Linear relationships between heart rate and oxygen consumption during exercise have been well documented (Arts and Kuipers 1994; Franklin *et al.* 1980), meaning that exercise intensities can easily be inferred from heart rate values.

In most individuals, average resting heart rates have been recorded at 60–80 beats/minute, while much lower levels have been found in trained endurance athletes. Immediately prior to exercise, the body usually reacts with an increase in heart rate, commonly known as the 'anticipatory response' – explaining why people might feel their heart rates going up even before they have got off the sofa! Similarly to oxygen consumption, heart rates also increase proportionally with exercise intensity (e.g. Whipp *et al.* 1981). Contrary to oxygen consumption, however, heart rate continues to increase proportionally until it almost reaches the individual's maximal capacity, at which point it starts to plateau. Maximum heart rates (HR_{max}) are recorded following an all-out effort at the point of 'volitional' fatigue. By the way, even though the term 'volitional' fatigue indicates that test subjects still have their wits about them to indicate when it is time to stop, the reality of an 'HR_{max} test' can be a lot less civilized, to the point of subjects nearly fainting and throwing up!

When exercise intensities are held relatively constant, heart rate at first increases rapidly; then it plateaus at a steady-state heart rate, the level at which circulatory function is optimally performed for that particular intensity of work. Once intensity increases, the heart rate will settle at a new steady state after approximately two to three minutes. The concept of steady-state heart rates, much like oxygen consumption, is a useful indicator of fitness: individuals with lower steady-state heart rates at fixed exercise intensity usually have better cardiovascular endurance capacities than individuals with comparatively higher steady-state heart rates. To improve such levels of cardiovascular endurance or 'fitness', it is therefore necessary to condition the body to be able to perform at higher intensity rates but with increasingly lower heart rates. Research proposes that exercising slightly below or around lactate threshold levels is the most effective at increasing cardiorespiratory endurance (Dwyer and Bybee 1983; Faria *et al.* 2005). In an ideal setting, this would mean determining individual lactate threshold and corresponding heart rate levels in a suitable laboratory before devising individual exercise programmes. Unfortunately though, this may not always be feasible. General guidelines stipulate therefore that, for unconditioned individuals, a heart rate of 60 per cent of their maximal heart rate is sufficient to improve endurance performance, while moderately trained people will need to up their workloads to at least 70 per cent of HR_{max} for exercise to have the desired effect (e.g. Howley 2001; Whaley *et al.* 2007). For individuals with higher levels of cardiovascular fitness, these intensities are unlikely to be of sufficient stimulus for fitness improvement (Wenger and MacNab 1975) and may thus need to be set at more ambitious levels. A study by Azevedo *et al.* (2011) suggested that, in highly conditioned men, exercise intensities may even need to be as high as 78–93 per cent of HR_{max}. Care must be taken when applying generalized training principles to female athletes (riders), as women generally have higher heart rate responses than men to submaximal exercise (see also reference box 'The battle of the sexes'). Before starting out on any exercise regimen, individuals should therefore, at the very least, be able to estimate their general levels of fitness to prevent exercise intensities from being too low or, worse, too high.

Rule of thumb for maximal heart rates

Performing an HR_{max} test can be somewhat unpleasant and even dangerous for some groups of people, most notably those who are sedentary or elderly or who have medical conditions. Researchers are continuously searching for a reliable, risk-free way of determining HR_{max}. The current most accepted way of calculating maximal heart rate without having to undergo gruelling levels of exertion is to subtract an individual's age from what is generally considered the highest heart rate the human body can achieve, namely 220 beats/minute. The relevant formula subsequently looks as follows:

$$HR_{max} = 220 - age \text{ (years)}$$

However, as Robergs and Landwehr (2002) argue in their review on the scientific history of the formula, it is far from precise, as it was developed on the basis of 11 references, using secondary, rather than primary data. Anyone using the above formula should do so with the necessary caution and should use any resulting datasets as approximate values only.

Settling the age-old question: is riding sport?

It will undoubtedly have become clear by now that the study of sport and exercise physiology is extremely complex and involves a considerable array of factors, some of which we have covered in the preceding text. To gain a thorough understanding of both the metabolic demands and the potential conditioning effects of equestrian sports, understanding the principles of sport and exercise physiology are, of course, vital. To date, some research efforts have been undertaken to investigate the physiological characteristics in equestrian sports in more detail. But, as with many other areas of rider-related research, there remains much to be uncovered.

In their extensive review on physiological and biomechanical parameters in equestrian sports, Douglas *et al.* (2012) quite rightly state that one of the difficulties in determining the metabolic cost of riding lies in the inherent differences of the various equestrian disciplines. Furthermore, as with other sports, variations in skill levels are likely to play a role in determining actual workload. Essentially then, the obvious question that presents itself in this: how physically demanding is horse riding?

At the walk

Let us start with the most sedate of equestrian activities, walking, and work our way upwards.[3] De Barros Souza *et al.* (2008) investigated metabolic and cardiovascular changes during walk in young female riders with no prior experience and a sedentary lifestyle. While the results provided evidence of some slight increases in oxygen consumption and cardiorespiratory parameters in the first five minutes of exercise, they were not indicative of particular physical strain on the rider. Similarly, in studies by Devienne and Guezennec (2000) and Westerling (1983), physiological parameters measured in participants riding at a walk only reached values indicative of light exercise. More specifically, at a walk, average heart rates were recorded between 102 beats/minute and 108 beats/minute (Devienne and Guezennec 2000; Westerling 1983) with VO_2 values of 0.64 ± 0.27 litres/minute (Devienne and Guezennec 2000). Riding at a walk therefore is unlikely to produce any significant conditioning effects in healthy individuals. Nevertheless, regardless of these low intensities in walk, de Barros Souza *et al.* (2008) argue, quite rightly, that engaging in activities with low physiological demands may be beneficial to populations with specific disorders or disabilities. Aspects relating to positive health implications of treatments using, for example, hippotherapy are also discussed in more detail in Chapter 6.

At the trot

The trot, on the other hand, is physiologically more demanding, with heart rates recorded by Westerling (1983) as 163 ± 19 beats/minute at a rising trot and as 170 ± 15 beats/minute at a sitting trot for experienced riders. Heart rates ranged from 130–145 beats/minute and 135–170 beats/minutes in female elite riders and 90 beats/minute and 100 beats/minute for one male elite rider. Devienne and Guezennec (2000) measured variables, such as heart rates, as ranging from 126–135 beats/minute and VO_2 values of 1.47 ± 0.28 litres/minute for experienced riders, with steady states for VO_2 being attained after one minute of trotting.

And at the canter

Not surprisingly, perhaps, even greater increases in physiological intensity were detected for canter, with mean heart rates of 172 ± 18 beats/minute for experienced riders. Values for female elite riders' heart rates ranged from 135 beats/minute to 172 beats/minute, with 98 beats/minute for the male elite rider in Westerling's study. Devienne and Guezennec also recorded higher values than in the trot, with heart rates at 144 ± 18 beats/minute and VO_2 levels of 1.90 ± 0.3 litres/minute for experienced riders. It seems, then, that an increase in equine speed also results in greater levels of exertion in riders, possibly because of greater demands on the rider's musculoskeletal system to stabilize the body.

Metabolic costs of different disciplines: who works hardest?

While the studies discussed so far investigated the metabolic cost of different equine gaits, the question that needs answering is how demanding different equestrian disciplines might be. There are a handful of studies that seem to provide at least a provisional answer. As we have seen, Devienne and Guezennec (2000) were able to show a progressive increase in oxygen consumption from dressage training in walk (0.7 ± 0.18 litres/minute), trot (1.47 ± 0.28 litres/minute) and canter (1.9 ± 0.3 litres/minute) to mean VO_2 values of 2.4 ± 0.35 litres/minute during the jumping of a course of 12 obstacles of 1.0–1.1 metres in height. These findings closely mirrored those by Westerling (1983), who showed that the heart rates of two riders over a course of show jumps almost immediately reached maximal values previously obtained during a bicycle ergometer test. Oxygen uptake was measured at 2.38 litres/minute and 1.73 litres/minute, representing 73 per cent and 78 per cent of the riders' maximal oxygen consumption. Showjumping riders in a study by Gutiérrez Rincón et al. (1992) also achieved heart rates above 90 per cent of their HR_{max}, with corresponding lactate levels that suggested the involvement of anaerobic pathways (4–8 mmol/litre).

A more recent study by Roberts et al. (2010) comparing the metabolic cost of the three phases in a one-day event (dressage, DR, showjumping, SJ, and cross-country jumping, XC) in female equestrians reached similar conclusions: oxygen consumption increased progressively from the dressage phase (DR: 20.4 ± 4 ml/kg/minute; $60 \pm 12\%$ VO_{2max}), via the showjumping (SJ: 28.1 ± 4.2 ml/kg/minute; $83 \pm 12\%$ VO_{2max}) to the cross-country phase (XC: 31.2 ± 6.6 ml/kg/minute; $93 \pm 19\%$ VO_{2max}), supported by increasing lactate levels (DR 4.8 ± 1.8 mmol; SJ 7.8 ± 2.4 mmol; XC 9.5 ± 2.7mmol) and heart rate (DR 157 ± 15 beats/minute; SJ 180 ± 11 beats/minute; XC 184 ± 11 beats/minute) levels. Interestingly, lactate levels seen in the showjumping phase were comparable to those seen in hurdlers (Beaulieu et al. 1995) and rugby players (McLean 1992), while values following the cross-country phase were similar to those seen in sprinters (Beaulieu et al. 1995) and speed skaters (Rundell 1996), providing strong evidence that riding should be considered a sport – unless anyone questions the nature of sprinting, rugby or speed skating!

The discipline of National Hunt races, whereby horse and jockey tackle solid obstacles at racing speeds, has also been shown to be of considerable metabolic cost, with recorded mean peak heart rates of 184 beats/minute and mean lactate levels of 7.1 mmol (Trowbridge *et al.* 1995). Researchers have reasoned that the forward position adopted by riders when going over jumps and riding at speed increases physiological demands on the body (Devienne and Guezennec 2000; Roberts *et al.* 2010; Trowbridge *et al.* 1995), owing to the greater muscular work required of legs, arms and back muscles.

To summarize, empirical evidence to date seems to indicate quite clearly that the discipline of dressage is, at least from a physiologically point of view, the least demanding, followed by showjumping, with eventing and racing clearly requiring the most from the rider in terms of aerobic and anaerobic fitness. It also remains to be said that, while it seems evident that riders require at least some levels of muscular strength, endurance and flexibility, in particular for coordination and postural stabilization (Terada *et al.* 2004), current research findings on these topics remain inconclusive, with inconsistent approaches to their measurement (Douglas *et al.* 2012).

Long-term benefits: does riding get you fit?

While we can agree that horse riding at higher intensities, and certainly at a canter, gallop and over obstacles, is physically demanding, there still remains the question as to whether participating in equestrian sports on a regular basis will improve fitness levels to any great extent. Anthropometric profiles of equestrian athletes might present some initial indications as to the effect of regular riding-related exercise. Several studies registered average body fat percentages of amateur competitive equestrians ranging between 23.4 ± 5.3 per cent (Roberts *et al.* 2010) and 28.6 ± 6.5 per cent in female collegiate riders (Alfredson *et al.* 1998). These values proved to be higher than in other sporting disciplines such as swimming, sprinting or cross-country skiing (Roberts *et al.* 2010). The comparatively high values of 28.6 ± 6.5 per cent detected by Alfredson *et al.* (1998) might give special cause for thought regarding the effectiveness of equestrian sport as practised at amateur level to improve overall body conditioning but this may be due to other issues, such as inappropriate nutrition. Following a 14-week equitation programme, Meyers (2006) found only non-significant decreases in body fat percentage from 25.1 ± 1.1 per cent before intervention to 23.5 ± 0.9 per cent post-intervention. Once again, however, the non-significant nature of the decrease might also be put down to other factors, including the duration of the programme.

In a study assessing general exercise responses in female collegiate riders, Meyers and Sterling (2000) investigated fitness parameters including VO_{2max}, pulmonary ventilation (VE_{max}, i.e. the amount of air taken in by the lungs per minute) and general strength and muscular endurance parameters. Collegiate riders scored lower than established norms for young females in the cardiorespiratory and strength variables, while achieving average to above average scores for muscular endurance exercises such as sit-ups and curl-ups. While Meyers (2006) found that after the 14-week equitation training programme of five hours/week at an average intensity of 68 per cent HR_{max} cardiorespiratory values, such as VO_{2max} and VE_{max}, increased slightly yet non-significantly. The only notable changes were recorded in muscular power output, arguably due to the intensity of the work of the legs in maintaining balance, posture and equine impulsion. Once again, the somewhat unimpressive nature of physiological changes may well be because of insufficient time spent training.

On the other hand, the previously discussed study by Westerling (1983) also investigated general fitness levels using standard testing equipment and proce-dures (e.g. bicycle ergometers and strength testing protocols). The metabolic cost of riding was investigated in experienced compared with elite riders. A group of physically active non-riders was also used as a control group for strength testing. Results showed that the two female elite riders had superior maximal aerobic capacity compared with the other two groups in the study, with VO_{2max} values of 48 ml/kg/minute and 57 ml/kg/minute. The one male elite rider was reported to reach maximum oxygen consumption at 58 ml/kg/minute. Still, even the experi-enced (female) riders, who rode 3–14 hours/week, reached slightly higher levels of maximal oxygen consumption (43.8 ml/kg/minute) than the standard values for women of the same age and weight. Similarly, elite riders also had lower heart rates at submaximal workloads than the experienced rider group. In view of the slightly superior fitness parameters of the elite riders and the comparatively better-conditioned experienced riders in the study by Westerling (1983) compared with the collegiate riders tested by Meyers and Stirling (2000) and Meyers (2006), initial conclusions may be drawn that intensive participation in equestrian sports at sufficiently high level is likely to result in improved cardiorespiratory endurance. However, the results must be interpreted with caution, as only two female elite riders and one male elite rider were tested. Considering that mean VO_{2max} values for male elite athletes from other disciplines are reported to vary between 57 ml/kg/minute and 86 ml/kg/minute, the cardiorespiratory endurance capacity of the male rider may be considered somewhat low. Female elite athletes' cardiorespiratory endurance levels have been reported to range between 48 ml/kg/minute and 62 ml/kg/minute, placing the elite female riders from Westerling's study in the low to middle rank. While it could be argued that elite riders might benefit from the higher workloads associated with a professional life with horses, fitness levels are still not comparable with those of elite athletes in other sports. More research clearly needs to be conducted to be able to draw valid conclusions about the broader equestrian population, as variations between riders are considerable. Devienne and Guezennec (2000) point out that at least some of the variability in physiological parameters might be attributable to differences in equine temperament. Their findings confirmed that those horses which required the most active work from the rider, also led to the highest metabolic costs. Furthermore, variations in how riding sessions are conducted are likely to have a considerable effect on overall metabolic costs. Riders who spend a large amount of their training time in walk are likely to stimulate cardiorespiratory systems a lot less than riders predominantly trotting or cantering.

Furthermore, it should be noted that the studies examined here (e.g. Meyers and Stirling 2000; Stirling 2006; Westerling 1983) used different testing modali-ties for determining fitness levels (e.g. cycle ergometers versus treadmill testing), which may distort reported levels of fitness parameters. There can be no doubt that additional studies are necessary to determine more definitely the conditioning and training potential of equestrian sports. However, in the meantime, riders are reminded of the fact that findings from studies involving extensive canter and jump training clearly show higher heart rates and lactate levels, indicating the potential for greater conditioning effects (Gutiérrez Rincón *et al.* 1992; Roberts *et al.* 2010; Trowbridge *et al.* 1995). Riders who decide that they wish to benefit from the more demanding elements of equestrian sports might choose to include regular jump and speed sessions into their training regimen – always bearing in mind the necessary safety and welfare precautions for themselves and their horses. But, in addition to any riding-related fitness regimens, riders of all levels would be well served to engage in additional sporting activities that stimulate sufficient levels of cardiorespiratory exertion. It should also be noted that before starting any kind of exercise regimen, individuals should consult a qualified medical practitioner to ensure that they are free from any adverse medical or health conditions.

Fitness and safety: not just an afterthought!

The question of whether horse riding is a sport can, on the basis of existing evidence at least, be put to rest. Riding in trot and canter may certainly be classified as moderate exercise, with jumping efforts demanding even greater cardiorespiratory exertions. The level at which participation in equestrian sports actually leads to the increase of levels of rider fitness is nevertheless dependent on the specifics of each training session, the temperament of the horse and, in all likelihood, the efficiency and effectiveness of the rider.

While it is therefore easily possible for riders to not work themselves into a sweat, there are some disciplines that can easily be considered high intensity. Showjumping (Gutiérrez Rincón *et al.* 1992), eventing (Roberts *et al.* 2010), National Hunt racing (Trowbridge *et al.* 1995) and even polo (Wright and Peters 2008) have been shown to require the involvement of anaerobic pathways. As a result, participating riders should, ideally, possess appropriate fitness levels to support optimal performance on the one hand and to ensure rider (and equine) safety on the other. Considering that riders have to balance themselves, help to balance their horses and be able to give horses clear, correct aids right until the end of a training session or competition, cardiorespiratory endurance should be sufficient to allow riders to perform to the same level of effectiveness and efficiency throughout the entire time they sit on their horses. Findings from a study investigating the relationship between the incidence of fall rates and physiological attributes in jockeys seem to be supporting such claims (Hitchens *et al.* 2011). Factors such as higher body mass index (e.g. weight/height ratios) and lower aerobic and anaerobic fitness were associated with an increased risk of falling. Higher fitness levels are therefore likely to prevent loss of balance and coordination from the untimely onset of muscular fatigue. Additional findings by Roberts *et al.* (2010) denoted mean fluid loss at the end of a one-day event, resulting in a decrease of 1.6 ± 1.1 per cent of bodyweight. Previous studies have found that weight loss of that extent is likely to cause deterioration in the capacity to perform high-intensity exercise (Nielsen *et al*. 1981). In a cross-country or jumping event, this may lead to the rider being unable to safely guide the horse through to the end of the course, with potentially serious repercussions. While the necessary care should be taken when generalizing findings regarding the relationship between fitness and safety on the basis of relatively few empirical studies, they should nevertheless be considered important pointers for riders and researchers alike. In the search for additional means to improve elements of performance, safety and equine welfare, particular attention should be paid to all aspects of rider fitness and training.

Disordered eating and performance: weighty issues in horse sports

It is a sad fact of modern, primarily Western, society that many women seem to have developed an unhealthy obsession with their physical appearance – a phenomenon that has been referred to as 'normative discontent' (Rodin *et al*. 1985). In a sport that, at least at amateur level, is dominated by women (e.g. Hedenborg and White 2012; Meyers and Sterling 2000; see also Chapter 6), any discussion on rider fitness and performance is therefore likely to turn sooner or later to the topic of body weight. The fact that, in a number of competitive equestrian disciplines, the appearance of either the horse–rider combination (for example, in Western or dressage) or the rider (for example, the vaulter in the discipline of vaulting) is likely to influence performance scores, adds a further incentive for participants to take care of their physical appearance. Furthermore, an increasing sensibility towards equine welfare might arguably lead to much more attention being paid to the impact heftier riders are likely to have on general equine health, soundness and locomotion.

To date, only a handful of studies have investigated the effect of weight on the workload and associated kinematic variables of horses. Thornton *et al*. (1987) found that a dead weight of ten per cent of the horse's own body weight attached to where a rider would sit caused a significant increase in metabolic cost, while Gottlieb *et al*. (1988) found similar effects in draught horses. Of course, these results are not all that surprising, as metabolic cost has been found to rise in direct proportion to the mass supported by the muscles (Taylor *et al*. 1980). So how much is too much for a horse? Historically, the cut-off point seemed to have been set at 20 per cent of the horse's weight (Powell *et al*. 2008). However, more recent research concluded that when trained endurance horses were required to carry additional loads of 20–30 per cent of their own body weight without corresponding increases in cannon bone circumference, an increased percentage of these horses suffered biomechanical failure (Garlinghouse *et al*. 1999). Powell *et al*. (2008) investigated the effect of additional weight loads and found no differences in heart rate, plasma lactate concentrations or indicators of skeletal muscle damage for horses when working with an additional weight of 15–20 per cent. Heart rate and work rate increased significantly when horses carried 25–30 per cent of their body weight, with plasma lactate concentrations and indicators of muscle damage significantly higher for horses carrying 30 per cent of their weight, leaving the authors to conclude that the lighter type of riding horse should not be required to carry loads in excess of 20 per cent of their own body weights, mirroring previously quoted traditional guidelines. However, future studies are needed to confirm the relationships between rider weight, equine welfare and performance.

In light of the combined factors of substantial female participation, aesthetic considerations and an ever-increasing concern with matters of equine welfare, one might assume that an obsession with being thin and associated disordered eating would be particularly prevalent among female equestrians. Indeed, in one of the very few studies on the topic, Torres-McGehee *et al.* (2011) found the prevalence of disordered eating to be at 42 per cent (38.5 per cent for English-style and 48.9 per cent for Western riders) in female American collegiate equestrians. These levels are comparable to those found among, for example, modern dancers (45.6 per cent) but lower than in gymnasts (50 per cent) (Black *et al.* 2003). Clearly, especially in view of the serious health risks associated with eating disorders (Smink *et al.* 2012), considerable attention must be paid to helping young equestrians develop a positive attitude to their bodies, fitness and health.

And yet, anecdotal evidence suggests that individuals at risk of disordered eating practices in equestrian sports are not only young, female riders but also male professional jockeys. One of the integral features of racing is the handicapping of horses, requiring them to carry a particular weight allocated on the basis of previous performances (Warrington *et al.* 2009). Jockeys are therefore required to 'make the weight' of the horse that they have been contracted to ride. While the racing industry and racehorse owners consider weight regulations an effective way to ensure fairness of the race, the health risks to jockeys are considerable. Weight restrictions are set by the relevant racing authorities but they generally range around 60 kg and 70 kg, including clothing and tack, for flat and National Hunt races, respectively (Cotugna *et al.* 2011; Warrington *et al.* 2009). To ensure that they do not top the scales above the permitted weight on race day, jockeys have been known to resort to a number of unhealthy practices. Excessive use of heat rooms, vomiting and measures to encourage dehydration (Cotugna *et al.* 2011), in addition to limiting the daily intake of calories in the days before a race frequently results in constant weight cycling. Literature investigating the effect of weight ranges in other athletic disciplines suggests that weight cycling can have detrimental effects on health and performance (Walberg Rankin 2006). Combined with the fact that races take place seven days a week, without a definable off-season (Cotugna *et al.* 2011; Warrington *et al.* 2009), jockeys are under continuous strain to conform to the restrictions placed upon them. Health implications associated with these severe weight-loss practices have been identified as low bone mineral density (Dolan *et al.* 2012; Warrington *et al.* 2009), low percentage of body fat (Warrington *et al.* 2009) and poor hydration practices (Cotugna *et al.* 2011; Warrington *et al.* 2009). Long-term effects are therefore likely to include damage to the kidneys and the heart (Cotugna *et al.* 2011), general impairment of performance and greater susceptibility to fractures, which, given the high-risk nature of racing (also see Chapter 5), can have particularly grave consequences. The level of personal risk that jockeys are being placed under by standard requirements and regulations of the racing authorities are astounding, not least in view of the high level of popularity of horse racing. While in the past concerns for the health and welfare of race horses have been raised (e.g. Evans and McGreevy 2011; McGreevy and Ralston 2012), serious attention should also be paid to the wellbeing of jockeys.

Concluding thoughts

Riders can rest assured that the activity to which they are committed and that they practice so diligently can, indeed, be considered a sport – at least if it is practized primarily at the higher intensities of trot and canter. What is more, disciplines involving jumping and galloping have an even greater metabolic cost and require considerable levels of aerobic and anaerobic fitness. However, while efforts have been made to kickstart scientific investigations of the physiological requirements for riding, there is still much that we do not yet know. Findings relating to the specifics of metabolic costs across all levels of ability and a wider range of equestrian disciplines, muscular strength and endurance and, more specifically, which muscles are primarily used during riding, as well as ranges of movement and flexibility, all still need to be investigated more thoroughly. Nevertheless, in view of existing empirical evidence, as well as anecdotal wisdom, that physical fitness might also help in preventing riding related accidents, a well-thought-out conditioning regimen should feature in every rider's training programme, with due consideration of relevant nutritional requirements.

Chapter highlights

1. The field of sport and exercise physiology and, by extension, rider physiology is concerned, on the one hand, with the different functions of bodily organs, systems and cells, and on the other with the structure of various body parts; i.e. anatomy.
2. The concept of 'homeostasis' describes the regulation and stabilization of the internal environment of a body to allow for optimal health and functioning. During physical exertion, the body needs to work harder to maintain homeostasis.
3. The first law of thermodynamics states that, while energy can be converted from one form to another, it can never be destroyed or created. This means that, in order to function, the body needs to take in energy in the form of carbohydrates, fats and proteins.
4. Carbohydrates are the most important energy source during exercise, with fats being used primarily during less intensive, but long bouts of exercise. Under normal circumstances, proteins are primarily responsible for sustaining the body's chemical reactions.

5. To produce adenosine triphosphate (ATP), the primary 'energy currency', the body engages in one of, or a combination of, three metabolic pathways, depending upon the availability of oxygen. The ATP-PCr (phosphocreatine) system and the glycolytic system do not require oxygen and are anaerobic pathways. In contrast, the oxidative system only functions when oxygen is present and is therefore considered to be an aerobic pathway.

6. The intensity of exercise or 'metabolic cost' can be analyzed using a number of physiological parameters. The measurements of oxygen consumption, heart rate and lactate accumulation are relatively straightforward and commonly used.

7. The metabolic cost of the three equine gaits increases more or less incrementally with their speed. The walk is not thought to produce any conditioning effects, while trot and canter can be classified as moderately to highly demanding, depending on additional factors such as riders' level of fitness and ability and characteristics of the horse.

8. Jumping and galloping activities such as showjumping, cross-country jumping, racing and polo have all been shown to be highly demanding, frequently involving the recruitment of anaerobic pathways.

9. To derive long-term conditioning effects from equestrian activities, riders should especially include faster gaits and jump training, while always taking the necessary safety precautions. Riders of all levels are likely to benefit from additional exercise regimens, assuming that they have cleared their intentions with a qualified medical practitioner.

10. In addition to associated health benefits, appropriate levels of cardiorespiratory fitness may also delay the onset of muscular and overall fatigue and help prevent horse and rider accidents.

11. Equestrian athletes, most notably those participating in aesthetic disciplines and horse racing, may be at risk of developing disordered eating practices. Attention should be paid to helping equestrians develop a positive attitude to their bodies, fitness and health.

3 Sport psychology in equestrian sport

Merely mind games?

Introduction: the problem of performing when it matters most

It is probably one of the most common problems of competitive riders in the world and across any equestrian discipline: in training at home, horse and rider perform admirably, with the horse reacting to the most subtle of aids, moving with elasticity and impulsion, clearing the most technical fences with height to spare, while the rider remains calm and in control throughout. But come competition day, the interaction between horse and rider frequently leaves a lot to be desired. The first signs of strain usually show in the warm-up arena. All of a sudden the horse fails to respond obediently, moving more stiffly or less 'through' than usual. Given a bit of time, the more competent or experienced riders might manage to resolve their most immediate problems, while their novice counterparts continue to work themselves and their horses into a frenzy. As soon as the combination enters the ring and the bell or starter gun sounds, things quickly deteriorate even further: the horse visibly tenses and either refuses to go or rushes forward, seemingly paying no attention to its rider.

Most of the time, riders still manage to somehow 'muddle through' and complete the dressage test, showjumping or cross-country course, or other competitive challenge. They might even be lucky enough that their apparent difficulties failed to show and they end up being rewarded with a decent score. Much more often, though, the competitive results do not reflect the kind of performance of which horse and rider are, in fact, capable. Considering the amount of time, money and effort that most riders spend to prepare themselves and their horses for competition, such outcomes are always frustrating and often enough simply devastating.

This particular scenario is only one example where horse–rider performance seems to be impaired by something other than riding ability, skill or experience. At competitive events, which, by their very nature are focused on performance output, the discrepancy between performing optimally and performing below expectation is particularly obvious. But there are a number of other situations in the daily life of a rider that, considered objectively, should not present a problem. Yet, due to the interpretation of circumstances by the rider, the relevant task turns into a challenge or, worse, a serious threat. A hack in the woods, for example, really demands nothing different in terms of riding skills than an outdoor menage surrounded by trees. However, to many riders, taking the horse into an environment that varies from their daily routine is a cause for alarm. The horse might, so they reason, spook at birds in the trees (which it might also do in an outdoor arena). It might fail to respond to the aids and either bolt or refuse to move (again, if the likelihood exists while out on a hack, chances are that the horse does not respond particularly well to the aids at home either). And so the list goes on: a training session with a well-known trainer the rider might want to impress; a different or higher obstacle in showjumping; taking the horse to a different venue for the first time; and so forth. These are all examples of situations which, depending on their level of experience, riders should be able to deal with, but which often enough do not go as well as expected. The reasons are manifold: riders are worried or apprehensive; they feel the pressure of expectation from those around them; they lack confidence in their own or their horse's ability; they lose focus at a crucial moment or aim for entirely unsuitable or unrealistic goals – in short, they often do not manage to develop an appropriate mindset to deal with the situation at hand.

Suffice it to say that the problems outlined above are not unique to the rider. Quite to the contrary, most athletes, no matter which sport they participate in, will have encountered the problem of not performing as well as they could have because of a suboptimal state of mind. It is therefore not altogether surprising that the scientific discipline of sport psychology has received considerable interest over the past few decades. As a way of definition, sport psychology is concerned with the investigation, analysis and evaluation of the impact of different psychological foundations, processes and consequences on sport-related performance. While published research on sport psychological concepts in equestrian sports is still relatively sparse, the psychological make-up of riders, including semi-stable personality traits and situation-induced mood and emotional states, is thought to impact considerably on the quality of the horse–rider relationship and on subsequent performance (e.g. Meyers *et al.* 1997; Pretty 2000a; Wolframm and Micklewright 2009, 2010a, 2010b, 2011a, 2011b).

This chapter therefore provides insights into some of the psychological processes likely to play a role in rider performance and how these might impact on horse–rider interaction. To that end, we will review existing sport psychological research, both in equestrian sport and other sporting disciplines, to support and explain relevant findings. Practical applications of sport psychology principles are discussed with a view to improving horse–rider interaction, both from a safety and a performance point of view.

Principles of horse–rider communication: the importance of consistency

Before discussing in more detail how aspects of sport psychology might assist in improving equestrian performance, be it at grassroots or elite level, some brief attention should be paid to principles of horse–rider communication.[1] There can be no doubt that horse sports are dependent on a functioning horse–rider dyad. Ideally, horse and rider should communicate effortlessly and should perform required movements, jumps or bouts of speed with ease and in harmony, without signs of stress, coercion or even force. To that end, riders must convey their wishes to their horses calmly, clearly and consistently.

Horses are commonly thought to be able to 'sense' a rider's emotional state, perhaps through their ability for keen observation of body language and sensitivity to touch (Williams 1999). Yet, to date, there is only little scientific evidence regarding precisely how horses react to changes in human physiology and subsequent behavioral expressions (e.g. increases in heart or respiratory rate, changes in posture and tone of voice). In one of the few studies on the topic, Keeling *et al.* (2009) were able to show that horses will indeed react with an increased heart rate to riders who reported experiencing anxiety. In their study, a number of horses were either ridden or led back and forth on a set 30-metre pathway in an indoor arena. Immediately before the horse–rider combinations set off on their fourth pass, the riders were told that an umbrella would be opened, designed to spook the horses. Even though the event itself never took place, the mere thought was sufficient to raise heart rates in riders and, so the authors concluded, the heart rate of their horses, providing initial empirical evidence that horses are likely to respond to physiological symptoms of their rider or handler.

But what are the implications of such innate sensitivities to horse–rider communication and, more specifically, riding and training of horses? In a nutshell, equine training is primarily, but not exclusively, based on principles of operant conditioning (e.g. McGreevy and Boakes 2006; McGreevy and McLean 2010; Murphy and Arkins 2007), which teach the horse to associate rider aids with changes in tempo or direction. In turn, this means that, for horses to perform optimally, riders need to be in control of themselves, both physically and emotionally: any cognitive or emotional changes in the rider brought on by, for example, competition 'nerves', fear of injury or even lack of motivation or tiredness, are likely to lead to, firstly, a lack of focus (Wolframm and Micklewright 2010b; 2011a), which might result in the inappropriate or inconsistent application of aids. Secondly, subtle changes in physiological parameters (Keeling *et al.* 2009), such as muscular tension, almost invariably lead to the impairment of fine motor control and changes in how aids are given (Symes and Ellis 2009). The horse, having come to associate one particular set of aids (the operant stimulus) to a particular movement (the operant response) is likely to react to this 'new' set of aids in a different manner. Yet most riders, while perhaps dimly aware of feeling 'different', will not notice the subtle changes in physiology and subsequent biomechanics. As a result, they are likely to interpret the response from their horses as a sign of uncooperativeness – an interpretation that might, in turn, lead to additional feelings of anxiety, frustration and even anger. A vicious circle of misunderstanding between horse and rider is invoked, which can be difficult to break.

Even if riders are able to prevent their horses from any extreme reactions, such as shying, bucking, rearing or bolting, any subsequent interaction will nevertheless be marred by tension and will almost invariably lead to a decrease in performance and, perhaps even more importantly, the safety of horse and rider. In addition to learning the relevant riding related skills and techniques, developing strategies to prevent or contain the emergence of disruptive thought patterns, moods and emotions while riding or dealing with horses becomes a must to aspiring horsemen and -women.

Rider traits: how personality affects performance

What is it that predisposes one rider to break out in a cold sweat at the thought of riding in front of a large crowd, while another relishes the thought? Why do some riders thrive on galloping at high speeds and jumping solid obstacles, while their best friends prefer the comparatively sedate pace and high levels of accuracy of a dressage test? Of course, past experience is one thing – a rider who has fallen off one too many times is likely to react differently to a situation than someone who has never so much as had a horse stand on their foot! This is where the study of personality finds its application, focusing on how semi-permanent 'traits' or 'dispositions' might impact on an individual's thoughts, emotions and subsequent behaviors. In personality research, 'traits' are considered basic units of study (Allport 1937). They denote relatively consistent patterns of behavior and are thought to be 'semi-permanent'; that is, unlikely to change very much over time (Winter *et al.* 1998). However, intuitively we might feel that our reactions and behaviors are not the same across different types of situations. Depending on previous experiences, physical or mental wellbeing or merely because of what someone just said to us, we might react happy and carefree on one occasion, while coming across as worried and pessimistic on another. Some early critics of the semi-permanent view of personality were adamant that more credit should be given to the impact of environmental factors on human behavior (Mischel 1968, 1976, 1977). To cut a long story short, modern personality research readily accepts the interaction between semi-permanent traits and external circumstances, which may cause individuals to experience more transient internal conditions known as 'states' (Funder 2006). Understanding, therefore, how individuals might be inclined to behave at a general level and how these dispositions are likely to interact with different environmental factors can go a long way towards developing appropriate management and coping strategies for riders during training and competition. While there is little research investigating personality components in equestrian sports, much of the work that has been carried out in other sports allows us to draw valid conclusions as to the impact of personality traits on rider performance, including horse–rider interaction. And even though the study of personality can in no way provide the team selectors of the next Olympics or World Equestrian Games with a failsafe method of procuring medals, it can at least shed some light on how riders' inherent dispositions might help or hinder their sporting success.

Unfortunately – in the context of this book at least – the field of personality research is too rich and diverse to cover in great detail here.[2] The following section therefore only provides a brief overview of the most important elements to the modern study of personality and what this might mean in terms of rider performance.

So where might all of this leave us? There are a number of personality components that should be examined more closely, as they may provide initial indications on how rider personality influences different aspects of ridden performance.

Extraversion: thriving on the thrill of the experience

The personality factor of extraversion composed of semi-permanent traits of sociability, impulsiveness, activity, liveliness and excitability (Eysenck 1967), has been shown to significantly influence activity preference (e.g. David *et al.* 1997; Eysenck and Zuckerman 1978; Furnham 1981). Considerable evidence suggests that athletes who participate in high-risk sports, such as skiing, mountaineering or motorcar racing, all exhibit personality traits related to extroversion, such as arousal-seeking or sensation-seeking (Gomá I Freixanet 1991; Kerr 1991; Zuckerman 1983). As will be discussed in greater detail in Chapter 5, equestrian sports may undoubtedly be considered 'high risk', with injuries as common as one per hour of riding (Silver 2002) and hospital admission rates for equestrian injuries more than three times as high as those from motorcycling injuries (Sorli 2005). Individuals participating in equestrian sports are, in all likelihood, aware of the risk involved in dealing with an animal that usually weighs in excess of 500 kg. However, depending on the type of discipline that riders engage in, the inherent risk might remain more or less containable. An unpublished study by Wolframm (2011b) examining the personality traits of 2,678 riders across different disciplines and different competitive levels, showed differences in scores on the 'rider liveliness' scale, which closely mirrors traditional definitions of extroversion. Dressage riders tended to score lower than either riders engaged in jumping or disciplines that involve facing less-predictable situations, such as endurance riding or horseball. In the discipline of dressage, horse and rider are primarily engaged in executing a number of predefined movements as accurately as possible. Disciplines such as eventing and showjumping are inherently more dangerous, as they involve jumping over obstacles, while endurance and horseball require that the horse and rider consistently need to adapt and adjust to changing environmental situations, such as undulating terrain or other riders. Indeed, studies investigating differences in traits relating to extraversion seem to come to similar conclusions. Endurance athletes, such as middle- and long-distance runners, tend to be more introverted than sprinters (Clitsome and Kostrubala 1977). Egloff and Gruhn (1995) propose that, because they experience hedonistic tone, that is, more pleasure at increased levels of sensory stimulation, extraverts seek stimulation through physical (or social) activity and are thus inclined to take more risk. Similarly, Young and Ismail (1978) reported that individuals with higher levels of fitness are characterized as adventurous, socially bold and unconventional. Considering that disciplines related to jumping and high speeds are both physically more demanding and contain a higher risk of injury (Devienne and Guezennec 2000; Gutiérrez Rincón *et al.* 1992; Roberts *et al.* 2010), extraverted individuals are likely to prefer equestrian disciplines that involve jumping or are somewhat less predictable.

Tough-mindedness and egocentricity: 'hard as nails'

Almost all successful athletes show a single-minded determination to succeed in their chosen sport 'at all costs', indicative of personality traits relating to nonconformity and egocentricity. Anecdotal evidence suggests that, to perform well, an athlete would need to spend a substantial part of the day training and tending to his own needs. Equestrian sports, of course, are notoriously time-intensive. Riders not only need to train their horses but also need to perform or supervise additional chores that ensure equine health and welfare. Particularly at the higher levels of the sport, even more time is spent training, leaving little time for anything else. Understandably, this frequently predisposes riders towards being less compliant with the wishes of others and prioritizing their own needs.

In a study examining levels of self-esteem and general self-efficacy in 642 primarily female horseback riders, Traeen and Wang (2006) note: 'the rider also learns to take control over "raw muscles and power" and to manoeuvre in critical situations. This provides coping experience, which is valuable in a society in which traditionally masculine qualities still dominate' (p. 443). Particularly at grassroots levels and in younger years, equestrian sports are dominated by female riders (Immes 1993), yet the personality traits of tough-mindedness and assertiveness are often associated with males. Considering horses' substantial weight and strength, combined with high levels of sensitivity and speed of reaction, riders need to be committed and assertive to train horses effectively – if for no other reason than to remain safe but also to be able to perform optimally. It therefore comes as little of a surprise to find that female riders tend to demonstrate traits that are connected to higher levels of assertiveness and confidence in their own abilities to get their own way. Traeen and Wang (2006) were able to show that female riders who owned their own horses (as opposed to riding a school horse now and again) considered themselves more masculine and self-assertive and expressed higher levels of self-efficacy. Similarly, in an earlier study by Kidd *et al.* (1983) horse owners were found to have high levels of assertiveness and self-concern but low levels of cooperativeness and nurturance. As most horse owners will readily admit, there comes a time when horses may be reluctant to execute particular movements or simply refuse to do what is required of them. Under these circumstances, the dispositional tendencies of a rider to not give in easily and to keep going in the face of adversity are likely to be considerable assets!

Anxiety: when fear rules

Undoubtedly another extremely important component when it comes to personality in equestrian sport relates to anxiety. The factor of 'neuroticism' predisposes an individual towards experiencing negative emotions, such as anxiety, more strongly and is composed of individual traits such as fearfulness, self-consciousness and depressive mood disturbances. Not surprisingly, high neuroticism scores are generally considered a disadvantage in all competitive situations (e.g. Jones 2003). Previous research investigating the relationship between trait characteristics and pre-competitive states also suggests that athletes scoring high on trait-neuroticism also tend to experience greater levels of pre-competitive (i.e. situation-induced) levels of arousal. A study by Trotter and Endler (1999) examined the validity of the multidimensional interaction model of anxiety (Endler *et al.* 1991) by measuring trait and state anxiety in adolescent female competitive riders. The authors found a significant interaction between trait anxiety and situational stress components to induce state (i.e. competitive) arousal. The authors concluded that competitive equestrian sports may lead to increased levels of state arousal due to stressors involving social evaluation. It should be noted, however, that the subject group of this particular study focused only on adolescents who may be more susceptible to the stressors associated with evaluation by others. Further research should therefore also investigate levels of arousal in adult equestrians. Nevertheless, recognizing and accepting the close relationship between measures of personality and situation-specific mood states (discussed in more detail below) must be viewed as an important element to improve safety and performance in equestrian sports.

While it is clear, therefore, that the study of personality does not offer the potential for 'crystal ball gazing' and thus cannot be called a straightforward method of predicting performance in equestrian sports, it might provide general indicators as to the choice of discipline and (competitive) competence level. Future research should focus more closely on this particular field of research. In terms of practical applications, this may mean that riders could benefit from recognizing their own dispositional tendencies and choosing to participate in the equestrian discipline most appropriate to them. Lastly, personality traits are semi-permanent and thus relatively resistant to dramatic change. However, understanding and subsequent modification of related emotional, cognitive and behavioral patterns by using appropriate coping strategies or mental skills may nevertheless be important to the improvement of horse–rider performance.

Mood matters: how states can be primary predictors of performance

Seeing that dispositional tendencies only provide indicative evidence regarding choice of discipline and, to some extent, competitive potential, sport psychology research turned to examining various mood and emotional states prior to performing. By way of definition, emotions are mental states of relatively short duration, often accompanied by a physiological response. Moods are also transient, yet longer in duration and generally involving more than one emotion (Lane and Terry 2000). With regard to equestrian sports, we can be fairly certain that emotional composure is a critical factor in the interaction between horse and rider. From an anecdotal point at least, most riders readily attest to their equine partners seemingly being able to detect and react to the mood states of their riders, lead-

The five-factor model of personality in equestrian sports: higher-order 'factors' and lower-order 'facets'

After several decades of using sometimes contradictory personality scales, researchers have now come to a preliminary consensus on a general taxonomy of personality traits. The various semi-permanent hereditary personality dispositions (i.e. 'traits') may be combined to form five replicable factors or higher-order personality 'types', referred to as the 'big five' (Costa and McCrae 1992; Goldberg 1993), which have been shown to be relatively stable across different cultures and languages. Most commonly used in modern personality research, each of these five factors, namely neuroticism, extroversion, agreeableness, openness to experience and conscientiousness, are subdivided further into six lower-order 'facets' and provide a relatively detailed analysis of an individual's personality. Tables 3.1 and 3.2 provide data on personality scores for elite, amateur, leisure riders and non-riding controls (Wolframm 2011a),[3] including all five factors and corresponding facets.

ing to changes in performance. Riders who remain in control of their emotional responses and are thus less likely to experience adverse physiological effects, such as an increase in muscular tension or increased heart rate, are also more likely to produce more consistent performances when in the saddle.

Differences in emotional control: a matter of experience

Put simply, equestrian disciplines differ from other sports because they depend on the participation of horses and humans in equal parts. Certain emotional parameters may therefore exist which facilitate horse–rider interaction at a general level. To that effect, research by Wolframm and Micklewright (2010b) investigated mood states displayed by advanced compared with novice dressage riders just prior to competition. The most important findings indicate that advanced riders show lower levels of confusion than novice riders. The mood state of confusion has been characterized by negative self-perception and effect (Prapavessis 2000), as well as bewilderment and uncertainty (Terry and Lane 2000). Previous research has also associated confusion with attention inefficiencies and poor information processing (Lane and Terry 2000). From an equestrian perspective, this means that riders who are unable to maintain their focus on sports-relevant tasks or to process information appropriately are unlikely to respond correctly to the different behavioral expressions displayed by their horses. In turn, this is likely to lead to riders giving inappropriate or no aids with a subsequent drop in performance. A decrease in performance might also undermine riders' levels of confidence, potentially resulting in even greater levels of confusion – and associated consequences. For the novice riders of Wolframm and Micklewright's study

Table 3.1 Rider personality domains (higher-order) scores including standard deviations

Level	Personality domains														
	Neuroticism			Extroversion			Openness to experience			Agreeableness			Conscientiousness		
	Mean	SD	(%)	Mean	SD	(%)	Mean	SD	(%)	Mean	SD	(%)	Mean	SD	(%)
Elite	71.1	28.3	36	119.8	13.7	69	111.4	21.5	55	105.8	105.8	105.8	129.6	14.8	65
Amateur	84.8	21.7	64	115.9	16.5	62	111.3	14.7	55	107.6	107.6	107.6	122.8	20.0	43
Leisure	85.2	19.0	64	119.9	16.3	69	124.0	13.7	79	113.8	113.8	113.8	127.0	18.9	58
Non-riders	80.0	23.9	53	108.4	18.3	48	113.9	19.4	55	120.8	120.8	120.8	117.6	22.1	36

Table 3.2 Personality domains (higher-order) and facets (lower-order) raw and percentile scores for elite, amateur, leisure and non-riders

	Elite			Amateur			Leisure			Non-riders		
	Raw score	SD	(%)	Raw score	SD	(%)	Raw score	SD	(%)	Raw score	SD	(%)
NEUROTICISM												
Anxiety	13.33	6.95	53	15.17	5.51	65	15.52	5.33	73	15.88	6.29	73
Angry-hostility	13.33	4.36	62	13.95	5.4	69	14.06	5.15	69	12.26	5.8	54
Depression	10.67	6.25	48	14.63	3.72	74	13.12	3.52	63	12.15	5.53	63
Self-consciousness	11.67	6.25	37	14.63	3.72	62	13.12	3.52	45	13.96	4.44	54
Impulsiveness	16.0	6.73	56	17.02	3.48	65	16.88	3.74	65	14.85	3.72	48
Vulnerability	6.67	3.94	21	11.27	4.16	67	11.65	3.59	76	11.26	5.01	67

EXTROVERSION											
Warmth	21.22	1.92	32	21.73	4.43	41	23.12	4.57	50	21.89	4.35	41
Gregariousness	15.22	5.07	39	17.80	5.17	62	18.94	5.10	71	18.11	4.85	62
Assertiveness	20.0	3.91	84	16.80	5.35	54	17.88	4.23	62	15.44	4.89	15
Activity	21.22	5.21	80	20.95	3.97	80	20.94	2.68	80	19.15	3.64	67
Excitement seeking	18.0	5	67	18.61	3.97	73	17.24	3.63	57	14.67	6.75	41
Positive emotions	22.33	4.77	70	21.10	3.6	60	21.76	4.24	70	18.59	4.81	41
OPENNESS TO EXPERIENCE											
Fantasy	15.56	4.9	51	18.02	4.98	65	20.0	4.41	78	18.52	5.02	72
Aesthetics	17.11	5.13	48	17.34	5.68	48	21.35	4.55	75	18.74	5.78	62
Feelings	22.0	4.33	71	22.83	3.61	79	23.65	3.37	85	20.63	4.58	62
Actions	16.44	5.34	51	14.49	3.04	29	17.35	3.57	61	15.48	4.11	40
Ideas	19.44	7.67	53	17.07	4.63	37	19.94	4.07	60	19.15	6.21	53
Values	20.89	5.11	58	17.71	4.63	28	19.94	4.01	48	19.15	6.21	38
AGREEABLENESS											
Trust	19.33	4.27	28	17.34	4.08	17	19.35	5.4	28	20.93	4.8	43
Straightforwardness	18.44	4.33	24	18.32	4.72	24	20.06	4.5	38	18.96	4.24	30
Altruism	20.78	3.07	43	22.17	3.52	55	21.76	3.36	55	22.85	3.1	65
Compliance	14.33	4.69	14	14.27	4.63	14	14.82	4.28	19	18.52	5.89	55
Modesty	16.0	6.96	26	17.51	4.05	43	17.18	3.52	33	18.59	4.73	53
Tendermindedness	16.89	3.02	17	18.93	2.88	37	20.65	3.33	60	20.96	2.67	60
CONSCIENTIOUSNESS											
Competence	23.0	2.83	62	20.68	3.55	51	21.35	3.1	51	20.33	3.1	38
Order	20.33	3.46	62	18.98	5.02	54	20.71	5.35	72	18.26	5.07	42
Dutifulness	22.89	4.83	51	22.63	2.91	51	23.70	3.51	61	23.33	4.11	51
Achievement striving	23.44	2.92	83	20.98	3.91	69	21.18	5.17	69	20.07	5.79	59
Self-discipline	23.56	2.4	74	20.78	5.02	41	20.94	5.17	41	20.07	5.79	32
Deliberation	16.33	3.57	40	19.15	4.90	66	19.18	5.8	66	17.93	4.89	57

(2010b) mood states of confusion were, not altogether surprisingly, positively correlated with tension, depression and anger, indicating that especially in less experienced riders, uncertainty and lack of confidence might be closely related to other negative mood states. In short, a vicious cycle of negative mood states, poor performance and lack of confidence might emerge which, incidentally, has been confirmed by research into other sports (e.g. Beedie *et al.* 2000).

Lower levels of confusion exhibited by advanced riders are indicative of improved information processing capacity and greater levels of task-focused concentration (e.g. Lane and Terry 2000). Advanced riders are therefore in a much better position to respond quickly and appropriately to behavioral cues given by the horse, which, in itself, is facilitative to improved performance and harmony.

On the dangers of feeling anxious

When discussing emotional and mood states, clearly the most prevalent of them, especially in equestrian sports, must be that of anxiety or 'stress'. In addition to being frequently perceived as unpleasant, most riders would probably also agree that the sensation of 'being stressed' is likely to have a detrimental effect on the interaction with the horse. Even though riders should, from a technical point of view, be able to ride a horse even while feeling anxious or stressed, effective horse–rider communication often goes awry. This, of course, is why anxiety is without a doubt one of the most important issues to tackle for riders hoping to perform in a competitive setting:

> The technical skills of the contestants, if the experiment has been set up correctly, cancel each other out. The sport experiment is not concerned with the particular technical skills the subject has brought with him to the contest. His [technical] skill is not really an issue – although he fervently believes it is – since his fellow contestants also have it; they have been screened and selected very carefully indeed to ensure that their [technical] skill compares with his. The deciding factor is not his [technical] skill, but his ability to perform it under stress.
>
> (Patmore 1986: 13)

Patmore's assessment of what makes an athlete successful may be considered a truism in all sports, including equestrianism. All athletes, regardless of their sporting background, face the same issue: come competition, what counts more than anything is not so much the level of skill or technique they have at their disposal but whether they are able to reproduce it there and then.

But even though attention is primarily paid to the detrimental effect of anxiety on elite performances, associated consequences are often equally as severe for leisure or amateur riders. While they may not have to deal with a low score in competition, feeling anxious might, in extreme circumstances, cause these riders to drop out of the sport altogether. Riders who are consistently worried about what their horses might or might not do, for example while out hacking or when schooling the horse on their own, will quickly lose confidence in their own abilities and those of their horse. Worse still, hesitation or indecision during moments where presence of mind is required invariably leads to accidents, for example out on the road, jumping a fence or reacting to the horse shying, bucking or bolting. The obvious questions that present themselves then are what, exactly, is anxiety? How does it affect the rider and what can be done about it?

Anxiety, stress and arousal: the same thing?

While most of us would probably readily attest to understanding the meaning of 'anxiety', 'arousal' and, in particular, 'stress', the lay literature tends to use these terms rather indiscriminately. No doubt, the intended meaning of all such associated synonyms is the negative emotional reaction with at its source an implicit or explicit threat to the individual's mental and/or physical wellbeing. At its most fundamental level, anxiety serves a protective function by signalling to the individual to prepare for a perceived threat. It is thus worth bearing in mind that anxiety can also be useful and serve to increase motivation (Eysenck and Calvo 1992) as well as task-relevant focusing (Carver and Scheier 1986). Essentially, during stressful events a control system is activated that enables an individual to cope with the demands of the situation (commonly referred to as the 'fight or flight response'.)

Yet, especially in more modern times, it sometimes seems altogether unclear why people react with stress or anxiety in certain situations, even though objectively they do not seem to pose any real threat to the individual. A hack in the woods, for example, certainly does not present much more danger to a rider with average experience than regular schooling in the arena. Still, many riders balk at the thought of taking their horses away from their usual environment. Why might this be and what are the different elements that interlink anxiety, arousal, stress and, ultimately, ridden performance?

Traditional definitions of stress are centred on Selye's (1956) behavior-based model of stress, which focuses primarily on the body's non-specific reactions during stressful situations. The three stages of reaction ('alarm', 'resistance' and 'exhaustion') describe the body's automatic response to any kind of external demand. As such, this type of definition does not always imply stress to be a negative response, yet it highlights the dynamic interaction between the individual and the environment. Throughout their theoretical musings, Lazarus and colleagues (Lazarus 1991, 2000; Lazarus and Folkman 1984) highlight two concepts as essential to our understanding of the relational nature of stress and anxiety. The 'appraisal stage' of a stress response revolves around evaluating the significance of a situation to the individual. The 'coping stage' is focused on the cognitive, emotional or behavioral adaptations that individuals employ to deal with the demands of a particular situation. Lazarus further distinguishes the appraisal stage into primary and secondary appraisal. Primary appraisal is thought to include aspects relating to how much an individual cares about a particular situation (also referred to as *goal relevance*), whether a situation is in line with a person's personal goals (*goal congruence*) and whether a situation might impact on, or be threatening to, an individual's self-image (*type of ego-involvement*). Secondary appraisal revolves around determining who is responsible for an event (*blame or credit*), an individual's evaluation of their ability to deal with a – personally relevant – situation (*coping potential*) and to what extent the outcome of an event is likely to be in line with the individual's own goals (*future expectations*).[4] Lastly, how individuals ultimately deal with the situation and their own primary and secondary appraisal are called coping efforts and they revolve around actual strategies employed to mediate their emotional response.

If, during primary appraisal, individuals evaluate a situation both as highly desirable but also potentially very threatening to their self-image and, during secondary appraisal, find their coping potential to be insufficient, the resultant emotions are likely to be negative and may be referred to as anxiety. For example, relatively inexperienced yet ambitious showjumping riders who are keen to prove their ability but are faced with a 1.20 meter course for the first time, might experience considerable anxiety. Primary appraisal reveals that successful completion of the course is something that they desperately want (i.e. goal relevance), and also think they need in order to advance in the sport (goal congruence). They might believe that failure to succeed will make them seem less of a rider in the eyes of significant others, such as team mates or their trainer (ego involvement). Yet secondary appraisal of the riders' own coping potential might make them realize that they do not possess the appropriate skills to 'get round' the course. As a result, the obvious reaction would be heightened levels of anxiety. Conversely, if primary appraisal reveals the situation to be important to an individual yet coping potential is found to be sufficient, the emotional response is likely to be one of excitement. Continuing with our showjumping example, this would be the case for riders who had previously jumped similar courses in training and competition, and know themselves and their horse to be up to the challenge.

Most importantly perhaps, the type of coping in which riders engage, following their respective primary and secondary appraisals, can be determined and greatly enhanced through psychological skills training. As will be discussed later on, relevant psychological strategies or 'mental skills' can assist riders both in evaluating their own coping potential more accurately and also in developing better coping strategies in times of stress or anxiety. However, it should have become obvious by now that how riders perceive a certain situation is dependent on a number of factors, such as riders' individual predispositions (e.g. personality), varying mood states, previous experiences, level of riding skill and, of course, their horse's level of skill. Any future research investigating levels of stress or anxiety in horse and rider must aim to bear the potential influence of these issues in mind.

Always or only sometimes: state versus trait anxiety

Researchers now commonly accept that anxiety is multidimensional in nature and comprises trait and state components, as well as aspects relating to cognitive and somatic anxiety. As discussed at the beginning of this chapter, the personality component of trait anxiety predisposes an individual to perceive certain environmental situations as threatening (Spielberger 1988). State anxiety, on the other hand, is defined as a temporal emotional response to a situation and characterized by apprehension, fear, tension and an increase in physiological arousal (Hanton *et al.* 2004b; Jerome and Williams 2000; Woodman and Hardy 2003). Such emotional responses usually occur prior to or during a competitive event, with temporal variants including several weeks leading up to the competition and several minutes before the start of the competition. From a practical point of view, helping riders to maximize their performance necessarily means understanding the relative impact, intensity and direction of different traits and states, particularly levels of anxiety, on components of emotional control.

Body and mind: somatic and cognitive components of anxiety

Cognitive anxiety

Researchers also agree that anxiety can manifest itself as two different components (e.g. Cheng *et al.* 2008). Cognitive anxiety refers, as the name suggests, to the 'thinking' elements, i.e. worry and concern. A rider experiencing cognitive anxiety might be inclined to think things like 'I am never going to manage to jump that fence' or 'I really worry that the changes won't come off in the test'. The relationship between cognitive anxiety and performance parameters is without a doubt extremely complex. Eysenck and Calvo's (1992) processing efficiency theory explains the relationship as follows: up to a certain point, cognitive anxiety is thought to lead to an increase in effort on the task at hand and to the appropriate allocation of mental resources, which will, in turn, lead to increased performance. However, beyond a certain point, too much memory capacity is allocated to task-irrelevant thoughts (i.e. worries) and the increased effort expended can no longer compensate for the lack of working memory available for the actual task. Especially for tasks that require 'brain rather than brawn' (i.e. they involve complex thought processes rather than mere physical exertion) increased cognitive anxiety is thought to have a debilitating effect. From an applied perspective, high levels of cognitive anxiety in a dressage test are likely to lead to comparatively poorer performances than in showjumping. While showjumping, of course, requires some working memory (for example memorizing the course), a dressage test lasts longer and can be considered more complex because of the changing floor patterns. Even though showjumping is arguably more dangerous and might thus invoke greater levels of cognitive anxiety, the relative impact of cognitive anxiety is likely to be greater in dressage.

Somatic anxiety

Somatic anxiety, on the other hand, refers to physiological symptoms, such as increased muscular tension, raised heart and respiratory rates or clammy hands. While it is clear that athletes and, in fact, people in general, suffer from either one or both components of anxiety, the extent to which they affect sporting performance, individually or in combination, has been subject to much research. It seems clear, however, that differences in effect can be expected depending on the discipline and on individual differences. Increases in somatic anxiety have been found to correlate, for example, with increases in Sargent jump performance (Parfitt *et al.* 1995) and perceptual-motor speed (Jones and Cale 1989). However, Gould *et al.* (1987) found a curvilinear relationship with somatic anxiety and pistol shooting performance, indicating that, once athletes' somatic anxiety went beyond a certain level, their performance started to decrease. Pistol shooting, much like horse riding, is dependent on fine motor control and, as such, is extremely sensitive to changes in physiological arousal. As anyone who regularly participates in equestrian sport or observes different riders will know, at an advanced level the aids given by a rider are barely visible. The horse seems to responds to the rider's thoughts alone when, in fact, rider signals have become so subtle that they are barely visible to the keenest of observers. While a certain level of physiological arousal is undoubtedly beneficial when dealing with an animal weighing in excess of 500 kg, any increase beyond 'optimum' levels of arousal are thus likely to disrupt the necessary motor control. In addition to changes in motor control, riders must also bear in mind the effect of physiological changes on the quality of the aids they give to their horses.

In light of this, it is perhaps not altogether surprising that advanced riders have been found to display lower levels of somatic arousal than their less experienced counterparts (Wolframm and Micklewright 2009). To perform at an advanced level, the horse must be trained in a consistent manner, with the rider being able to apply the correct aid every single time, thus facilitating the progression in training. More elevated levels of somatic arousal, often experienced by less skilled riders, are likely to lead to a disruption of the fine motor control necessary to perform more complex movements. A rider experiencing muscular tension may still be able to communicate with a horse on a basic level, getting the horse to perform simple changes in pace and direction. Yet the interaction between horse and rider is unlikely to be as harmonious as one would wish. Riders – often inadvertently – end up pulling in their horses' mouths, bouncing up and down in the saddle (owing to tension in their lower body) or even bracing themselves in the saddle against the movement of the horse (as frequently seen in medium or extended trot). Quite simply, this is often caused by a lack of sufficient fine motor control as a result of high levels of physiological arousal. While lower levels of somatic arousal are undoubtedly also a key factor in other sports requiring fine motor skills, the sensitive nature of the horse and its ability to react and respond to arousal levels from the rider seem to make it all the more important that riders learn how to control unwanted physiological symptoms.

Does it help or hinder? Perceptions of anxiety and arousal

Many researchers now agree that different components of anxiety should not be considered individually but need to be examined in light of their interactive effect and subsequent joint impact on performance (Burton and Naylor 1997). As suggested by a number of researchers, symptoms of arousal may just as easily be indicative of positive emotions such as joy or excitement or, indeed, negative ones, such as anger or fury (Cheng *et al.* 2008; Jones 1995). However, it has also been pointed out that positive emotions do not always lead to facilitative effects on performance (Hanin 1997). The relatively common fault at the last fence in a showjumping course might be considered a case in point: having ridden fault-lessly throughout the entire course, many riders might breathe an inward sigh of relief when approaching the last fence, thinking something along the lines of 'nearly there, not much can happen now'. Feelings of relief or even excitement at the thought of having ridden 'clear' up to that point are undoubtedly positive emotions. Yet, while they may be positive in nature, they are also distracting and frequently cause riders not to pay attention to the task at hand – leading to a fault at the last. From a pragmatic standpoint, it could therefore be argued that what matters most is whether symptoms of arousal experienced by riders are in fact helpful, i.e. facilitative, during the actual performance or whether they are unhelpful, i.e. debilitative, and prevent them from performing as well as they could. Indeed, researchers have suggested that even negatively toned emotions can be facilitative to performance (Hardy and Parfitt 1991) as long as athletes are able to convert these emotions into relevant task related behaviors. Essentially then, the impact of emotional responses on performance depends primarily on whether riders interpret them as facilitative or debilitative regardless of whether the emotions are positive or negative in nature.

The sky's the limit: feelings of self-confidence

The 'million dollar question' that probably most of us would like to have answered is what, in fact, causes riders to interpret symptoms of arousal as facil-itative to performance. In fact, the answer is relatively straightforward: the concept of self-confidence has been shown to be the key on numerous occasions.

In fact, both facilitative interpretations of symptoms of arousal and feelings of

---

What's what: self-confidence and self-efficacy

Interested students of sport psychology often come across the terms 'self-efficacy' and 'self-confidence' and might notice that they are frequently used interchangeably. At a conceptual level, self-efficacy may be defined as the perception that one's coping resources are sufficient to meet situational demands. It entails an individual's notion of being able to perform a specific task successfully or deal with a particular situation (Bandura 1977a) and as such can act as a moderator to feelings and interpretations of anxiety. Self-confidence, on the other hand, is generally considered a non-specific concept of self-belief, referring to strength of trust in one's abilities, with-out specifying what these abilities are referring to (Bandura, 1997). However, both sport psychological research and laymen's literature frequently use the term self-confidence rather than self-efficacy. We will therefore follow suit and use the term 'self-confidence' unless specified otherwise.

self-confidence are considered the two most important qualities for success in competition (Hardy 1996a). Research has consistently shown that individuals with higher levels of self-confidence interpret levels of arousal as facilitative (Jones *et al.* 1994; Jones and Swain 1995). Additional research by Jones and Hanton (2001) and Mellalieu *et al.* (2003) showed that athletes who interpreted arousal symptoms as facilitative overwhelmingly indicated their mood state as 'confident'. The close interaction between directional interpretations of somatic arousal and mood states as experienced by athletes may also assist in explaining the role of self-confidence in moderating the effects of arousal on performance. A number of studies confirmed that superior athletes interpret symptoms of arousal as more facilitative than less-successful athletes, despite no differences in intensity of arousal (e.g. Hanton *et al.* 2004a; Jones *et al.* 1994; Jones and Swain 1995; Jones *et al.* 1993). At the same time, they reported higher levels of self-confidence, lending further support to the notion that:

- the facilitative interpretation of pre-competitive arousal symptoms seems to be an important predictor of superior performance; and
- self-confidence is likely be one of the most important variables moderating the interpretation of arousal.

A lack of confidence by less-skilled performers led to a loss of perception of control and subsequent loss of focus. As a result, symptoms of arousal were interpreted negatively, and thus called competitive anxiety.

In one of the first studies investigating sport psychological concepts in equestrian sports, Meyers *et al.* (1997) found that elite riders scored significantly higher in anxiety management than non-elite riders. Recent studies into pre-competitive states of equestrian dressage riders showed that experienced riders exhibited more facilitative pre-competitive mood states (Wolframm and Micklewright 2010b), lower somatic arousal and greater self-confidence scores than less experienced riders (Wolframm and Micklewright 2009). By way of explanation, Bandura's (1997c) model of self-efficacy purports the notion that beliefs regarding self-confidence are determined by mastery enactment, modelling, persuasion and perception of one's own physiological state. In advanced, experienced riders, it is likely that previous successful performance and greater levels of skill and experience heighten levels of self-confidence, which, in turn, allow for the enhanced ability to control symptoms of arousal and/or anxiety. This, in turn, may lead to more facilitative and thus performance-enhancing interpretations of arousal. Empirical evidence therefore seems to support the notion that, in equestrianism, the ability to control symptoms of anxiety is, similar to other sports, one of the contributing factors to superior performance.

The implications of the current state of equestrian-related research into situational states may thus be considered as two-fold: firstly, high levels of confidence and low levels of negative mood states such as anxiety, confusion, depression, fatigue and tension are generally considered facilitative to performance. Secondly, in addition to such 'generic' mood states, riders should also ensure that they are aware of the frame of mind that assists them in performing at their best. While certain athletes and, indeed, riders may be performing optimally under low levels of arousal or pre-competitive emotions, others require moderate or even high emotional stimulation to be able to excel in training or competition (e.g. Hanin 1997, 2000). Riders would therefore be well advised to monitor closely their own emotional/mood states and their effect on performance, both at home and in competition.

Through thick and thin: confidence in the equine partner

As previously discussed, an athlete's assessment of the demands of the competitive situation is likely to affect both the cognitive and physiological components of arousal on the one hand, as well as the activation of regulatory resources such as coping strategies on the other. According to Lazarus and Folkman's (1984) transactional approach, individuals will interpret the environment according to how pertinent it is to their personal welfare. Personal factors, such as the importance of an event and the environmental factors that pertain to the novelty, predictability and timing of that event, will play a role in determining whether a situation will be judged as stressful by the individual.

However, unlike other sports, this process for equestrian riders is also likely to include an appraisal of their horse's ability to cope with the demands of the competitive situation. Equestrianism is a sport that by its very nature is dependent on a functioning horse–rider dyad. Yet the fact that the horse has a will and motivation of its own and, as a prey animal, is also prone to powerful reactions when faced with seemingly threatening situations, makes horse riding at times rather unpredictable. How a rider perceives his horse and his relationship to that horse is likely to be of considerable influence on levels of arousal and relevant coping capacities prior to competing. Indeed, levels of self-confidence (referred to as self-efficacy by the authors) have been found to be closely related to riders' perceptions of their horse's ability to perform (Beauchamp and Whinton 2005).

Additional research has also shown that the perception of equine temperament traits seems to correlate both with the interpretation of arousal and ultimate performance (Wolframm and Micklewright 2010a). The study in question investigated riders' responses to unfamiliar horses that they had to ride as part of a student competition. Temperamental traits, such as excitability or a temperamental and spirited nature, seemed to elicit an increase in arousal intensity and interpretation. The riders did not know the horses and thus would have found it difficult to make a valid assessment of their own 'coping potential' in dealing with these rather spirited equines. The element of potential threat, both to their physical safety and goal attainment (namely not achieving a good score because of a horse that is difficult to control) would have led to both feelings of increased anxiety and lack of perceived coping (e.g. less self-confidence). Nevertheless, even when riders do know their horses well, more temperamental horses might frequently lead to greater levels of anxiety, quite simply because they seem to demand more from the rider in terms of perceived coping skills.

Equally, Wolframm and Micklewright's (2010a) study also showed that those equine character traits mostly considered positive, such as carefulness, trustfulness and lack of dominance, but also fearfulness, resulted in better performance scores. Riders who believe their horses to be fully submissive to their aids are likely to come across as more confident and in control. In showjumping, riders who perceived their horses as trustful, careful, smart and less dominant also achieved a higher overall showjumping score. Especially in showjumping, a good horse should be able to show a degree of 'independent thinking' – to be bold and smart enough to still jump even if the rider makes a mistake. Equally, carefulness is a treasured trait, as it usually means that the horse will try to avoid touching the poles and thereby reduce jumping faults. The perception of these traits is likely to increase the rider's confidence in their four-legged partner, which, according to Beauchamp and Whinton (2005), may positively influence behavioral enactment of the rider towards successful performance. In short, therefore, ridden 'performance', be that in the show ring or at home, is likely to be correlated not merely to rider self-confidence but also to the rider's perception of the horse's ability.

Taking it to the next level: psychological skills

We are able to witness it regularly at the top end of the sport: riders who are able to 'hold it together' even in situations of extreme pressure. Just think of the German eventing rider, Michael Jung, who, at the time of writing this book, is the only rider in the history of the sport to hold the title of Olympic, World and European Champion. While many people had expected Jung to add the 2012 Olympic title to his collection well before the Games had even started, he still needed to make good on the day, having to claw his way back from 14th position after the dressage phase. Only nerves of steel enabled him to complete first a clear round cross country with another two clears in the showjumping arena (one for the team medal and one for the individual). Equally, Pippa Funnell's tremendous achievement of winning eventing's most coveted prize, the Rolex Grand Slam in 2003 remains as yet unrivalled. As this feat involves winning the three four-star events of Kentucky, Badminton and Burghley in the same year, the mental strain of winning, not one but three of the toughest competitions that exist in the sport of eventing, is tremendous. While there are undoubtedly many riders who really know how to train horses, it is the ability to cope with the competitive pressures placed upon them that make them truly exceptional from a performance point of view. In a nutshell, riders at the very top generally manage competitive stress considerably better than the 'also-rans' or amateur riders. Yet even among elite athletes, considerable differences between the ability to 'cope' exist and become apparent in situations of extreme pressure (Gould *et al.* 1993b). Unfortunately, as is the case with many other aspects relating to sport psychology in the rider, few research studies have been conducted investigating coping skills in riders. To develop a better understanding of the potential role of coping skills in equestrian sports, a brief outline of the relevant theoretical concepts as related to other sports is necessary.

Psychological skills to enable coping

Lazarus and Folkman (1984) define the concept of 'coping' as the cognitive and behavioral efforts of an individual to manage the internal and external demands encountered during a competitive situation. Coping is considered to be the mediating process between stressful events, such as a sporting competition, and a person's psychological and physiological symptoms of health (Folkman *et al.* 1986). Other researchers hold that appropriate coping strategies, such as psychological skills, can protect the individual against the potentially psychologically and physically damaging qualities of stress (Anthony and Liberman 1986).

Previous research on coping and the use of related psychological skills in sport have shown that athletes usually employ a mix of different psychological strategies to cope with the changing demands of a sporting context (Compas 1987; Folkman and Lazarus 1985; Gaudreau and Blondin 2004). Gould *et al.* (1993b), for example, investigated the link between sources of stress and coping in figure skaters. Their findings supported the idea that coping is a complex process; a 'one fits all' style that can be employed successfully in all types of stressful situations does not seem to exist. The authors distinguished between eight broad coping strategies or psychological skills, such as rational thinking and self-talk, positive focus and orientation, social support, time management and prioritization, precompetitive mental preparation and anxiety management, training hard and smart, isolation and deflection and ignoring the stressors. A similar study by Gould *et al.* (1993a) showed that Olympic-level wrestlers used a combination of thought control, task focus, behavioral changes and emotional control. Findings further revealed that coping automaticity was strongly related to coping effectiveness and superior performance. Research by Holt and Hogg (2002) investigating the coping styles of participants in the 1999 World Cup Finals in football found that players used reappraisal techniques such as positive self-talk, problem-solving following a mistake and recalling past mistakes. They also relied on the use of social resources such as encouragement and support, effective performance behaviors and blocking out irrelevant stimuli.

Preparation is key: effective routines

But while coping strategies may vary somewhat depending on the individual, there seems to be a number of psychological characteristics that distinguish the successful from the unsuccessful athlete and the elite from the non-elite. As Bertollo *et al.* (2009) would have it: 'To become successful, the athlete needs to be committed, dedicated, motivated, mentally tough, and able to pursue achievement goals in a rational way. All these attributes may be developed or improved by using psychological skills' (p. 245).

One of the key elements in allowing athletes to feel that their coping resources are sufficient is the focus on improving mental preparation routines (Greenspan and Feltz 1989; Murphy and Martin 2002). Athletes of a lesser calibre can be assisted in reaching their personal bests through teaching them appropriate psychological skills and preparation routines (Bertollo *et al.* 2009), while even more experienced athletes can derive benefit from honing relevant psychological skills. In a study investigating mental strategies of elite modern pentathletes, which includes a showjumping phase, Bertollo *et al.* (2009) presented findings that indicated the importance of displaying attitudes such as perseverance, consistency and commitment in training leading up to competition. Furthermore, psychological skills, such as goal setting, emotional control, behavioral routines, attentional strategies and mental practice, were viewed as instrumental in allowing these athletes to control negative affect and achieve top performances. Gould *et al.* (2002) found very similar characteristics in a group of Olympic champions. These high achievers scored on measures of confidence, freedom from worry, goal setting, mental preparation and focus/concentration. Indeed, in an extensive review on the subject, Williams and Krane (2001) were able to identify a number of psychological characteristics and mental skills prevalent in highly successful athletes: self-regulation of arousal, high confidence, concentration and focus, an 'in control but not forcing it' attitude; positive imagery, self-talk, high determination and commitment, goal setting, thought control and preparation routines. Taken together, the research findings strongly indicate that the elite or more successful performer indeed shows a pattern of psychological skills and characteristics more pronounced than that of lesser-performing athletes.

The equestrian elite: how do they do it?

Anecdotal evidence suggests that what holds true in other sports is no different in the world of equestrianism. Riders at the very top of their game demonstrate time and again that, in addition to excellent riding ability, they also have superior psychological skills to cope in the most difficult situations. But, while riders of all levels are usually quick to emulate the superstars of their chosen discipline, when it comes to sport psychology training, many riders at the amateur, non-elite levels seem reluctant to invest in the training of these 'soft' skills. A closer look at data (Wolframm 2011a) from interviews with both elite and non-elite riders might shed some light (see Table 3.3 for more detailed results). It seems that, in general, elite riders consider mental skills to be considerably more important than do non-elite riders. While elite riders readily acknowledge the importance of attitudes and mindsets such as achievement striving, determination, dedication and remaining emotionally relaxed, as well as the ability to cope under pressure as instrumental in order to reach the top, non-elite riders particularly highlight external factors such as financial means, training opportunity and time to train. Even more telling is the fact that non-elite riders indicated that psychological skills were not of particular importance to them 'right now'. They felt that these only came into play at higher competence levels. In all likelihood, then, non-elite riders make little effort to try to improve their psychological skills. Elite riders, having recognized the value of psychological skills, seem to spend more time developing relevant strategies and, as a result, are better able to use them in competition.

Table 3.3 Differences in mental strategies between elite and non-elite riders, as portrayed during semi-structured interviews

Skill	Difference in mental strategy
Perceived differences between elite and non-elite riders	Elite riders considered certain attitudes and mindsets such as achievement striving, determination, dedication and remaining emotionally relaxed, as well as the ability to cope under pressure, to be particularly important. Non-elite riders sporadically acknowledged a distinct set of personality characteristics but highlighted external factors such as financial means, training opportunity and time to train as the key difference. Elite riders also considered differences in riding-specific ability to be a key factor, with talent as the most important aspect.
Perceived importance of psychological skills	Elite riders considered psychological skills to be extremely important to success, rating them with a 9.6 (out of 10), while non-elite riders thought that mental strategies only came to be important at the more advanced levels, rating them with a 7.8 (again, out of 10). Non-elite riders felt that, at their level, psychological skills did not play an important role.
Type of psychological skills used	Both elite and non-elite riders considered focusing skills and goal-setting abilities as particularly important, while elite riders named general coping techniques, cognitive restructuring techniques and positive self-talk to be of additional value. Both elite and non-elite riders mentioned the need for relaxation skills, yet they did not feature prominently during interviews.
Pre-competitive preparation routines employed	Both elite and non-elite riders considered preparation of equipment an important aspect of preparing for a competition yet elite riders also stressed the importance of the horse being in shape and the rider mentally prepared. Non-elite riders emphasized in particular the need to be at a competition in plenty of time, as well as getting to know the competition grounds and having significant others with them for support. Elite riders particularly stressed the importance of anticipating demands of the competition and training the horse accordingly, sentiments which were mirrored, albeit to a lesser extent, by non-elite riders.
Dealing with mistakes	Elite riders highlighted the importance of not dwelling on mistakes and retaining task-relevant focus, while non-elite riders admitted to regularly losing focus and getting tense following a mistake.
Dealing with unforeseen events	Non-elite riders indicated that unforeseen events caused them to get stressed and to have negative thoughts, which they would try to cope with through relaxation and problem solving. Elite riders stressed problem-solving skills, focusing and perspective taking but also the importance of preparing for the eventuality of a mistake beforehand, for example through training in different environments.

Table 3.3 continued

Skill	Difference in mental strategy
Dealing with competitive anxiety	Elite riders generally considered the symptoms of anxiety as facilitative and as a signal to compete rather than something that would impair their performance. Elite riders also mentioned the use of positive self-talk, focusing skills, solution-focused thinking and relaxation techniques to deal with competitive anxiety. High-frequency counts indicated that getting tense was a particular issue for non-elite riders when experiencing anxiety. Their most prevalent coping strategies included relaxation and self-talk.
Regaining confidence	Elite riders referred to using cognitive restructuring, positive self-talk, solution-focused thinking (by assessing which elements in the ridden performance needed improving) and scaling down the demands, 'going back to basics', when faced with loss of confidence. Non-elite riders only referred to using repetitive practice and being successful in an event as their preferred method of regaining confidence. Interestingly, a number of elite riders referred in their interviews to the fact that many riders, once they have lost confidence, would merely revert to repeating exercises over and over. But because no actual analysis of what went wrong in the first place had taken place initially, riders would subsequently fail to 'fix' the problem and thus were less likely to regain confidence.

When comparing the type of coping strategies employed by elite and non-elite riders, it appears that elite riders primarily employ task-orientated, problem-focused coping strategies. Non-elite riders, especially when faced with situations over which they have no control, such as unforeseen events or making a mistake, seem to focus on their emotional response instead. As elaborated by Skinner *et al.* (2003), individuals who perceive themselves to be in control of a situation (e.g. have the necessary resources to deal with the circumstances at hand) are more likely to use task-orientated coping strategies. In contrast, individuals who feel that there is 'nothing they can do' are likely to become disengaged and tend to avoid the problem. Arguably, elite riders do have more experience and greater skill to deal with a particular situation. In all likelihood, they are better able to develop relevant solutions, resulting in increased levels of confidence. Nevertheless, even a non-elite rider competing at novice to intermediate level should have the appropriate skills to deal with (most) situations arising at a competition. Yet it seems that non-elite riders do not use their own levels of skills and expertise to the most effect. Non-elite riders indicated that one way of regaining confidence was to practice a particular movement over and over again. In fact, elite athletes indicated that one of the greatest mistakes committed by non-elite riders was that, following a mistake, they (the non-elite riders) would keep repeating the same movement without reflecting on and subsequently correcting what had gone wrong. As a result, they would end up never improving the situation, nor increasing their levels of confidence. While it could be argued that non-elite riders lack the experience to know what had gone wrong, correctly employed coping skills would at least allow them to ask someone more experienced for appropriate feedback.

Mental skills training: mind games do work!

The positive effect of psychological skills on attaining optimal levels of emotional control during sporting performance has been documented widely over the past few decades (Bertollo *et al.* 2009; Gould *et al.* 1993a, 1993b, 2002; Holt and Hogg 2002; Mahoney and Avener 1977; Williams and Krane 2001). Such skills generally include goal setting, which refers to the structured planning and setting of sporting goals to attain a certain performance outcome (Gould *et al.* 1993a); thought control, describing the ability to allow only performance enhancing, positive thoughts to enter the conscious mind; and arousal management, which helps an athlete to control physiological symptoms of anxiety (Bertollo *et al.* 2009). Furthermore, concentration and focusing skills are considered very important, as they allow athletes to focus only on performance-relevant tasks and actions, rather than getting distracted by other environmental factors (Williams and Krane 2001). Lastly, the mental skill of imagery is very popular among athletes and has been found to be particularly effective in both the acquisition and performance of motor skills (Hall *et al.* 1989), as well as in enhancing motivational functions (Callow *et al.* 2001).[5] In one of only a handful of studies investigating psychological skills in equestrian sports, Callow and Waters (2005) measured the efficacy of visual (i.e. seeing oneself performing an activity in one's own mind) and kinaesthetic (i.e. feeling oneself performing an activity) imagery to improve self-confidence in three flat-race jockeys. Results of the study showed a significant increase in self-confidence for two of the three jockeys, while the increase in confidence of the third jockey was approaching significance. In fact, the authors note specifically that, for this particular jockey, even though statistical results were non-significant, he felt that the intervention had substantially increased his confidence.

But, while interventions involving a single psychological skill appear to facilitate sporting performance, their effectiveness might be limited by individual differences and preferences (Blakeslee and Goff 2007). Multimodal psychological skills programmes that combine different mental skills techniques may in fact be more effective in helping athletes to develop appropriate coping strategies for a variety of situations (e.g. Hanton and Jones 1999; Mamassis and Doganis 2004). In one of the first studies of this kind in an equestrian setting, Bloom and Stevens (2002) investigated the effects of a multivariate team-building programme with an intercollegiate equestrian team. Interventions focused on leadership and communication skills, setting team norms and standards and coping with competitive pressures. While statistical analysis only indicated a trend towards greater team cohesion, participating riders did report improved coach–rider relationships and rider–rider relationships. Despite the authors not focusing on teaching performance enhancing mental skills, nor measuring direct performance outcomes at competition, the study nevertheless served to provide first indications of the value of sport psychological interventions.

Along similar lines, Blakeslee and Goff (2007) examined the effect of a four-week mental strategies training package on a group of eight competitive collegiate equestrian riders compared with nine controls. The intervention consisted of relaxation skills, mental imagery, self-talk and goal setting taught in an initial two-hour session and followed up by half-hourly sessions once a week. While a significant performance improvement could be detected over time, this occurred both in the mental strategies group and the control group. The authors noted that, even though the control group received no formal mental skills training, they did in all likelihood communicate with the intervention group and benefitted indirectly from mental skills training.

A more recent study by Wolframm and Micklewright (2011b) explored the effect of a multimodal psychological skills training, including goal setting, self-talk, concentration training, relaxation and imagery on dressage performance and emotional composure in ten dressage riders. Following a six-week intervention programme, dressage riders performed significantly better, compared with initial competitive dressage scores, which were gathered six weeks before the study began, as well as in comparison with competition scores immediately before the intervention. Despite manipulation checks throughout the study to ensure that positive results were not only the result of a learning effect, obvious study limitations exist, especially regarding the size and nature of the participant group. Nevertheless, the study provides additional support to existing notions that multimodal intervention designs assist athletes in achieving optimal performances (Hanton and Jones 1999; Mamassis and Doganis 2004; Thomas *et al.* 2007).

The question presents itself as to how the combination of different psychological skills might serve to improve equestrian performance. The psychological skills of goal setting, self-talk and focusing skills all aim to increase task-relevant focus and to decrease the danger of distracting thoughts. Goal setting allows athletes to map out their plan of action via short-term goals, which has been shown to enhance task-specific focus. It also is thought to enhance motivation, as it enables riders to continuously assess their progress (Locke and Latham 1985). Sport psychology researchers have suggested that self-talk helps to combat negative, task-irrelevant thoughts. These are particularly likely to encroach on a rider's thought processes under conditions of high cognitive load (Dugdale and Eklund 2002). A dressage competition where riders have to remember their dressage test, the time schedule and preparation routines for their horses might thus elicit negative thought processes in riders unable to employ relevant mental skills. Positive, affirmative self-talk statements with either task-specific or motivational content are likely to inhibit interfering thoughts and have been shown to facilitate performance in both precision and power tasks (Hatzigeorgiadis *et al.* 2004). Positive self-talk is therefore likely to be particularly beneficial in equestrian sports, where precision in the application of aids is of vital importance to ensure effective horse–rider communication. Lastly, the application of relevant cue words has been shown to increase attentional focus, as verbal cues can assist in redirecting attention towards task-specific actions (Johnson *et al.* 2004; Landin 1994). Drawing on the combined evidence of other sporting activities and equestrian sports, it may be concluded that the combination of goal setting, self-talk and attentional focus is likely to increase a rider's task-relevant focus, which in turn is likely to improve performance.

Research into other sports has also shown that athletes using a combination of progressive muscle relaxation (Jacobson 1938), mental practice and imagery were able to perform significantly better than imagery-only or attention-control groups (Weinberg *et al.* 1981). For riders to be able to perform 'as one' with their horses, relevant aids must be as subtle and refined as possible, demanding the necessary levels of fine motor control and accuracy. As referred to throughout this chapter, heightened muscular tension and increased respiratory and heart rates are likely to impact on riders' ability to execute the necessary aids in a timely and accurate manner. Especially in times of increased physiological arousal, such as in competitions or in novel situations, riders frequently 'grab hold' of the reins, while also 'blocking' the movement of their horses with their seat. This means that, even if the horse was to respond correctly to the initial cue given, said response would unlikely be reinforced by the immediate release of the aid (i.e. the associated pressure of the hands, legs and seat). Such lack of reinforcement might result in the horse 'offering' various other behavioral responses, which generally are not desired by the rider. In fact, the horse might even resort to behaviors such as bucking, rearing or refusing to move, seeing that all other alternatives have previously been ignored by the rider (usually unconsciously).

The result, once again, is a vicious circle: the rider is tense and unable to remove the pressure associated with a particular aid; the horse whose attempts at offering the correct response are being ignored and will thus start displaying undesirable behaviors. And the rider by this point is likely to experience even more tension. The combination of relaxation techniques together with the mental skill of imagery (in itself a technique that improves levels of relaxation) is likely to assist in the regulation of physiological arousal and to help riders to experience optimal bodily responses while they envisage themselves performing relevant equestrian activities. This, in turn, is likely to lead to more refined horse–rider interaction, improved performance and, ultimately, greater levels of safety.

Concluding thoughts

Sport psychology, the study of how aspects such as dispositional tendencies, emotional attributes and the ability to control 'mind over matter' can impact on sports performance, has been acknowledged as important in many, if not most, sports. In equestrian sports, where the interaction between horse and rider depends on fairness, consistency and level-headedness, the way the rider thinks, acts and feels is of the utmost importance. Perhaps not altogether surprisingly, current studies investigating different psychological aspects such as arousal control and anxiety management, self-confidence and mental skills training, mirror the findings in other sports: debilitative interpretations of anxiety are likely to impede performance, while self-confidence seems to be an important moderator. Riders at the top of their sport have been shown to exhibit more effective coping skills and mental strategies, even though mental skills are likely to have a positive effect on riders of all levels of expertise. Nevertheless, there is a clear need for additional research illuminating the role that sport psychological components may play in helping riders to achieve the frame of mind necessary to get the best out of themselves, their horses and their relationships – both from the point of view of performance and that of safety.

Chapter highlights

1. Equine training is based on learning theory. The horse learns to associate certain 'aids' from the rider with different movements through principles of negative and positive reinforcement. Riders subsequently need to be in control of themselves, both physically and emotionally, to be able to consistently and concisely apply relevant aids.
2. Understanding how the combination of semi-permanent dispositional factors (i.e. personality traits such as extroversion, or neuroticism) and transient conditions caused by external conditions (i.e. mood and emotional states) affects individual rider behavior is the first step towards developing appropriate coping strategies.
3. Mood states before or during an event, such as feelings of confusion or uncertainty, have been associated with attentional inefficiencies, poor information processing and, thus, suboptimal levels of concentration. Advanced riders are thought to exhibit lower levels of confusion than their novice counterparts.
4. Anxiety is multidimensional in nature, involving somatic (i.e. physical) and cognitive ('thinking') elements. Individuals may also have an anxious disposition ('trait anxiety') or may feel anxious for a short period of time because of situational factors ('state anxiety'). Both anecdotal and empirical evidence suggest that feeling anxious or 'stressed' can have serious negative repercussions on horse–rider interaction and on ridden performance.
5. Self-confidence (also frequently referred to as self-efficacy) is an important moderator of anxiety and is also thought to play a vital role in optimal performance. Self-confidence is developed through levels of mastery, feedback, vicarious experiences and positive interpretations of physiological arousal.
6. In equestrian sports, confidence in the equine partner is likely to be almost or even as important a factor as confidence in the rider's own skills. At the same time, rider perceptions of equine temperamental traits are likely to influence rider confidence and anxiety.
7. Psychological characteristics, such as perseverance, commitment and determination, as well as mental skills such as imagery, self-talk, self-regulation of arousal, goal setting and thought control (among others), have shown to

be important indicators of performance in sport. These findings also seem to be mirrored in equestrian sports: higher-achieving riders also show greater psychological skills than their less successful counterparts.

8. Multimodal psychological skills interventions are likely to have a positive impact on horse–rider interaction, ridden performance and, ultimately, horse–rider safety.

4 Coaching riders

From a different perspective

Introduction: the best possible coach

It undoubtedly holds true for just about every sporting discipline, including equestrian sports: every athlete (and every rider) hopes for the best possible coach. At times, that might even mean going to the immediate competition.

The news that emerged on 31 January 2012 set the world of competitive dressage on fire and the upper echelons of the Dutch and German national federations into a frenzy! It concerned one German rider, who some time ago had taken on the ride of possibly one of the world's most famous horses. Allegedly he was to be trained by the then Dutch national coach. Concern and disbelief could be heard on both sides of the German–Dutch divide. Considering that 2012 was an Olympic year and that the German and Dutch teams were both vying for medal positions, the Dutch National Federation considered that the coach in question should at least wait to train his new charge until after the Olympics. Following confirmation shortly afterwards that the coach in question had indeed agreed to postpone commencement of his new working relationship, the issue seemed to be off the table – for the Dutch! The German dressage world, on the other hand, sprang into action, with many of their representatives dismissing the coach's training method as being contrary to their vision of correct and appropriate dressage training. Several official statements by the German National Federation made it clear that the young rider's choice of new trainer was not looked upon kindly. The German rider, however, held firm with his choice of new coach, believing him to be the best for the job. In the end, the issue was resolved almost by itself: owing to illness, the rider was unable to contend for a spot on the Olympic team. Following the 2012 Games in the summer, the coach did not prolong his contract with the Dutch national federation, leaving him free to pursue other activities, such as training the young German, without any perceived conflicts of interest.

For one, this particular issue highlights many of the sensitivities of top international equestrian sport, ranging from conflicts of interest to training principles. More importantly in the context of this book, it also highlights the significance of another aspect in equestrian sports: finding the right kind of coach.

Traditionally, the riding and training of horses has always been about the direct interaction between horse and rider or horse and handler. There can be little doubt that riders only develop the necessary 'feel' for the horse by actually riding and handling the horse. Yet even the most advanced rider is aided by regular feedback on how and whether the skills they are applying to the horse actually result in the correct response. Therefore the 'eyes on the ground', which is how many riders often refer to their coaches, form an essential prerequisite to developing, first of all, appropriate skills and, ultimately, top performances. What is more, several equestrian disciplines, predominantly 'pure' dressage and the first phase of eventing, several Western disciplines, vaulting and some showjumping classes, rely on outside observers, i.e. judges, to assess performance. This means that, from a performance point of view, the overall 'picture' of the horse–rider combination as perceived from the ground may be almost as important as what the rider experiences in the saddle, especially in the final stages of competition preparation.

Even though the emphasis with regard to achieving athletic performance is placed squarely on the shoulders of the athlete, being a coach is no easy task either: first and foremost, it is the coach's responsibility to ensure that athletes learn both the appropriate skills and the appropriate behavioral and psychological components necessary to perform to the best of their ability in their chosen sport. More challenging still, coaches are frequently charged with inspiring their athletes to pursue athletic excellence, by imparting their ideas and vision to their athletes (Schinke *et al.* 1997). If all that were not enough of a challenge, coaching in the equestrian disciplines is made even more complex by the triadic interaction between coach, rider and horse (Cumyn 2000; Maw 2012).

In short, equestrian coaches should not only be able to instruct, motivate and inspire their human charges but also need sufficient skill to both guide the rider's training of the horse and, preferably, to get into the saddle themselves should the need arise. All in all an interesting and challenging topic, which, to date, has only received little empirical attention. However, much of the existing literature in other sports, combined with applied knowledge of equestrian culture, might go some way towards furthering our understanding of equestrian coaching. This chapter summarizes and discusses current knowledge relating to 'involved observers' (i.e. coaches and parents in sport) and how this may be used in the development of appropriate skills, attitudes and mindsets in equestrian sports. In view of the scarcity of the evidence relating directly to equestrian coaching, we will draw on the evidence available in other sports, while making an informed link to horse sports.

Definitions of coaching: the name of the game

Throughout the chapter, we will use the term 'coaching' with a view to sports, as opposed to other models of coaching, such as life or career coaching. Coaching in this context may then be defined as aiming to improve riders' physical, technical, tactical and psychological skills and abilities to allow them to cope with the demands of the different equestrian disciplines. Related terms such as 'training', 'teaching' or 'instructing', which are also frequently used in equestrian circles, are implied and incorporated in such a definition of coaching. It should also be noted that, in many professional sports settings, the (head) coach usually acts as the focal point in any coaching team, which consists of specialists in other fields, such as nutritionists, physiologists, psychologists, sports doctors, and so on. While it would be unrealistic to ask a coach to be an expert in all of these fields, they should at least have a general appreciation of the importance and impact of any of these adjacent fields of expertise. Quite clearly, coaches need to have a broad basis of knowledge, a clear 'roadmap' for their riders and an open mind to guide their athletes towards the final outcome.

When aiming to clarify the ins and outs of coaching in equestrian sports, the questions that arise immediately are, first of all, what is sports coaching and perhaps more importantly, what do coaches actually do? Secondly, how does coaching in equestrian sports differ from coaching in other sports and what are the subsequent implications for coaches in horse sports?

Researchers in the field of coaching science have been trying to define the first set of questions, i.e. those relating to coaching in a more generic sense, for the past three decades (Abraham and Collins 2011). While the subject matter itself is complex, the reasons behind the difficulties in coming up with a distinct set of coaching competences are relatively straightforward: there simply are too many contextual variables (i.e. requirements and idiosyncrasies of the various sporting disciplines, different settings for training and competition, sociopolitical aspects, individual differences of coach and athlete; environmental components). As a result, many of the coaching models that have been developed by researchers within the field (e.g. Abraham *et al.* 2006; Chelladurai 1990; Côté *et al.* 1995a; Lyle 2002) are thought to be too theoretical to be applied in practical settings (Abraham and Collins 2011). In the following section, we therefore investigate existing knowledge regarding coaching practice primarily from an applied point of view, and attempt to place empirical findings into the appropriate practical context. The second set of questions, namely those relating to the peculiarities of equestrian sports, are discussed in the context of horse–rider–coach interactions and compared with other sporting disciplines.

The most pragmatic approach to identifying the most important elements of coaching would be to look at the common denominators of different coaching programmes being taught across the world (Smith and Smoll 2005). Specifically, it seems that most coaching programmes focus on developing competencies related to either sport-specific components or performance-related knowledge and skills (Smoll and Smith 2006).

Sport-specific components generally include skills, techniques and strategies pertaining to the sport in question, while performance-related knowledge will include biomechanics, exercise physiology, nutrition, sports medicine, growth and development and sport psychology (Smoll and Smith 2005). A good, and most definitely an outstanding, coach should have soundly developed competences in either field, being able to draw on a broad basis of both practical and theoretical know-how, interspersed with an understanding of pedagogy, time and risk management.

In equestrian sports, coaches should therefore be able to impart to their (human) charges the relevant technical requirements of the sport, e.g. how to position the body while in the saddle and how and when to give the correct aids, while also being able to – ideally – advise riders on how to maximize their performance, for example through additional physical conditioning, appropriate nutrition, and mental skills. What is more – and this is where equestrian coaching differs substantially from any other sporting discipline – they must also have sound knowledge and competences in equine physiology, biomechanics and psychology. For example, the last few years have witnessed the emergence of a buoyant field of equine learning behavior and its application to training horses. Yet a number of researchers in the field lament the fact that these scientific under-pinnings have, as yet, been integrated in very few professional training systems, to the detriment of both welfare and performance of horse–rider combinations (e.g. Creighton 2007; McGreevy 2007; McLean and McGreevy 2004). A study based in Australia by Warren-Smith and McGreevy (2008) was able to indicate that only a minority of the participating coaches was able to explain correctly the use of positive reinforcement (2.8 per cent), negative reinforcement (11.9 per cent) and punishment (5.4 per cent) in horses. Seeing that the education of riders begins with the tuition they receive from their coaches, it seems clear that good equestrian coaches must have thorough understanding of the principles underpin-ning rider *and* horse performance.[1]

Coaching processes: how do they do it?

While definitions of coaching provide interesting food for thought from an academic, theoretical point-of-view, the manner in which coaches do what they do (i.e. coaching processes) is doubtlessly more interesting, if not more relevant, from an applied point of view. The actual process of coaching might feasibly be divided into the broader, but by no means exclusive, categories relating to:

- conveying information;
- structuring practice;
- administering feedback (e.g. Lawrence and Kingston 2008); and
- encouraging appropriate behaviors and the development of personal compe-tencies (e.g. Coatsworth and Conroy 2007; Keegan *et al.* 2009).

Conveying information: what's what?

The process of conveying relevant technical information, might, at first glance, be considered to be the most important aspect of any coaching set-up. After all, the inherent nature of equestrian sports coaching revolves around teaching riders both the physical and motor skills relevant to riding a horse. At the heart of any coaching trajectory lies the inherent hope that performance of a particular set of motor skills will improve with time. The psychological concept of the 'learning performance distinction' (Salmoni *et al.* 1984; Schmidt and Lee 2011) stresses in particular the distinction between mere motor performance (i.e. isolated incidents of movements performed) and motor learning (i.e. the performance of movement that is sustained over time). Rather than merely being able to execute certain movements during their practice sessions, athletes (riders) presumably wish to be able to reproduce learned movements consistently and over time. In addition to 'mere' technical instructions, coaching also extends to the imparting of additional, 'tactical' information. Riders should, for example, be trained in different ways of riding a test or a course. For instance, at which point in the cross-country course should riders aim to take the long route at a combination of fences? When should they try to make up time or go for a clear round instead? A similar example might be the manner in which endurance riders try to pace their horses so as to present them in the best possible condition at the vet gate. Dressage riders might need to be taught how to ride their horses just before entering the arena, considering that judges might already be watching and forming an – albeit unofficial – opinion. In the same vein, learning how to walk a showjumping course before a competition is in many ways as important as the ability to present the horse to the fence accurately. Lastly, horse sports all share the additional aspect of dealing with an animal. The information conveyed by an equestrian coach therefore also needs to include important elements relating to the nature of horses, their behavior, physiological and biomechanical attributes and how they are likely to interact with their riders.

Structuring practice: a question of timing

Modern research on motor skill acquisition unequivocally agrees that, while certain coaching practices clearly lead to an immediate improvement of motor performance, they might not necessarily foster long-term motor learning (Kantak and Winstein 2012). In fact, when teaching multiple motor tasks (e.g. A, B, C), motor performance is enhanced when said tasks are performed in a blocked order (e.g. AAA...BBB...CCC) as opposed to a random order (e.g. ACBCABCAB). Long-term retention, i.e. motor learning, on the other hand, improves if motor tasks are practised in a random rather than in a blocked order (Kantak and Winstein 2012). The reasons for this have been attributed to the phenomenon of 'contextual interference' (Shea and Morgan 1979), which indicates that a high variability of contextual variables decreases the quality of motor performance. This means that after having learned tasks in a blocked-order structure, performance may be highly localized and context-specific and not easily transferable to different environments. Conversely, while performing motor tasks in a random design might initially attenuate motor performance, context-independent learning is likely to increase. Especially in view of the difficulties that riders have in performing equally well at competition as they do at home, this concept is particularly important. Coaches should make sure that they structure their training sessions to initially include blocked sessions, to increase feelings of competence and motivation, but at a later stage also teach using randomized designs to make sure that the rider can still perform under different contextual variables (i.e. at a show).

Providing feedback: praise where praise is due

The learning of both complex motor tasks and tactical know-how is of course not merely achieved by the appropriate structuring of sessions. Athletes (riders) also need to know when they have executed a movement correctly, by receiving appropriate feedback and reinforcement. Coaching feedback may generally be categorized into either positive forms of feedback, such as encouragement, support, instruction-orientated or negative coaching feedback strategies, such as punishment or ignoring of athletes (McArdle and Duda 2002; Smith *et al.* 1979, 2007; Smoll *et al.* 2007). While there can be no doubt that providing any kind of feedback plays an important role in the coaching process, providing the right *kind* of feedback and at the right *time* is an even more important element and should be considered to be a vital aspect to the appropriate structuring of coaching sessions. In fact, Horn (1985) suggested that appropriateness and timing of feedback are likely to influence the positive development of athletes much more significantly than the amount or frequency of feedback provided. Technical feedback, which relates to error correction or adjustment in technique or strategy, and positive reinforcement, such as praise or providing external rewards, can go a long way towards increasing motivation, self-confidence and enjoyment in athletes. We therefore discuss a number of aspects relating to the effect of coaching feedback in athletes in more detail below.

Encouraging appropriate behavior: fair's fair

In more recent years, the additional dimension of coaching with regard to important psychological variables is being considered much more frequently and has become increasingly important. The reasons for this are, in fact, strikingly straightforward. To progress to a more advanced level in any given activity, considerable time must be spent on repetition and error correction. Yet the degree of repetition and 'deliberate practice' (i.e. training units that are structured around and aimed at improving specific elements of performance) required at more advanced levels is often not inherently motivating (e.g. Ericsson *et al.* 1993; Oliver *et al.* 2010). This means that coaches must also spend considerable time trying to motivate athletes, promoting their adherence, engagement and positive states of mind. In addition to what we might wish to call 'skill-related' variables, therefore, coaches undoubtedly play an important role in providing valuable psychological guidance and support, teaching their athletes important behaviors ranging from social and life skills (Gould and Carson 2008), optimal functioning (Jowett 2007; Jowett and Cockerill 2003), maintaining sports participation and preventing drop-out (Fraser-Thomas and Côté, 2009; Weiss and Gould 1986) and positive psychological attributes such as self-esteem, motivation, decreased anxiety, sport competence (Halliburton and Weiss 2002), and sport-specific self-confidence (Magyar and Feltz 2003).

In a recent study investigating the perceptions of elite coaches of important behavioral components in athletes, Oliver *et al.* (2010) identified eight clusters of behaviors that were considered important predictors of athletic progress: professionalism; motivation; coping; commitment; effort; seeking information to improve; concentration; and negative behaviors. It may be worthwhile to consider some of these constructs with the distinct nature of equestrian sport in mind. Professionalism refers to the athletes' general approach to training sessions, including turning up on time, being prepared and wearing the right kit. Coaches would expect athletes to show respect towards coaches and staff but also towards facilities and equipment. Applied to equestrian sports, the dimension of professionalism undoubtedly also includes a respectful and kind attitude towards the horse, its training and general care. Equine welfare and an ethical approach to training plays an increasingly important role in all aspects of equestrian sports, ranging from strict stewarding at competitions to the zero-tolerance rule of doping. Only riders prepared to adhere to a strict code of professionalism can, rightly, hope for long-term success in their chosen sport. The component of motivation included aspects relating to the drive to succeed focused on achieving goals and being driven to be the best. Again, while these are no doubt important attributes in any aspiring athlete, it remains the responsibility of the coach to temper aspirations whenever they might endanger the health and wellbeing of the horse, the rider or the horse–rider combination. The category of coping included elements relating to how to deal with and maintain a positive attitude following failure, as well as how to respond appropriately following success. The importance of relevant coping skills has already been discussed in detail in Chapter 3. However, it remains to be said that it is the nature of dealing with horses that success one week might easily be followed by failure the next. Once again, therefore, it is one of the responsibilities of the coach to ensure that riders learn that ups and downs are all part and parcel of the sport.

The construct of commitment related to an athlete's willingness to pursue and invest themselves in the sport for an extended period of time, while 'effort' was indicative of athletes who were prepared to work hard and 'go the extra mile' to achieve their goal, even if that meant enduring physical discomfort. It is important to note that, in equestrian sports, the construct of effort might, in many ways, be a double-edged sword. While ambitious riders undoubtedly must show their willingness to exert extra effort, they are also restrained by what their horses are able to accomplish. Even if riders might be perfectly willing to push themselves to their physical limits, they must also remain aware of, and not be tempted to ignore, their horses' physical limitations. Especially in a rider's formative years, it falls to the coach to shape that rider's attitude towards the fine balance between the desire to achieve and their horse's welfare. Furthermore, the behavioral construct of seeking information to improve sees athletes asking questions, being reflective and self-evaluative and using criticism as feedback. Especially in the equestrian disciplines that are dependent on outside observers (judges) the willingness to use feedback to improve cannot be underestimated. The concept of concentration and maintaining focus involves an athlete's ability to pay attention throughout a session, as opposed to being easily distracted or switching off. Again, in equestrian sports, the behavioral component of paying attention is particularly important, considering that riders not only have to listen to their coach but also to communicate with their horses. Being able to remain alert and listening to the horses' signals is undoubtedly essential, both from a performance and a safety point of view.

Quite clearly then, in addition to those coaching processes that refer to the more technical aspects of sports performance (i.e. conveying of information, structuring practice and providing feedback) coaches arguably have as important a role to play in conveying and encouraging appropriate behaviors.

Go(o)dly coaches: what they do when they do what they do best

From a conceptual point of view, coaching processes might seem relatively straightforward. Yet the real world of sports has taught us that there remain a number of qualitative determinants that separate the good from the mediocre or even poor coaches. In the following sections we look more closely at some of the factors that make for 'great' coaches and foster effective coach–rider relationships.

Outstanding coaches can make (or break) riders and, of course, horses. They are revered, both within and often even beyond their immediate environment. Especially at international events, be it World and European Championships or the Olympic Games, attending coaches frequently seem to take on the role of ambassadors, striving for their own country's recognition and glory on the international stage. But while the potential repercussions, both good and bad, are exponentially greater at international shows, the charisma of an outstanding coach, no matter which sporting discipline, can be felt at the smallest of village competitions. Yet, as most riders are likely to know from their own experience, not all coaches are good, let alone outstanding. So what is it that makes an outstanding coach tower head and shoulders above the rest of the sporting world? In the following section, we look at some of the structural and behavioral components that have shown to be important characteristics in outstanding coaching.

What makes a coach an outstanding coach?

How should we define 'outstanding' coaching? Many coaching texts and, indeed, the previous pages, imply that outstanding coaches are those that achieve the best results at the highest level (Horn 2008). Two problems with such a definition immediately spring to mind. Firstly, what about the countless coaches who spend their days teaching beginners or novices in a chosen sport, infusing them with joy, motivation and confidence, yet failing to ever coach an Olympic athlete? Does the apparent qualifying criterion of having coached at the highest level make Olympic coaches any better than those who haven't? Secondly, the fact that coaches achieve results does not necessarily mean that they are truly great (in fact, they might simply have been lucky). They might perhaps be effective in teaching their athletes the necessary skills but focus little on the overall psychological development of their athletes, resulting in a host of problems at a later stage of that athlete's career. What we can take away from that, both for equestrian sports but also applied more generally, is that any coach, no matter whether they are active at grassroots or international level, can be an outstanding coach.

Nevertheless, early coaching research relied heavily on those coaches who were effective (i.e. achieved many wins) and therefore in the public eye because of exposure at the highest level (e.g. Smith *et al.* 1977; Tharp and Gallimore 1976). Being influenced by 'mainstream' developments in psychology, many of these early studies were based on behaviorism and, not surprisingly, measured only observable behaviors of successful coaches (Smith *et al.* 1977; Tharp and Gallimore 1976; Williams 1978). Yet results soon showed that winning and losing coaches often exhibited the same kind of behaviors (Claxton 1988; Model 1983), leading to the conclusion that a purely performance-based differentiation might not be the most effective. Furthermore, the same kind of behavior might be interpreted differently by different athletes, leading to equivocal results (Smith *et al.* 2009).

The realization that effective coaching is more than the sum of accumulated results combined with advances in cognitive psychology led to what has loosely been termed the 'social cognitive' approach (Gearity and Murray 2011) and has focused more on elements of thoughts and knowledge. This line of research has been able to demonstrate that effective coaches know much about the techniques, skills and tactics necessary in their chosen sport (Côté *et al.* 1995a), develop and implement effective planning (Gallimore and Tharp 2004), foster their athletes' level of sport-specific and generic levels of self-confidence and motivation (Côté *et al.* 1995a; Potrac *et al.* 2002) and individualize their own communication strategies to each athlete, thus facilitating the development of effective relationships (Gallimore and Tharp 2004; Jones *et al.* 2003; Potrac *et al.* 2002).

The path to success: career development in coaching

No matter what the sporting discipline, researchers in the field of coaching science agree that elite, outstanding coaches who have made it to the top in their chosen sport all share certain attributes and will, to some extent, have followed similar 'career' paths. A number of independent researchers have shown that top performers, including coaches, generally follow similar developmental stages. Those individuals who end up as top coaches usually start out as novice, yet highly motivated athletes, progressing through more advanced athletic participation, followed by an introduction to coaching and finally culminating in coaching at the more advanced level (e.g. Bloom 1985; Berliner 1988; Gilbert and Côté 2003; Salmela 1994; Schinke *et al.* 1995). Coaches quite clearly 'grow into' their professional status through previous experiences as athletes (Bloom *et al.* 1995; Jones *et al.* 2003; Salmela 1994; Schinke *et al.* 1995). Indeed, if nothing else, simple mathematics provide indicative answers: many researchers now agree that, to reach expert status, whether as a coach or athlete, at least 10,000 hours or ten years of deliberate, focused, goal-orientated, practice is required (Côté *et al.* 1995b; Jones *et al.* 2003; Potrac *et al.* 2002).

During their initial participation in some form of organized youth sport, coaches will have come to understand the special idiosyncrasies of their particular sport through years of active experience and engagement (Sage 1989; Salmela 1994). They will have learned from their own coaches, by means of observation and modelling their own coaches' behavior. These principles of social learning theory (Bandura 1977b, 1986; Boesch and Tomasello 1998; Hancock *et al.* 2011) that have allowed humans to develop their own culture in a much wider setting (Causey and Bjorklund 2011) also explain how certain characteristics of a sports culture are passed on through generations of athletes and coaches alike. Sage (1989) coined the concept of 'organizational socialization', which describes how, in addition to becoming familiar with important technical aspects of being a coach, such as teaching specific skills, neophytes are also indoctrinated with the 'true essence' of that particular sport.

There is little formal empirical evidence mapping the background and educational development of the world's foremost equestrian coaches. However, anecdotal findings certainly seem to indicate that they, too, have gained much of their knowledge through a lifelong affiliation with horses that, generally, started in early childhood. As expressed by Latimer and Birke (2009) in their work examining people's associations with horses: 'Riders ... need to be 'educated' when young by being with horses from an early age and by progressing through different kind of riding experiences, and up the scale of different kinds of activity and horse' (Latimer and Birke 2009: 12). Findings from a study by Pummel *et al.* (2008) investigating within career transitions in the young event rider seem to provide some support of this notion, suggesting that strong family traditions in equestrianism led to riders taking up the sport at a young age. Previously unpublished data from the doctoral thesis of Maw (2012) on coaching practices in equestrian sports suggest an 'inseparable association between riding and teaching riding' (p. 137). Of the 41 participating riding coaches that Maw interviewed for her thesis, 39 had started riding as a child, with 78 per cent having been introduced to competition in their youth as well.

A previously unpublished preliminary survey investigated different aspects relating to the career development of equestrian coaches,[2] such as their age of first involvement with equestrian sports, their highest level ridden at and highest coaching level achieved. Findings strongly supported the notion displayed in other sports that early involvement in equestrian sports is an important prerequisite for equestrian coaches, especially those at the top level (Table 4.1).

Regardless then, of whether the ultimate goal is to become a top coach or a top athlete, long-term investment and commitment is a necessary requirement. Incidentally, while it does not seem strictly necessary that top coaches should have been elite performers themselves, they must, at the very least, have enjoyed a thorough grounding in the practical skills, theoretical knowledge and cultural underpinnings of the sport (Jones *et al.* 2010). In equestrian sport, the additional dimension relating to the quality of the horse complicates the question of performance level even further. Without a doubt, success in any equestrian discipline is, at least in part, dependent on the quality of the horse. While there may always be exceptions to the rule, talented horses do not come cheap and not all talented riders might be in a position to have access to such quality. Many

Table 4.1 First involvement with equestrian sports in relation to highest coaching levels
(*N* = 124)

Age (years)	Highest coaching level (n)					Total
	Unofficial/no competitions	Novice to medium	National talent development programmes	National under-21 squads	Semi-professional/ professional	
< 6	3	21	1	1	14	40
6–10	7	27	3	3	11	51
11–14	5	6	5	1	3	20
15–18	0	3	0	0	3	6
19–29	2	0	0	1	2	5
> 30	1	0	0	0	1	2
Total	18	57	9	6	34	124

excellent coaches might therefore not have competed at Olympic or World level themselves, a notion that is again supported by quantitative data relating to career development in equestrian sports. There are clearly a number of coaches who end up teaching at a level higher than the level at which they competed themselves, undoubtedly because of a lack of sufficient funds or the opportunity to ride 'better' horses. However, national governing bodies charged with devising equestrian coaching programmes should make sure that coaches have a thorough theoretical understanding of the technical requirements of how to structure the progressive training of both horse and rider. Furthermore, coaches should also have fundamental practical experience to convey the necessary information to their charges. (Table 4.2).

How we do things: sport-specific knowledge

We have already established that the process of conveying sport-specific information is one of the key requirements of coaching in sports. However, when it comes to differentiating the good from the average coach, the quality of the information that coaches impart on their charges plays an even more important role. We mentioned it in the previous section: researchers investigating excellence in sports agree that, to reach expert status, performers must devote approximately ten years or 10,000 hours to the deliberate practice of a particular sport or discipline (Ericsson and Charness 1994). In practice, this means training for three hours per day, every day, for a period of at least nine years – including holidays and weekends! But according to Ericsson *et al.* (1993), the key to excellence is not simply the number of training hours that develops true expertise. Rather, relevant training units must be structured around appropriate levels of difficulty and should include informative, i.e. content-driven, feedback and the opportunity for repetition and error correction. Only under those conditions will repetitive practice also lead to marked improvement in performance.

Table 4.2 Highest level at which equestrian coaches have ridden/are riding, compared with the level at which they are coaching (*N* = 124)

Highest level at which coaches competed (n)	Highest coaching level (n)					Total
	Unofficial/no competitions	Novice to medium	National talent development programmes	National under-21 squads	Semi-professional/ professional	
Unofficial/ no competitions	10	5	1	0	0	16
Novice to medium	7	32	6	1	4	50
National talent development programmes	0	2	2	0	2	6
National under-21 squads	0	4	0	0	0	4
Semi-professional/ professional	1	14	0	5	28	48
Total	18	57	9	6	34	124

What do these findings mean to (equestrian) coaches? While it is ultimately the athlete (rider) who needs to be sufficiently committed to achieving a status of excellence, the coach undoubtedly plays an instrumental role in creating the type of environment that allows for such training to occur. Any coach with the aspiration of producing top performers must have the kind of theoretical and practical knowledge to be able to provide appropriate instructions and feedback before, during and after each training unit. Equally importantly, coaches must have the necessary experience to develop long-term training programmes that allow athletes to progress through the relevant levels within an optimal timeframe. In equestrian sports, much like any other sporting discipline, this quite simply means that coaches need to have the necessary experience to teach and provide appropriate feedback at, and preferably above, the level at which the rider is performing. There will be only very few, if any, coaches who are able to guide their charges through the different developmental stages without having first mastered these stages themselves.

Indeed, the need to receive good quality instruction and feedback throughout their career might mean that, at some point, riders 'outgrow' their coaches. The improvement of athlete (rider) skill has been shown to be part and parcel of expert development (Bloom 1985; also see section on athlete development below) and it is again a hallmark of good coaches to recognize when it is time for the rider to be moving on to someone with more or better-suited experience. Equally important is that once the decision to move on to someone else has been made, the coach behaves 'gracefully' and does not consider the rider's decision to be personally motivated.

Yes, you can: developing self-esteem and self-confidence

While the ability to impart the relevant information relating to sport-specific skills and tactics is no doubt of utmost importance when teaching athletes, developing psychological components such as self-esteem and sport-specific confidence is likely to come a close second. As we have already seen in Chapter 3, the concepts of self-confidence, self-esteem and self-efficacy have long played an important role when discussing sports. Frequently, though, these concepts are being used interchangeably, even though they denote somewhat different phenomena. Self-esteem must be viewed as a global concept defined as internal reflections on one's own abilities, competence and self-worth (Malim and Birch 1989; Rosenberg 1965). Self-efficacy, or the more commonly used term of sport-specific self-confidence, entails an individual's notion of being able to perform a specific task successfully or deal with a particular situation (Bandura 1977a; also see Chapter 3). As discussed in Chapter 3, self-confidence has been found to be one of the very few psychological constructs consistently linked to improved sporting performance (see a meta-review by Woodman and Hardy 2003). Furthermore, the idea that sport participation increases levels of self-esteem, i.e. feelings of self-worth (Coopersmith 1967; Rosenberg 1979) also seems to be firmly ingrained in society and is frequently used to encourage athletic participation. What is more, considerable evidence exists to suggest that, in equestrian sports, both self-esteem and self-confidence are important moderators of performance (e.g. Beauchamp and Whinton 2005; Meyers *et al.* 1997; Traeen and Wang 2006; Wolframm and Micklewright 2009, 2010a, 2010b). The role of coaches in fostering and sustaining levels of self-esteem and self-confidence must therefore not be underestimated.

It seems, however, that self-esteem does not necessarily increase directly or immediately with sports participation. Rather, a number of contextual variables exist that seem to influence the development of global and specific measures of confidence. Generally speaking, levels of self-esteem are likely to increase if coaches show high levels of support, social acceptance, loyalty, trust and feedback that is accurate and positive (Harter 1999; Leary and Baumeister 2000). Research has identified several dimensions relating to overt coaching behavior that proved to be indicative of athlete satisfaction, including the quality of coach–athlete relationships and team cohesion (e.g. Curtis *et al.* 1979; Smith and Smoll 1990). Aspects such as coach supportiveness (i.e. reinforcement and mistake-contingent encouragement) and instructiveness (comprising technical instruction and mistake-contingent technical instruction) were associated with the most positive outcomes, while punitive behavior (e.g. punishment and punitive technical instructions) showed very strong negative correlations with athletes' attitudes.

More specifically, there are a number of coach-training programmes designed to enhance coaching behaviors, which, in turn, are believed to positively influence the development of confidence in young athletes (e.g. Brown and Butterfield 1992; Martens 1997; Seefeldt *et al.* 2001; Smith and Smoll 1996). One of the key components constitutes the emphasis on learning, effort, personal growth and improvement over objective, normatively evaluated success of the athlete (rider). Coaches are encouraged to use reinforcement strategies, rewarding correct skill deployment, encouragement and technical instructions rather than reverting to punishment or aggressive strategies when athletes fail to perform (Smoll *et al.* 1993). While, to date, no research exists examining these types of strategies in equestrian sport it may be assumed that optimal coaching behaviors apply equally to riding coaches. To increase riders' levels of self-confidence and self-esteem, equestrian coaches should create an environment that stimulates personal growth and skill development above more objective measures of success.

More specifically, this means that, during training, coaches should encourage athletes to 'keep trying', while also providing relevant technical instructions. All too often, riding coaches are quick to admonish what is incorrect ('Your horse needs to be softer in the hand' or 'You need to get it to react better to your leg') yet provide no further instruction as to how to proceed. While such comments may provide initial feedback for less-experienced riders, at a more established level, riders will have already felt through their legs, seat and hands what the coach has highlighted. Many riders might now adopt a 'trial-and-error' strategy for solving the problem but may eventually become disillusioned and uncertain of their own level of skill. In time, this may lead to a decrease in, first of all, sport-specific confidence and, if left in a negative spiral, in more global levels of self-esteem. Positive reinforcement, through praise, of the correct skills displayed and of the correct reaction of the horse will both increase riders' feelings of self-efficacy and their own ability to 'feel' the horse's correct response.

Day after day: developing motivation

The development of psychological parameters such as self-confidence and self-esteem can rarely be considered in isolation but almost invariably go hand in hand with motivational factors. Researchers tend to view motivation as a social cognitive concept, rather than mere physiological arousal (Roberts 2001). This means that levels of motivation are generally determined through the goals behind a chosen activity and are thus primarily concerned with the 'why' of a particular activity (Deci and Ryan 2000). Self-determination theory (Deci and Ryan 1985, 1991) broadly distinguishes between intrinsic and extrinsic motivation. It argues that the three intrinsic needs of achieving competence, autonomy and 'psychological relatedness' (i.e. satisfaction) are instrumental in achieving psychological health and wellbeing. Engaging in behaviors that are intrinsic and therefore authentic, derived from an individual's own perception of wishes and needs, has been found to lead to enhanced performance, persistence and creativity (Deci and Ryan 1991; Sheldon *et al.* 1997). Externally motivated factors, such as threats, punishment, imposed direction, forced goals and competence evaluations decrease intrinsic motivation (Deci and Ryan 1985). On the face of things, it seems apparent that athletes would fare much better in terms of psychological health, satisfaction and, ultimately, performance, to be motivated by intrinsic as opposed to extrinsic goals. Yet how individuals determine their own goals, i.e.

their personal definitions of why they engage in an activity, is heavily influenced by how they define personal success, which, in turn, may be dependent on environmental factors, such as coaching style, parental influences and, in later years, peer climate.

Achievement goal theory has contributed considerably towards the definition of success at a theoretical level and generally distinguishes between task involvement and ego involvement (Nicholls 1984, 1989). Task-involved individuals define success through personal levels of accomplishment, which are *self-referenced*. They feel successful when they have mastered a new task, witnessed personal skill improvement or have given their best effort. Most importantly, they are still likely to feel successful even if, at an objective level, they possess fewer skills than others. Ego-involved athletes, on the other hand, measure their own levels of success against others, i.e. they are *other-referenced*. Their main aim is to demonstrate superiority over others (generally competitors), which is also referred to as approach ego-orientation, or to avoid being seen to be inferior to others (avoidance ego-orientation) (Elliot and Church 1997). During their formative years, young athletes will develop relevant goal orientations through the concepts and interpretations of success that they perceive in significant others, i.e. coaches or parents. It is hardly surprising to note that task-orientated athletes will engage in more adaptive achievement strategies, and will be focused on learning new skills and personal improvement. Motivational problems and maladaptive behavior primarily occurs in environments with a 'winning at all cost' attitude and where mistakes are punished, social comparisons are drawn and athletes with higher ability are paid more attention and receive better resources (see Duda and Whitehead 1998; Harwood *et al.* 2008 for reviews on this topic).

Creating appropriate motivational climates in a sports setting clearly is one of the coach's key responsibilities. However, in line with Guba and Lincoln's (2005) interpretative approach to coaching, how athletes perceive their coaches' behavior has a pertinent effect on the type of motivational climate that is created. What is more, effective coach leadership and athlete performance are dependent on preferred and perceived coach feedback being congruent (Chelladurai 1984). Research by Stein *et al.* (2012), investigating youth ice-hockey players' perceptions of coach feedback, showed that athletes generally preferred more positive informational feedback, less punishment and less non-reinforcement behaviors of good performance or effort than they felt they had actually received. Results also showed that the more frequently coaches used punishment or ignored (i.e. did not reinforce) good performance, the more perceptions of an ego-involved motivational climate increased. Athletes felt that they were performing in a climate wherein social comparisons and performance outcomes were rewarded above personal development and effort. This is particularly worrisome in light of the fact that ego-involved motivational climates have been linked to increased levels of anxiety, tension, perceived performance pressure and maladaptive coping strategies (Treasure and Roberts 1998). The emphasis on task orientation, personal development and learning was perceived to be strongest when athletes felt that their coaches provided informational feedback, such as praise in response to successful performance, as well as encouragement and technical information in response to mistakes.

It seems clear, therefore, that coaches should pay particular attention, on the one hand, to the types of behavior they display when coaching athletes and, on the other, how their behaviors are perceived and interpreted by their athletes.

Where does this leave equestrian coaches in their search for creating motivational climates that help riders to develop or retain intrinsic, task-orientated motivation? In addition to the points that can be gleaned from previous sections, it may be useful to highlight some of the most salient methods that have been developed in the academic realm of coaching science (Ames 1992; Dweck 1986; Epstein 1989; Smoll and Smith 2006; Stein *et al.* 2012) and apply them to the equestrian context.

Coaches should emphasize the development of self-referenced, short-term mastery goals that are novel, challenging and help the rider to engage both with the task at hand and with their horse. Equestrian sports differ from other sports in the additional sense that riders will usually spend considerable time with their horses outside of any formal training contexts and are thus likely to do a lot of training on their own. This means that it is all the more important that riders remain involved in the structuring and decision-making processes of their training programmes. Riders should claim shared ownership of any achievement targets that may be set, while also being encouraged to engage in self-monitoring and self-management tools (see below).

Throughout the daily or weekly training, coaches should focus on personal development, progress and mastery, while acknowledging effort exerted. As such, both effort and progress should be positively reinforced, while mistakes should be followed up with instructional information. Most importantly, social comparisons should be avoided in favor of individual progress. No doubt this can be a challenging task in a competitive environment, yet it has also been recognized to be an important prerequisite to good coaching. A number of equestrian disciplines, such as dressage, reining or vaulting, are dependent on external judging, which is, by its very definition, dependent on more or less subjective assessments by outsider observers (Plessner and Haar 2006). As such, it is only too easy to measure and evaluate progress both in comparison to others and others' perception of performance. Especially in disciplines that are based on certain judging criteria, riders should be encouraged to set goals and to assess performance in view of their personal achievement. However, these principles equally apply to other, more objectively measured, disciplines. Any competitive sport inherently requires the comparison of athletes' skill and ability, whether such assessment is based on objective criteria such as time or poles knocked down or relatively subjective measurements such as judging scores. This means that, particularly in preparation for competition, coaches should encourage riders to focus on achieving optimal levels of communication with their horse and on working on what they know they need to do to get the best out of their horse. Scores or placings should only be viewed as secondary feedback to how the training is progressing, rather than being perceived as an end in itself.

In the eye of the beholder: the importance of interpretation

More recently, researchers in the field of coaching science have paid additional attention to how athletes perceive and interpret their coaches' behaviors (e.g. Cumming *et al.* 2007; Stein *et al.* 2012). The 'interpretative approach' to coaching (Guba and Lincoln 2005) is based on the assumption that, for behaviors to have meaning and value, athletes need to interpret them in the way they are intended. A study by Becker (2009) investigating athletes' lived experiences of great coaching developed six themes that were thought to play a role in how the coach was perceived. Four of those themes, namely coach attributes, relationships between coach and athletes, the coaching environment and the coaching system, remained stable throughout great coaching experiences. The coaches consistently perceived as great presented themselves in the same manner (coach attributes), maintained relationships in a clear, consistent and predictable way (relationships), provided an environment that was perceived as stable and thus 'safe' (coaching environment) and stuck to the same training system (coaching system). Essentially, this meant that athletes knew precisely what they could and could not do, allowing them to focus on their coach's actions, their own development and sporting performance (Becker 2009). Importantly, however, coaches are not always accurate in rating their own behaviors. In fact, research indicates that it is generally the athletes who are much more accurate in the assessment of their coaches' behaviors. Two important lessons can be drawn from such findings: Firstly, coaches should attempt to be as consistent as possible in their overall approach to training and communicating with their riders. Secondly, and perhaps even more importantly, coaches should also work on their own reflective skills, making sure they are aware of the types of behaviors they display and how these are perceived by their riders.

Under pressure: coaches' behavior in competition

And yet, despite considerable theoretical and practical knowledge regarding appropriate coaching behaviors, a different picture regularly emerges come competition time. Stern faces, raised voices, critical or even downright negative feedback minutes before a combination enters the ring are unfortunately still relatively commonplace. In a study investigating the frequency of negative comments made by coaches in a variety of children's team sports (rugby, netball, soccer and touch), Walters *et al.* (2012) found that more than one in five comments by coaches during the match were negative. While the authors rightly commented on the fact that the sporting culture and what might be associated as acceptable behavior is likely to contribute considerably towards how coaches behave, they also noted that the negative comments tend to undermine a positive sporting environment. In fact, the punitive behaviors displayed by coaches might even lead to feelings of resentment from athletes, rather than inducing performance enhancement, and might in the long run contribute towards athlete drop-out from sport (Smoll and Smith 2006). In addition to the detrimental effects on the human athletes, equestrian coaching science also needs to take into account the indirect effect on the horse – tense and anxious riders, who are lacking in self-confidence, are unlikely to coax a relaxed, confident performance from their horses (e.g. Wolframm and Micklewright 2010a, 2010b, 2011), resulting in what might be called a 'double whammy' of negative coaching effects.

What is more, the literature investigating motivational factors for children to participate in sport has consistently identified fun and excitement, skills development, action and challenges (Barber *et al.* 1999). Coaches, who are driven to engage in negative behavior, shouting at the riders or even punishing them, are unlikely to increase either motivation or effort in their charges. Especially in younger riders (up to the age of 11–12) such behaviors might go a long way towards undermining their enjoyment of the sport. Children in their pre-teens are only just beginning to develop the kind of cognitive skills that allow them to understand the reasons behind their coach's outburst. Furthermore, hypothetical deductive reasoning, which helps children to understand that, to achieve their future goals, they might have to put up with unpleasant situations in the short term, generally only starts to emerge during the teenage years (Piaget *et al.* 1969). The reasons why coaches might be inclined to react negatively in a competitive setting have been put down to perceived pressure for coaches to perform themselves or to show competence (Mageau and Vallerand 2003). It therefore stands to reason that, in situations where coaches might themselves feel that they have to 'deliver the goods', their coping mechanisms result in negative or punitive commentary towards their charges. From an anecdotal point of view, this kind of behavior might also be observed in overzealous parents, who seem to be bent on seeing their children become successful at all cost. Again, empirical data are needed to further investigate the role that parents play in equestrian sports. In the meantime, however, parents might be well served to take into account the general principles applicable to good coaching practice.

While there clearly are a number of 'cultural' differences between equestrian sports and team sports, some immediate lessons can be drawn. Even in the competitive 'heat of the moment', when coaches feel that a lot may be gained by outstanding performances, the type of feedback they give and how they behave towards their charges should mirror what is displayed during training. That way, the likelihood of invoking the same kind of behavioral and emotional responses from the riders, as well as creating a motivational atmosphere that stimulates enjoyment of competition, increases considerably. In fact, research by Erickson *et al.* (2011) showed that the coach–athlete interactions of a successful swimming team were characterized by more consistent, structured communication and feedback patterns than those in a less-successful team. While there can be little doubt as to the complexity and unpredictability of the coaching process (e.g. Bowes and Jones 2006; Jones and Wallace 2005), Erickson *et al.* (2011) argue that the most successful coaches respond in a structured, predictable manner, thus providing athletes with a 'safe' environment that fosters appropriate athlete behaviors, e.g. professionalism, motivation, commitment, concentration and effort (Oliver *et al.* 2010) not only in training but also in competition.

Coach–rider relationships: match or mismatch?

Accurately interpreting behavior is difficult at the best of times, however. As we have already discussed in Chapter 3, much of how and what we think, feel and perceive is shaped and influenced by our own personality traits. In that sense, most of our interactions with others and the immediate environment will be shaped also by their various personality traits. Research investigating the effect of personality traits on relationships has found strong support for the notion that the degree of similarity between two individuals shapes the quality of their relationship. More specifically, it has been suggested that similarity in personality traits can assist in reducing conflict, reinforcing one another's behaviors and characteristics, increasing levels of attraction, facilitating communication patterns and increasing consensus (e.g. Barelds and Dijkstra 2007; Selfhout *et al.* 2009). While there is limited evidence available regarding the effect of personality concurrence between athletes and their coaches, a study by Jackson *et al.* (2011) showed that, especially regarding the personality traits of extraversion and openness to experience, dissimilarity patterns tended to undermine perceptions of dyadic quality. High levels of extraversion, for example, are indicative of active communication patterns and high levels of activity, as well as personal disclosure and engagement in social support. Coaches and athletes with similar levels of extraversion are therefore likely to comply with each other's need for certain types of communication patterns, while dissimilar individuals are likely to get frustrated if the other does not respond as they would wish. Again, similarity in openness scores also provided an important basis for relationship quality. Openness is generally associated with preferences for discussion, diversity in opinion, innovation and flexibility (McCrae and Costa 1997). The coach–athlete relationship is by its very nature defined by striving to improve performance of the rider, which may be achieved through different means and training methods. To develop training strategies that suit both members of the dyad in terms of innovativeness, flexibility and room for discussion, both athlete and coach should be 'singing from the same hymn sheet'.

Depending on the level of training, the way in which rider and coach come together might vary. In riding schools, there is little opportunity for riders to pick and choose their coaches, short of changing stables. Nevertheless, if at all feasible, riding schools might spend time trying to match riding pupils with instructors who are similar in terms of temperament and attitude towards the sport. At present, riders who perform at a higher level, and thus invest in individual coaching lessons, usually consider first and foremost a particular coach's training style – which training philosophy they follow and what training principles they apply. However, to derive the most benefit, motivation and satisfaction from training sessions, which, as we have seen, will ultimately lead to increased levels of confidence, riders should spend some time in determining whether a coach also suits them on a personal level.

Models of athlete development: coaching through the (riders') ages

Compared with most other sports, horse riding may be performed into late adulthood. In fact, a number of elite athletes may reach their peak in their 30s, 40s or even 50s. At the same time, horse sports are very popular with children and teenagers, who might benefit from specific talent development initiatives (Elferink-Gemser *et al.* 2011). As a result, equestrian coaches and instructors teaching at different levels and across different age groups should be aware of different stages of cognitive and emotional development, in particular in their younger clients, and be able to apply pedagogical techniques accordingly (Lyle 2002). In his seminal work on child development, Piaget (summarized in Piaget *et al.* 1969) conceptualized his periods as 'four periods of development', which greatly help to understand the differences in approach that might be required in teaching, for example, a six-year-old as opposed to a 12-year-old.

In addition to normative cognitive development in children and young adults, a number of athlete development models have been conceptualized, mapping different transitional periods within sporting careers (e.g. Bloom 1985; Côté 1999; Wylleman and Lavallee 2004). Among existing models, the developmental model of sport participation (Côté 1999) has been acknowledged as the most prominent among modern athlete development literature (Bruner *et al.* 2010). This model asserts that athletes pass through three stages of sports development during their sporting career: the 'sampling stage', which typically occurs between the ages of 6 and 12, during which children will 'sample', i.e. participate in, a number of different sports and engage in activities that are less structured and designed to maximize inherent enjoyment (Côté and Hay 2002). The 'specialization stage' (ages 13–15) will see the young athlete participating in fewer disciplines, while at the same time expending greater effort with a view to improving 'specialized' performance. During the 'investment years' (age 16+) athletes will traditionally engage in large quantities of deliberate practice activities, which are characterized by being highly structured, requiring effort, generating no immediate reward and aimed at improving performance (Ericsson *et al.* 1993).

During the years of equestrian participation, i.e. pre-operational and concrete operational stages, coaching strategies should therefore be focused on enjoyment of the sport, with young riders ideally receiving much positive feedback and stimulation from the coach or instructor. While requiring some basic levels of expertise and an inherent sense of safety for child and pony, a riding coach teaching at the initial stages of athletic development should also have the necessary didactic and motivational skills, being able to emphasize the 'fun' elements rather than merely focusing on skill development. Most importantly at this stage, the emphasis should be on 'sampling' different disciplines. While parents or coaches might themselves have a preference for a certain discipline, they should allow their child to experience the full range of equestrian activities, ranging from flatwork to jumping, from mounted games to hacking out in the woods. Early diversification has even been shown to develop lifelong enjoyment and participation of different sporting activities (Côté and Hay 2002; Kirk 2005), while early specialization, on the other hand, is associated with performance anxiety, injuries, increased pressure from parents and coaches and burnout (Hecimovich 2004; Wiersma 2000). In equestrian sports, it stands to reason therefore that a thorough grounding in a variety of different disciplines helps the young rider to develop confidence across a variety of horse-related situations, as well as laying the foundation for potentially more versatile equine training systems in future. Dressage riders who are capable of and enjoy jumping their horses on occasion are likely to feel more secure in the saddle, even when their horses are proving to be 'high spirited'. Showjumpers with a good grounding in the principles of dressage, on the other hand, are likely to have better schooled, and thus potentially safer, horses to jump.

One of the key requirements at this point is, of course, the provision of the appropriate four-legged companion. While anecdotal evidence abounds of young riders 'learning together with their pony', an inexperienced mount is generally highly unsuitable for a young child still learning.

The 'specialization years' and the next important stage of the development of the young rider are defined through increasing commitment and self-direction. This should be matched by an increase in commitment and specialization from the coach who, in turn, should have sufficient expertise in any particular discipline to further the young rider's desire to learn. The relevant style of instruction thus also becomes more skill-orientated and technical. However, while this is the period during which riders might decide to specialize in one particular discipline, coaches (and parents) are well served to continue to include elements of other equestrian disciplines: a study by Wall and Côté (2007) showed that hockey players who later dropped out had started specialized training significantly earlier than other players (mean age of 11.75 years for drop-out players as opposed to 13.8 years for active players). Even though straight comparisons between these two rather different sporting activities are difficult at best, the results by Wall and Côté should nevertheless be viewed as a warning against early specialization in equestrian sports until proven otherwise.

During the final, i.e. most advanced, stage of athlete development, namely the investment years, riders show total commitment to their chosen discipline and their own development. Any coach should now be able to provide the rider, no matter what their age, with the necessary guidance in terms of technique and skill to support them on their road to success. Throughout the investment years, talented riders (and other athletes for that matter) are likely to undergo additional career transitions, as they make their way from grassroots to regional, national and, ultimately, international level, a process which in itself is likely to bring along with it its own inherent challenges and difficulties. In a study investigating career transitions in three-day eventing, Pummel *et al.* (2008) found that transition-related changes in riders are comparable with those of other athletes. Semi-structured interviews with riders progressing from club to regional level showed that, even though the sport of eventing had itself become increasingly more enjoyable, riders also showed significantly more investment, sacrifice and effort. A multidimensional support system, which helped meet emotional, esteem, tangible and informational needs of the riders, was key throughout the transitional process. In line with previous research into athlete development (Côté 1999), parental support was considerable and 'leading' in the initial stages of the riders' eventing careers but was eventually superseded by the supporting role from coaches and peers, who were better able to provide technical, sports-related advice. Nevertheless, and perhaps in contrast to a number of other sports, parents continued to play an important supportive role. Equestrian sports in general, and eventing in particular, are very time-consuming and cost intensive and 'a young rider is unlikely to be able to progress in the sport without such support' (Pummel *et al.* 2008: 442). The authors identified organizational issues to be a particular source of stress, which may be alleviated somewhat through a strong support network of significant others, i.e. parents, peers and coaches. Furthermore, the study also highlights that intensive involvement in sport, especially if it also involves the transition towards more advanced levels, can also impose challenges on other areas of life, such as at the social or academic level (Wylleman and Lavallee 2004). From a coaching perspective, this means that coaches should be prepared not only to provide technical and skill-related support but also to help their riders to develop relevant coping skills for dealing effectively with the challenges of career development.

To summarize, the continuous development of a rider in terms of skill and ability from beginner to advanced level means that the requirements on coaching behavior and didactical skills also change. In addition to the necessary technical, motivational and didactical requirements, a flexible and open attitude towards the changing needs of the rider thus forms an absolute must of the equestrian coach. See Table 4.3 for a brief description of the four stages of development (Piaget *et al.* 1969) and the developmental model of sport participation (Côté 1999) with their potential application to equestrian coaching. For the purpose of completeness, Table 4.3 also lists the first, sensorimotor, stage, despite it not being strictly applicable to coaching.

Table 4.3 Stages of theoretical child and athlete development with applications to equestrian sports

Age (years)	Four periods of development[1]	DMSP[2]	Application to equestrian sport
0–2	SENSORI-MODEL During their first stage of development, young infants begin to develop sensorimotor skills function and become aware of how they might interact with the world. Towards the end of this period, infants come to understand 'object permanence'; i.e. they learn that just because objects are no longer within their field of perception, they do not cease to exist.	No equivalent	The infant develops the capacity for simple problem solving towards the end of this first period and ambitious parents might thus decide to sit their offspring on the back of a pony. It should be clear, though, that seeing that the infant lacks the necessary motor and cognitive skills to control the animal, any such activities should only be attempted under close (parental) supervision, with an adult holding on to the child at all times.

Table 4.3 continued

Age (years)	Four periods of development[1]	DMSP[2]	Application to equestrian sport
2–6	PRE-OPERATIONAL The child is starting to be able to use mental representations of actions, meaning that they are able to imitate actions previously observed and to engage in symbolic play.	EARLY BEGINNINGS SAMPLING STAGE (see below for details)	Any coaching that occurs at this age should be focused on playful activities only rather than any type of formal instruction and should invoke the child's new-found sense of imaginary play.
6–12	CONCRETE OPERATIONAL At this stage of development, children begin to engage in 'operations', a system of internal mental representations that underlie logical problem solving. Relational reasoning and classification also start to develop.	SAMPLING STAGE Children should be allowed to engage in numerous sporting activities, including various equestrian disciplines. The main focus should be on deliberate play activities.	With children learning to ride in the early stages of the concrete operational stage, the focus of any coaching should still lie primarily with 'fun' elements. Coaches should therefore be primarily supportive and encouraging, with activities aimed at experiencing enjoyment. Once the child develops the ability for relational reasoning, more structured teaching can be employed. A note of caution: younger children quite frequently seem to engage in new activities without any fear. However, once the capacity for relational reasoning begins to develop, children also might become aware of the potential consequences of their actions, meaning that a previously brave child might all of sudden become much more easily frightened.

Table 4.3 continued

Age (years)	Four periods of development[1]	DMSP[2]	Application to equestrian sport
12– adult	FORMAL OPERATIONAL During the next few years of development, the teenager develops the ability for hypothetical deductive reasoning: starting with the idea of a possible outcome and working its way back towards what this might mean regarding current behavior or actions. Teenagers and young adults are now able to reflect on their own actions, set goals and modify their own behaviors towards achieving those goals.	SPECIALISATION STAGE (13–15) Young riders should now engage in fewer disciplines and should increase the number of deliberate practice activities. INVESTMENT STAGE (16 +) At this stage, the rider will have chosen a particular discipline and will primarily engage in deliberate practice activity.	Coaching becomes the amalgamation of appropriate technical, motivational and didactical skills. Coaches (and parents) should beware of asking riders to specialize too early. Instead, the importance of learning different equestrian-related skills and activities should be highlighted, both from a motivational and a safety point of view. Once riders have taken the step towards discipline specialization, coaches should support athletes throughout the transitional periods by helping riders to develop appropriate coping skills.

Notes:
[1] Adapted from Piaget *et al.* 1969.
[2] Developmental model of sport participation (adapted from Côté 1999).

The value of reflection

It should have become clear by now that outstanding coaching is extremely demanding, both in terms of content and process. To improve existing skills and to develop greater insight into coaches' own levels of functioning, scientific investigations are now focusing on how knowledge in coaching is generated (Knowles *et al.* 2006) and the role reflective practice might play throughout (Ghaye and Ghaye 1998). In fact, this is now being recognized as an important tool in improving both content and process of coaching. Even though early literature suggests that coaches should be able to develop solutions to the different issues they encounter during coaching practice based on their theoretical knowledge (Schön 1983, 1987), the 'real world' of coaching is hardly ever as clear cut as that. Issues that might have appeared simple and easy to navigate in a classroom become much more complex in a field setting, through a combination of different circumstances (Anderson *et al.* 2004; Galvin 1998).

The practice of reflecting on their own actions and decisions can help coaches to understand why they did what they did, enabling them in turn to develop confidence in their own coaching style even when under pressure (Kidman 2001). While there can be no doubt that the process of reflection in any guise is likely to be of benefit, engaging in it in a structured manner with an understanding of the underlying framework involved will reap the most rewards (Platzer *et al.* 1997).

In addition to the benefits attached to the written reflective process associated with, for example, journal writing (Scanlon and Chernomas 1997), the more open exchanges of reflective conversations are likely to trigger even greater development and progress. One medium that has recently been developed to allow for an individual reflective experience and to encourage the reflective conversation with likeminded others is the reflective card ('R-card') (Ghaye 2008). R-cards have been designed to enable coaches to reflect quickly and in a focused manner on any decisions or behaviors displayed while in action. The cards include the five coaching skills or 'competencies' of judgment, communication, decision making, team working and observation (Ghaye 2008) and encourage a coach to engage in the act of 'noticing' their own performance in one or several of these core competencies while in action. All that is required is for the coach, while engaged in any coaching activity, to choose any one particular competency and complete the R-card on the spot. Later on, following the coaching session, a more detailed reflection sheet may be completed and in-depth reflection on skills displayed and decisions taken is enabled.

In one of the few published studies that focus on coaching in equestrian sports, Hughes, Lee and Chesterfield (2009) investigated the potential of R-cards in equestrian coaching. Especially in a sport such as equestrianism, which is deeply steeped in tradition, a rather novel approach to improving practice might take some 'getting used to'. However, results indicated that equestrian coaches found the R-cards a useful means to reflect on and improve their own coaching practice. Despite the fact that the cards were used in a slightly different context to how they were supposed to be used, namely following a training session, rather than during, they nevertheless triggered the kind of thought processes that reflective practice aims to encourage (Hughes *et al.* 2009). Even though further research is required to support existing findings of the usefulness of the reflective process that occurs, there can be no doubt that, in equestrian sports, in which a coach is charged with overseeing and guiding the development of the rider, the horse and the horse–rider combination, regular reflection must remain paramount.

Not only coaches but also riders themselves should strive to engage in regular reflective practice regarding their own progress as riders, especially if they are not in a position to have a coach at their side at all times. Especially at grassroots level, few riders are able to afford daily coaching and training. Yet they should still be able to monitor their own training, to recognize mistakes made and continue to strive for improvement. Monitoring strategies, such as using a training diary, reflective analysis, video analysis and using sport science tools (discussed in more detail in the conclusion to this book, Chapter 7) have been found to help Olympian athletes, including equestrians, in achieving excellence

(Bradbury 2001). The general concept of self-coaching, i.e. applying the principles of performance analysis and evaluation to an individual's own riding, might
therefore provide an important tool for riders at all levels.

Coach–rider–horse 'triad': the third partner

In addition to important attributes and behaviors displayed by coaches,
researchers also acknowledge the importance of the different contextual factors
and their contribution to the coaching context (Côté *et al.* 1995a). We have
already discussed this earlier in the text. With regards to equestrian sports, the
presence and innate unpredictability of the horse must surely be considered the
most important contextual factor and, as such, can only be considered as a moderating variable in the coach–athlete relationship.

While relatively little research exists investigating effective communication
patterns in horse sports, there exist a number of indicators that coaching in equestrian sport is considerably more complex than in other sporting disciplines. For
her Masters' thesis, Cumyn (2000) investigated communication patterns during
dressage coaching. In addition to the more commonly used communication chan-
nels of visual and verbal, she argued that equestrian coaching also relied
considerably on kinaesthetic and auditory feedback given by the horse to facilitate the learning process. Not surprisingly then, the level to which the horse is
trained necessarily impacts on the type of coaching employed. Cumyn identified
six contexts characterized through different levels of experience in horse and
rider. While the coach–rider interaction featured strongly throughout the six
different contexts, the focus of the coach on either teaching the rider, helping the
rider to teach the horse or teaching the horse changed. For example, in a
horse–rider combination where both horse and rider were inexperienced, a coach
would focus both on improving horse and rider. A combination of experienced
horse and inexperienced rider, on the other hand, would be taught with the main
focus on the rider. While Cumyn's study only employed three coaches and six
riders, her model serves as an important starting point of reflection for equestrian
coaches. It almost goes without saying that, regardless of the type of sport or
discipline, coaches should always aim to tailor their sessions to the ability, skill
and experience of the athlete. In equestrian sports, however, it is not merely the
rider but also the horse's level of experience and ability that the coach must take
into account. As such, equestrian coaches continuously need to be aware of both
their human and equine charges and the level of interaction that goes on within
the coach–rider–horse triad.

Incidentally, at this point, readers may have noted a certain analogy between
effective coaching strategies of riders (humans) with the appropriate training of
horses. When discussing how they train their horses, most (top) riders will agree
that good horse management starts with planning training and competition sched-
ules. Furthermore, even though a concept such as 'self-confidence' remains
questionable in the horse as a non-reflective animal,[3] most riders at the top of their
game will spend considerable time teaching their horses the skills necessary to

compete at a certain level. They will also be very much aware of providing their horses with regular diversion and distraction by way of, for example, relaxing hacks through the countryside. Most importantly perhaps, almost all top riders consider adapting their riding and training systems to fit individual horses' needs as an essential prerequisite to performance (Wolframm 2011a; Wolframm and Meulenbroek 2012). One might therefore be drawn to conclude that, at least on some level, the effective coaching of riders is underpinned by the same principles as the effective training of horses.

Equestrian judging and bias: taking a different angle

Competitive sport depends by its very definition on performance assessment. Depending on the type of sporting discipline, this can be done objectively, such as in poles knocked down in showjumping, the winning time in a trotting or galloping race or the number of goals scored in a polo match. Equally, there are a number of other disciplines that rely on a system of points or scores, given by either one judge or a panel of judges on technical and aesthetic components. In fact, modern sports depend to some considerable extent on performance judgment: one-third of sports recognized by the International Olympic Committee use judging to assess performance (Stefani 1998). While there can be little doubt that judges try to evaluate athletes as objectively as possible, their judgment is prone to being influenced by other factors than pure performance criteria (Plessner and Haar 2006). To the competing athletes, as well as to the spectators, such judgments might, at times, even come across as biased or 'unfair'.

In the equestrian sport of dressage, inconsistent scoring and considerable variations among high-ranking judges at international events have caused considerable concern among riders, horse owners, sponsors and spectators. Seeing that competitive results not only influence individual and team standings but also impact on the market price of the horse, developing judging systems that are transparent and objective has become imperative, both from a sporting and an economic perspective. However, to be able to develop any such systems, an appreciation and understanding of how judges come to make decisions is paramount. While the current volume does not allow for sufficient space to discuss the issue of judging, perception and bias in equestrian sports in full, a brief overview of some of the most important issues relating to biases in judging is provided here, to stimulate further debate on the topic.

Even though it would be desirable for judges to use all the information available, human processing capacity is limited (Plessner and Haar 2006). People in general and, in the context of this section, judges in particular, are strongly inclined to employ decision-making 'heuristics' (they make use of easily accessible information that they believe to be reflective of the entire situation to come to a decision). A number of studies investigating bias in competitive sport have shown that panel judging is very susceptible to non-performance based factors (e.g. Boen *et al.* 2006). They reason as follows (in general terms): even though judges are usually given detailed descriptors of movements to be performed, the judgment process is nevertheless frequently influenced by a number of biases. The following six biases are commonly identified in the sport psychological literature:

1. The 'patriotism effect' refers to the tendency to favour athletes from one's own country (e.g. Ansorge and Scheer 1988; Fenwick and Chatterjee 1981; Seltzer and Glass 1991; Ste-Marie 1996; Whissell *et al.* 1993).
2. The 'halo effect' refers to the tendency to generalize impressions of an athlete's performance in one dimension to a number of other dimensions (Borman 1975; Moormann 1994).
3. The 'order effect' refers to the tendency to expect a good or bad performance by the athlete as a function of the rank order in which the performance takes place (e.g. Ansorge *et al.* 1978; Moormann 1994; Plessner 1999; Scheer and Ansorge 1979, 1980).
4. The 'memory-influenced effect' refers to the tendency to be influenced by specific prior performances (Ste-Marie 2003; Ste-Marie and Lee 1991; Ste-Marie and Valiquette 1996; Ste-Marie *et al.* 2001).
5. The 'reputation effect' refers to the tendency to found one's evaluation on the reputation of that athlete (Findlay and Ste-Marie 2004).
6. The 'conformity effect' refers to the tendency to adapt one's scores to the scores of judging colleagues (Scheer *et al.* 1983; Vanden Auweele *et al.* 2004; Wanderer 1987).

For equestrian disciplines that are based on subjective performance assessments, such as 'pure' dressage, the dressage phase in eventing, vaulting and several Western disciplines, these judging effects seem to have several important implications. Open feedback systems are likely to increase conformity among judges, based in turn on normative or informative influences. The relative stability of the conformity effect over time also implies that, even on a day when a particular horse–rider dyad does not perform as expected, judges might still be inclined to adhere to previous norms. Taking into account both reputation and memory-influenced effects, this may mean that longitudinal judging remains relatively stable, sometimes even regardless of actual performances. The most immediate implication is that judges should be rotated at least for championships, a decision that has already been implemented by the FEI for all their major championships.

In addition to these most immediate issues, judges might also tend towards certain biases depending on their personality disposition. Scheer *et al.* (1983) argued that judges succumbed more easily to the conformity bias if they scored low on personality traits such as dominance and autonomy. Interestingly, Scheer and colleagues also discovered that conformity seems to be more prevalent when scoring is negative. This may mean that individuals in positions of influence, such as judges, may feel that critical comments may support their position of authority and expertise more easily than granting higher marks. Future research should aim to investigate in more detail the prevalence of judging bias in equestrian sports, as well as the impact on psychological aspects, such as how dispositional traits or situation-induced mood states affect the tendency towards certain types of biases. From an applied perspective, it seems evident that additional efforts must be taken to increase transparency and applicability of judging systems, with particular focus on effective judge training and educational schemes.

Concluding thoughts

There is no doubt that coaching and training not only support the development of appropriate levels of skill but may also play a major role in preventing accidents and subsequent injuries in horse–rider combinations. While the literature investigating coaching strategies in equestrian sports is currently relatively sparse, much can be gleaned from studies into other sports. Indeed, many of the principles that apply to effective coach–athlete relationships are equally relevant in equestrian coach–rider combinations. However, the nature of equestrian sports demands structural investigations relating to the nature of effective coaching of the horse–rider dyad.

Chapter highlights

1. Coaching may be defined as aiming to improve riders' physical, technical, tactical and psychological skills and abilities to allow them to cope with the demands of the different equestrian disciplines.
2. Compared with other sports, the task of an equestrian coach is even more complex: in addition to supporting riders on their way to achieving excellence, coaches should also have the relevant knowledge and skill to (help) train riders' horses.
3. A definition of a definite set of coaching competencies is difficult to achieve, owing to the great variety of contextual variables, including the requirements and idiosyncrasies of the various sporting disciplines, different settings for training and competition, sociopolitical aspects, individual differences of coach and athlete, and environmental components. This means that coaches need to be well versed in the specific demands of their own coaching contexts.
4. Generally speaking, coaching competencies relate to either sport-specific components, including skills, techniques and strategies or performance-related knowledge such as biomechanics, exercise physiology, nutrition, sports medicine, growth and development and sport psychology.
5. The process of coaching might feasibly be divided into the subcategories of conveying of information, structuring of practice, administering feedback, and encouraging appropriate behaviors and developing personal competencies.
6. There is more to being an outstanding coach than merely achieving results at the highest level. More importantly, outstanding coaches should focus on the overall optimal psychological, physical and technical development of their riders.
7. The concept of 'organizational socialization' describes how the important 'cultural' aspects of sport are passed on through generations of athletes and

coaches. The careers of equestrian coaches are generally thought to develop from an early age and through active participation, allowing coaches to really understand the true nature of the sport.

8. Among other factors, outstanding coaches should possess relevant sport-specific knowledge. They should be able to develop and encourage self-esteem, self-confidence and self-efficacy and know how to nurture motivation in their riders.

9. Consistency in their overall approach to training and coaching, combined with reflecting on how coaching behaviors might be perceived by riders are important attributes in coaches and mirror in essence the type of training principles riders should apply when training their horses.

10. To derive the most benefit, satisfaction and motivation from coaching sessions, coaches and riders should also be well-matched. Evidence suggests that those coach–rider combinations who share certain personality dispositions are better suited to one another.

11. Considering that equestrian sport is enjoyed by a broad range of people, from very young children to elderly adults, coaches must be flexible in their didactical approach and tailor their coaching sessions to every individual rider's needs.

12. The nature of the coach–rider–horse triad dictates that the level to which horse and rider are trained impacts on the type of coaching employed.

13. Judging in equestrian sports presents an additional challenge, as limits of human processing capacity might lead to certain types of biases, such as the so-called patriotism effect, halo effect, order effect, memory-influenced effect, reputation effect and conformity effect.

5 Injuries in equestrian sport

Dealing with it or part of the deal?

Introduction: a bittersweet story – the tale of Courtney King-Dye

As an Olympic dressage rider with many successes at the top level to her name, Courtney King-Dye had everything going for her. A yard full of talented horses, plenty of ability and a thirst to become the best she could possibly be, the young American was living her childhood dream. But on 3 March 2010, everything changed.

Courtney was schooling a six-year-old, cantering down the long side of the arena, when the horse tripped and fell, trapping Courtney underneath him. She was not wearing a helmet. By her own admission, she had been in a hurry to get to a show and did not bother to put on the protective hard hat. As a direct result of her fall, Courtney suffered a skull fracture and a traumatic brain injury that left her in a coma for four weeks, unable to do the simplest of physical tasks for many months afterwards. While her cognitive abilities were not affected, walking, talking and, of course, riding, had turned into the ultimate challenge.

Yet the personality characteristics that helped Courtney get to the top of her chosen sport would prove equally important on the long road to recovery. In April 2012, Courtney had recovered sufficiently to qualify for the US Paralympic selection trial. She ended up not participating, as her horse, Make Lemonade, was deemed unsuitable as a therapy horse. However, her spirit and competitive streak seem unbroken, as she continues in her aim to be the best she can be and compete in the 2016 Paralympic Games in Rio de Janeiro, Brazil.

Courtney King-Dye's story underlines the importance of safety in equestrian sports, as she herself continues to expound in the Riders4Helmets Campaign (www.riders4helmets.com) that was sparked by her tragic accident.

As almost every rider is likely to attest, riding and being around horses is dangerous and accidents unfortunately do happen. Common adages in equestrian sports frequently focus on the theme of riders parting company with their horses: 'Riding is falling and getting up again' or 'You need to fall off seven times to become a rider'. Many of us have fallen off whilst out on a hack, during a showjumping round, going cross-country or 'backing' a young horse. But even more 'sedate' daily schooling activities or simply interacting with horses from the ground can be associated with very serious injuries, as evidenced by the tragic case of Courtney King-Dye.

Even though many of us might think of horses as 'gentle giants', the reasons why horse riding is potentially extremely dangerous are – almost – intuitive. Seeing that horses rely on their bodies to transmit and receive information, they are highly skilled at reading (and using) body language. Such awareness on the part of the horse implies that any minute changes of body position, muscular tonus, respiration and even heart rate from the rider might be picked up and reacted upon by the horse. Combined with the horse's considerable size and strength including a mind of its own (Brandt 2004), equestrian sports may be considered as some of the most dangerous, with fatalities or severe injuries, especially in the discipline of eventing, being as common as one injury for one hour of riding (Silver 2002). More conservative estimates place the rate of injury at one accident per 350 to 1,000 hours of – non-competitive – riding (Bixby-Hammet and Brooks 1989; Firth 1985). On the basis of these statistics, horse riding can be classified as higher risk than automobile racing, motorcycling, skiing and rugby (Buckley *et al.* 1993; Macnab and Cadman 1996). Yet, regardless of the dangers of the sport, horse riding has lost little of its appeal, with participation rates continually on the increase (Hawson *et al.* 2010). As we expand on in Chapter 6, the bond between horse and human is much more than simply 'sport'. Frequently, riding horses becomes a choice of life for riders and subsequently forms an important part of who they are. In addition to the more serious consequences of equine-related accidents, such as broken bones, head or internal injuries or even loss of life, less-severe physical impairments might nevertheless result in a – at the very least temporary – loss of a rider's identity. Not being able to compete, train or even be around the horse upsets routine and can also disrupt the existing relationship between horse and rider. It becomes clear therefore that preventing accidents and, as a result, injuries in horse sports becomes of primary importance. This chapter draws together current findings on injury rates, most common injuries and existing knowledge regarding injury prevention, while also providing recommendations on how to safeguard the health and welfare of riders in different situations.

Injury rates and types of injury: a dangerous game

Accepting that equestrian sports are dangerous is one thing. But riders may ask themselves, why they should torture themselves with the gruesome statistics of it all, trying to understand the rationale behind horse-related injuries. The horse remains a horse after all and it is the combination of speed, power and unpredictability that provides for much of the thrill of riding. Might it not be much better then to stick one's head in the proverbial sand and simply hope to be spared from serious injury?

In his textbook on human motor control, Rosenbaum (2010) argues that understanding a system means being able to predict, ultimately control and, in the case of equestrian sports, avoid it. At this point, we are still a long way away from being able to reliably predict rider accidents, let alone avoid them. Yet the mere process of identifying what causes accidents, their severity and which factors are instrumental, might lead to the equestrian community creating a safer environment for horse sports.

The incidence and severity of injuries tend to vary somewhat among different countries, making identification of key factors and direct comparisons difficult. In her review on equestrian injuries, Havlik (2010) rightly notes that equine-related incidents are influenced by the equestrian culture and, by extension, the type of equestrian activities in which people engage. Nevertheless, equestrian sports seem to feature at the very top of any list of dangerous sports. An early study by Firth (1985) found 20 times more accidents in horse riding than in motorcycling, with more accidents occurring per hour, while a review 15 years later by Sorli (2000) identified the hospital admission rate from equestrian injury rates as more than three times as high as from motorcycling injuries. Studies by Pounder (1984) and Paix (1999) identified equestrian sports as the activity with the highest mortality rate of one per one million participants. However, other researchers have noted that absolute frequencies of injuries in horse-related activities are no higher than other risk sports such as wrestling, football, track and field (Havlik 2010), yet the risk of severe injury catapults equestrian sports above and beyond other high-risk sports such as motorcycling, American football and automobile racing (Havlik 2010; Lee and Steenberg 2008; Smartt and Chalmers 2009). Of all riders who had incurred an injury, females generally outnumbered males, ranging from 53 per cent (Hobbs *et al.* 1994) to 84.6 per cent (Moss *et al.* 2002). In their review on equestrian injury patterns, Hawson *et al.* (2010) further reported that females were represented more frequently in younger age groups. Even though male riders were underrepresented, their injuries were generally more severe (Jagodzinski and DeMuri 2005; Cuenca *et al.* 2009), which might perhaps be due to a greater willingness to take risk. Future research committed to identifying underlying causes of accidents undoubtedly needs to investigate the relationship between different dispositional tendencies, attitudes and behaviors on injury rates.

The statistical tendencies found in adult riding populations are mirrored in young riders. Studies by Cuenca *et al.* (2009) and Kiss *et al.* (2008) note that 25 per cent of all lethal sports injuries in paediatric patients (children) are caused by horseback riding, with a final mortality rate of 2.5 per cent. Ghosh *et al.* (2000) also note that the incidence of riding-related injuries is almost twice as high in girls as it is in boys, again reflecting the popularity of equestrian sports in the young female demographic.

Not surprisingly, perhaps, the most common way of sustaining an injury is by falling or being thrown off a horse, with reported statistics ranging from 39.2 per cent (Ekberg *et al.* 2011) to 80 per cent (Loder 2008). Reviews on the topic by Hawson *et al.* (2010) and Havlik (2010) both found kicks from a horse to be the second most common way to be injured. Veterinarians even report kicks as the most frequent manner of being injured (Lucas *et al.* 2009) and other studies report kicks as the number one cause of injuries when handling horses from the ground (Abu-Zidan and Rao 2003; Iba *et al.* 2001). Being crushed, trodden on, bitten or dragged while leading the horse also featured as common causes for injuries (e.g.

Hobbs *et al.* 1994; Moss *et al.* 2002). Individual studies further identified additional aspects such as being struck by an obstacle while mounted (Chitnavis *et al.* 1996), being knocked over by the horse (Lloyd 1987), the horse falling (Ekberg *et al.* 2011), being injured by equipment or falling off a horse-drawn vehicle (Smartt and Chalmers 2009). But in order to place the occurrence and severity in the correct context, it needs to be noted that most of the published results were collated in a hospital setting. There are undoubtedly many more incidents of riders or horse handlers being injured, yet the individual felt that a trip to the doctor or local hospital was not warranted. There may thus be additional ways in which riders or equine handlers might have been injured that have not, as yet, been reported in the published literature.

Body parts: you can 'leave your hat on'

On the road towards true understanding of accidents in horse sports, realizing how injuries occur and which body parts are affected necessarily go hand in hand. Once people begin to appreciate the mechanisms behind injuries, they will be able to initiate a multi-pronged approach towards controlling the inherent dangers of equestrian sports. The literature relating to equestrian injuries is, at least compared with other topics on equestrians, extensive. Owing to space restrictions, we will therefore concentrate on key issues. Readers interested in the topic are advised to consult additional references. Interestingly, in recent years, the overall pattern of injury sites has been shifting, possibly reflecting the development of more sophisticated protective equipment (Havlik 2010) and greater awareness and willingness to wear said equipment. While studies from the 1970s and 1980s still reported frequencies of head injuries of 66 per cent (Barber 1973) and 50 per cent (Lloyd 1987), more recent findings identify percentage rates of around 25 per cent (e.g. Craven 2008; Cuenca *et al.* 2009; Kiss *et al.* 2008; Loder 2008; Smartt and Chalmers 2009). The reasons behind these changes have been theorized to be a direct result of an increased use of helmets (Bond *et al.* 1995). These current trends are certainly very encouraging and an increasing number of riding establishments and competitive venues make the wearing of hard hats obligatory. Indeed, the FEI has followed suit and on 1 January 2013 made the wearing of protective headgear compulsory at all FEI events. Dressage riders, Western riders, and vaulters are exempted from this rule when in the show ring, where they are allowed to wear their usual attire. However, there still remain many amateur and professional riders who refrain from wearing a hard hat when not in competition. Considering the status of many professional riders as role models, safety implications for the younger generation of riders are considerable, as young riders may be prone to copy the behavior of those they admire. Bond *et al.* (1995) succinctly summarized the inherent dangers of riding without the appropriate head gear: 'The injury severity, and mortality associated with being thrown from a horse without a helmet was comparable to that of being struck by a car' (p. 488). This is further supported by findings by Sorli (2000) which indicated that, of those riders who eventually succumbed to their injuries, 60 per cent died of a head injury as a direct result of not wearing a hard hat. In support of the severity of the issue and its application to children, Bixby-Hammet (1992) showed that head injuries in children were the most frequent cause of death resulting from equestrian activities. A study by Ghosh *et al.* (2000) supported this with similar findings of the main cause of death in children with equestrian-related injuries being damage to the central nervous system, including skull fractures. So, even though some recent research findings seem to be encouraging, the continuous development of better headgear must remain at the forefront of industrial activities in equestrian sports. A study by Rueda *et al.* (2011) used finite element modelling, a technique designed to observe the loads on brain tissue during helmeted impact, making it possible to quantify the forces to which the rider's brain is being exposed during a fall. It can only be hoped that manufacturers will be able to use such findings and modify equestrian helmet design accordingly. No doubt, the initial cost of technologically advanced riding equipment is likely to constitute a considerable financial burden but surely there is nothing as valuable as protecting a rider's or child's head. More importantly still, riders and, in particular, young children must be encouraged to wear a helmet at all times. To that effect, Worley (2010) argues for the inclusion of equestrian sports in injury prevention programmes, with healthcare personnel being encouraged to play a particularly active role in promoting the wearing of safety helmets. Lastly, the function of role model that many top riders may play who choose to wear a hard hat both in training and competition also should not be underestimated. Although referring to a somewhat different context, the immortal words of Joe Cocker clearly serve as a mantra to all equestrian riders around: while mounted, you can (and should) 'leave your hat on'!

Even though we have seen some positive developments relating to a decrease in head injuries, injuries to other body parts continue to feature in accident reports, possibly in part because other protective gear is not as frequently worn (Havlik 2010). According to Havlik's (2010) review, orthopaedic injuries (i.e. afflictions to the upper and lower extremities) are currently claiming the number-one spot in most lists of equestrian-related injuries. In their study investigating the nature and circumstances of injuries in New Zealand equine sports, Smartt and Chalmers (2009) determined that collectively, injury to the limbs, limb extremities and girdles accounted for almost half of all injuries (48 per cent). A straight fall from a horse (also referred to as a 'simple' fall) resulted predominantly (58 per cent) in fractures and dislocations of limbs and girdle bones, while a fall from a horse with additional trauma due to the horse kicking or crushing the rider (a 'complex' fall) resulted in 45 per cent of all cases in injuries to limbs or girdles. An American study by Loder (2008) using a large nationwide database from the years 2002 to 2004, found injuries to the upper extremities in 29.7 per cent and lower extremities in 16.4 per cent of all cases. The author noted that fractures were the single largest cause for admission, findings that were mirrored in research by Smartt and Chalmers (2009). Loder (2008) goes on to admonish that protective gear such as wrist, knee and elbow guards, should be considered for equestrian sports to mirror the cautionary approach taken for roller and line skating. Chitnavis *et al.* (1996) admonish that a number of contusions, abrasions and even digital amputations could be at least ameliorated by avoiding entrapping fingers or hands in the reins, lunge rein or leading ropes and wearing non-slip protective gloves, a sentiment supported by Regan *et al.* (1991). Ceroni *et al.* (2007) argued in their paper on the prevention of equestrian foot injuries that a number of soft-tissue injuries and fractures of the lower extremities might also be avoided altogether by the wearing of appropriate, namely sturdy, footwear that prevents the heel from slipping too far into the stirrup, as well as the use of safety stirrups. Particularly in children, other papers have also noted an equally high or higher incidence of contusions and abrasions compared to fractures (e.g. Bixby-Hammet 1992; Hawson *et al.* 2010). In all likelihood, this is because parents or adults present during a riding incident will be much quicker to have a child admitted to hospital, even if the injury only appears to be relatively minor. However, it might also be that children are not as ready to wear the appropriate protective gear when dealing with their four-legged friends and are frequently less aware and quick to react around horses. Additional body parts commonly affected, in particular by falls from the horse, are the torso, including injuries to the back, the abdomen (i.e. involving the spleen, liver, kidneys and testicles) and pulmonary systems (e.g. Havlik 2010; Hobbs *et al.* 1994; Moss *et al.* 2002).

No doubt, fatal injuries are feared the most by those involved in equestrian sports. A very close second, however, are injuries that render a rider permanently impaired. Possibly one of the most famous victims of a debilitating riding accident was the American actor, Christopher Reeve, who, by what seems like a particularly cruel twist of fate, shot to fame in his role as Superman. Having taken up horse riding in 1985, Reeve ended up falling from his American Thoroughbred, Eastern Express, when the horse refused to jump a fence during the cross-country phase of the Commonwealth Dressage and Combined Training Association finals in Culpeper, Virginia, in 1995. He landed head first and shattered his first and second vertebrae, an injury that left him quadriplegic and dependent on a breathing apparatus for the rest of his life. He died in 2004 from cardiac arrest, believed to have been caused by an adverse reaction to antibiotics. Reeve's tragic accident was, of course, an extreme example of a spinal cord injury. These are not common among riding-related accidents (Roe *et al.* 2003). Lloyd (1987) determined that of 234 patients admitted with horse-related injuries, only five of those suffered from a spinal injury, while Loder (2008) noted a spinal injury rate of 2.4 per cent. Yet even if a spinal injury does not result in neurological impairment, it will have serious repercussions on the lives of the afflicted riders. Research seems to indicate that injuries to the lower spinal regions (i.e. the thoracic and lumbar parts of the spine) are more frequent than the upper region, the cervix, which is the more vulnerable part of the spine (Silver 2002). This allows for the speculation that there are two types of mechanisms involved when falling off a horse (the main cause of spinal injuries). In the jockey or jumping position, whereby riders sit forward with their buttocks out of the saddle, the risk of falling off with the head leading, thereby sustaining a cervical injury inevitably combined with a head injury, is greatest. In the classical dressage style, whereby riders sit back in the saddle, a thoracic-lumbar fracture is more common as riders are thought to land on their buttocks. In fact, Silver (2002) argues that these types of injuries are almost exclusive to equestrian sports. Bearing these findings in mind it seems clear that, in addition to hard hats, which now seem to have become more commonly accepted, the wearing of body protectors and even so-called air-vests and air-jackets, designed to inflate the moment a rider impacts on the ground, protecting the neck, torso and hip region, should be recommended.

In summary, even though studies do differ somewhat as to the frequency and type of injury, most authors do agree on the body parts most at risk: head, neck, upper and lower limbs, spinal cord and internal organs (Moss *et al.* 2002).

The dangers of horse sports: the reasons behind them and what to do about them

The reasons why horse riding is dangerous are in many ways as straightforward as they are difficult to overcome: horses weigh on average 500–600 kg, are capable of reaching speeds of up to 65 km/hour and can produce forces of up to 1,000 N in a single kick (Havlik 2010). In addition to their impressive physical attributes, horses are also flight animals and, by their very nature, are inclined to flee first and 'ask questions later'. In many ways, such a combination of equine traits constitutes a recipe for disaster and is probably also one of the main reasons why accidents among riders are common and sometimes severe. And yet, despite the obvious importance of the topic, there is still much that needs to be gleaned relating to the cause of accidents on the one hand and the means of avoiding them on the other. While we are primarily focusing on rider safety for the purpose of this book, the additional aspect of equine welfare must not be ignored. To many riders and equine handlers, integrating rider safety and equine welfare seems to be quite a challenge: in their quest to exert full control over the horse, hoping to increase safety, people still resort to measures not in line with equine welfare requirements but which in fact might even lead to greater safety concerns. Horses may not be turned out regularly for fear of injury to the horses themselves or others around them; they may only ever be ridden in an enclosed environment to prevent the horses from 'spooking', while regular exposure to new stimuli might help desensitize the horse. Equally, the use of coercive training methods frequently leads to increased levels of resistance in the horse, culminating in a vicious circle of unsafe behavior and inappropriate attempts to control – rather than retrain – the horse. In view of the original aim of developing true understanding of accidents related to equestrian activities, we now investigate some of the factors that might impact on the frequency and/or severity of injuries.

Rider variables: making a difference

Is it possible to determine higher risk groupings in riders? Does rider experience confound injury frequency or is it professionals in particular who suffer more accidents? Despite or perhaps because of the relatively wide array of data, it is not always easy to determine which rider variables impact on injuries. One element that warrants hardly any debate is the fact that female riders are injured much more frequently than males, with ratios ranging from 62 per cent females compared with 37 per cent males (Ghosh *et al.* 2000) to 84.6 per cent females to 15.4 per cent males (Moss *et al.* 2002). This, however, is likely to be a mere reflection of gender distribution in equestrian sports (e.g. Ghosh *et al.* 2000; Havlik 2010).

Regarding rider experience, findings vary across different studies and, at times, even seem to be contradictory. Havlik (2010) concluded that novice riders seem to have a higher overall risk of injury, while professional (i.e. advanced) riders seem to suffer from more serious injuries. Interestingly, Paix (1999) found an increase of injury rates among riders at the highest levels. These findings undoubtedly relate to the facts that, at more advanced levels, demands on horse and rider are much more challenging, proportionally increasing the associated risk of injury. In contrast, research by Mayberry *et al.* (2007) showed that, while accumulative injuries increased over the years and with experience, the incidence rate of average and serious injuries declined with increasing skill level. In fact, the authors found the highest incidence rate of injuries in the first 18 hours of experience, with an 80 per cent drop by 100 hours, and the stabilization of injury rate near zero at around 5,000 hours (Mayberry *et al.* 2007). These results might not be universally representative, as the authors relied on participants' recollection of injuries, which may not always be accurate. Yet they nevertheless portray an important message: while the career risk of injury is considerably higher for professionals and advanced riders, owing to the cumulative effect, beginners or novice riders face a more immediate risk of incurring an injury, as they are unlikely to possess the relevant skill, balance and speed of reaction to deal with the sometimes unpredictable nature of horse sports.

Data relating to age of riders essentially mimic the results relating to experience: younger riders (primarily female) are generally at greater risk of sustaining an injury. More specifically, Moss *et al.* (2002) report the highest incidence of injuries in teenagers between 10 and 15 years, with a gradual decline until the age of 30, after which injury rates tended to rise again slightly. However, Chitnavis *et al.* (1996) found the greater number of injuries in the 20–30-years age group, closely followed by riders of 10–20 years. The study by Loder (2008) identified the age group of 10–19 years as being by far the greatest at risk. The reasons why younger riders are particularly prone to injuries are, in all likelihood, a combination of several factors. Firstly, children have, on average, spent fewer cumulative hours in the saddle, making them generally less skilled and experienced. On the other hand, children and young teenagers have not yet developed the cognitive ability to assess the consequences of a situation, (see Chapter 4 for an explanation of cognitive development in children), meaning that they might seek out potentially dangerous situations simply for the 'fun' of it. Lastly, a study by Hawson *et al.* (2011) determined that pony behavior that was considered to be unsafe led to a decrease in price. Considering that the purchase of a pony constitutes a considerable expense for many (most) parents, it may be that they end up buying a pony that is unsuitable for a child. Misbehavior from the pony, combined with the inexperience of the child, might well lead to an increased rate of injuries.

The implications of the findings relating to immediate rider variables are clear. No doubt even professional and advanced riders need to remain vigilant, especially as the sporting demands will increase proportionally with competitive level. Furthermore, professional and advanced riders are also the ones to take on young, untrained horses that are by definition a greater safety hazard. However, particularly in the early stages of a rider's career, necessary measures for injury prevention need to be taken by raising awareness, training appropriate skills and drawing the rider's attention to the dangers of different disciplines. The various aspects that might play a role in increasing safety in equestrian sports are discussed in the following section.

Equine ethology, behavior and learning theory: what riders need to know

There can be little doubt that most riders develop a close affinity with horses in general and with their own horses in particular (we discuss the topic of horse–rider relationships in more detail in Chapter 6). Riders seem to associate emotional concepts such as friendship, support and even love with their horses (Keaveney 2008). It is therefore not altogether surprising that people long for the kind of connection with their horses in the same way that they would with a human friend. Anthropomorphic notions, whereby people attribute animals with human emotional and cognitive traits (Kidd and Kidd 1987), still abound in many forms of horse–human relationships.

While perhaps intuitively appealing to many horse lovers, assuming that horses think and behave similarly to humans can have serious repercussions and can pose a considerable safety risk. Preconceptions that horses might signal submission to their riders out of deference or respect, or that they are carrying out their riders' command out of a motivation to please, assume that horses have the superior cognitive capacities to understand and evaluate the consequences of their behavior (McGreevy *et al.* 2009). By extension, this would imply that horses might be able to distinguish between 'correct' and 'incorrect' behavior and, indeed, behavior that is safe or dangerous. Riders who implicitly rely on and trust their horses to make these kinds of decisions potentially place themselves in considerable physical danger.

Any initiative to improve safety measures in equestrian sports should therefore necessarily begin with a thorough understanding of equine ethology, with a particular emphasis on how equine behavior is shaped according to the principles of learning theory (rather than on the basis of reasoning and higher cognitive faculties) (e.g. McGreevy and McLean 2007; McGreevy *et al.* 2009; McLean 2008; McLean and McGreevy 2010). A horse that is reacting to a particular cue from a rider or handler in the desired manner is likely to do so because the behavior has been reinforced appropriately, either through a positive stimulus (such as a treat or a scratching at the withers, i.e. positive reinforcement) or, more likely, through the removal of pressure indicative of negative reinforcement (such as the release of pressure on the reins during a half-halt once the horse has slowed). A ridden horse that spooks at an unfamiliar object and runs away reacts in the first instance on instinct. To improve rider (and horse) safety, there are two aspects that need addressing. Firstly, while it is impossible to completely eliminate the intrinsic flight response of horses, the deliberate habituation of horses to novel stimuli can help to inhibit their fear response (Christensen *et al.* 2006). Secondly, once a horse has been consistently trained to respond to the tightening of the contact by slowing down, using principles of negative reinforcement, it will also be more reliable to stop. The key, however, to effective negative reinforcement training is that the rider releases the applied pressure as soon as the horse has started to slow. Many riders, especially in a situation which might be anxiety inducing, actually fail to release the pressure, even once the horse has started to slow. Instead, anxious riders continue to hold on to the reins extremely tightly, thus, in essence, 'denying' the horse the reward for showing the behavior that the rider had intended (namely slowing down). The next time the horse is placed in a similar – frightening – situation, the previous experience will have taught it not to immediately slow down to the pressure of the rein (as the 'reward' i.e. the release of pressure, was withheld). It is easy to see how this kind of situation might end up resulting in a vicious circle of the horse spooking, the rider desperately clinging on to the reins to stop the horse yet failing to reinforce actually slowing down and the horse thus essentially learning to ignore the rein aid. The dangers of 'confusing' the horse by applying inconsistent signals have also been raised in a study by Hockenhull and Creighton (2012; also see below), which showed an increased risk of horses exhibiting extreme conflict behaviors if they were ridden regularly by three different riders. As it was impossible to determine a definite causal effect the authors offered two possible explanations. It may be that the main rider/owner was unable to cope with their horse's unruly behavior and thus needed support by perhaps better qualified riders. However, it may also be the case that inconsistency in the training approach and, more specifically, the application and effective release of the aids, led to the horse exhibiting extreme forms of conflict behavior.

Clearly, one of the primary issues of improving aspects of safety in equestrian sports is therefore a thorough understanding of the principles of learning theory and how these apply to equine ethology in particular. Once again, space issues prohibit a more detailed account of the subject. However, students are strongly advised to consult the works by leading researchers on the topic (e.g. McGreevy *et al.* 2004; McGreevy and McLean 2010a; McGreevy and McLean 2007; McGreevy *et al.* 2009)

Keeping horses the safe way

While ethology might be considered one side of the equine behavioral coin, general management practices are clearly the other. The way that horses are kept, handled, ridden and generally managed will undoubtedly impact on their behavior, with concessions to equine welfare potentially causing serious safety implications. Keeping horses stabled for a majority of the day, preventing them from exercising regularly, feeding them too much concentrate and too little forage, allowing them no access to conspecifics and working them using aversive training methods are only some of the examples of where inappropriate management might result in horses being difficult to handle and/or ride and thus presenting a real safety hazard (e.g. Hausberger *et al.* 2004, 2009; Heleski *et al.* 2002; McGreevy and McLean 2005; Fureix *et al.* 2010). More specifically, research seemed to indicate that young horses kept in individual stables showed more undesirable behaviors, such as bucking or jumping around, than horses kept in groups at pasture (Rivera *et al.* 2002). A study by Lesimple *et al.* (2011) was able to produce similar findings. Riding school horses kept in individual boxes demonstrated more active locomotive patterns when released into an indoor arena. Incidentally, studies have shown that equine breed, especially in conjunction with environmental factors, might also impact on emotionality and learning ability (Hausberger *et al.* 2004; Lesimple *et al.* 2011), which might be taken into account when deciding on suitable mounts for different types of riders. However, covering the topic of modern equine management and welfare is once again beyond the scope of this book and the interested student might wish to consult existing literature (e.g. Fraser 2010; Waran 2002).

In the following sections a number of issues identified in recent research are highlighted which might have particularly salient implications for rider safety.

The human(e) approach: handling horses safely

In addition to the principles of equine training and management, there are other, perhaps even more basic, considerations that might affect the way in which horses react to humans. A review on the subject by Hausberger *et al.* (2008) noted a number of shortcomings of existing studies relating to the appropriate definition of direction of gaze, posture, positioning and speed of approach. Considering the long history of horse–human relations and the obvious dangers involved, the dearth of research investigating how aspects of human body language might impact on equine behavior, in particular flight responses, is surprising. A study by Birke *et al.* (2011) was one of the first to study the phenomenon of a potential egocentric spatial barrier (Graziano and Cooke 2006), which might elicit a flight response in horses. Mirroring the results of a study by Austin and Rogers (2007), Birke *et al.* (2011) were able to determine that a flight response in both experienced and naïve horses was triggered following an approach by an unfamiliar person at a distance of approximately 2.5 metres. The authors also noted that a greater approach speed elicited a more pronounced flight response, while eye gaze seemed to have little effect. In fact, gazing away from the animals elicited an earlier take-off point than focusing on the animals. While especially the naïve horses in the study did habituate within a short period to the presence of the researchers, it is still important to note that a 'startle' response is likely to be initiated even in horses that are used to being handled if they are being approached at speed. According to Saslow (2002), such reactions are a likely consequence to the distribution and organization of ganglion cells and retinal structures typical to prey animals, making them highly sensitive to the perception of movement and acceleration. Practical implications aimed at preventing potential injuries are that, when approaching their horses, humans should aim to control and slow down their movements. While the risks of being hit by a flying hoof or being run over if horses are startled are high, even in an open field, they increase exponentially if the horse is essentially trapped in an enclosure, such as a stable, trailer or veterinary examination room.

In many ways, these findings are supported further through research conducted by Keeling *et al.* (2009) as discussed in Chapter 3. Horses tended to show an increased heart rate at times when their handlers or riders also experienced an increase in heart rate. It is possible that horses reacted to a quickening of step of their handlers or to excessive muscular tension of their riders. While the exact mechanisms of possible co-variations in heart rate between horse and riders/handlers are as yet not fully understood, practical conclusions may be drawn. Riders experiencing higher heart rates owing to physiological arousal might be eliciting a similar response in horses. According to Gautier and Cook (1997), aroused animals are likely to exhibit their startle response more easily. They thus might react in ways that pose a danger to the rider or the horse–rider combination. While frequently much more easily said than done, riders would be well served to practice mental skills techniques (as outlined in Chapter 3) that assist them in controlling physiological and psychological arousal.

Even more practical applications regarding how equine handlers might wish to ensure a safe environment were addressed in studies by Hausberger and Muller (2002) and Hartmann *et al.* (2012). For instance, Hausberger and Muller (2002) found that the behavior of horses towards unfamiliar humans might be affected by the person taking care of them on a daily basis, indicating the possibility for generalization. While additional research is required to confirm these findings, possible implications are that horse owners who are unable to care for their horses themselves should try to ascertain how their horses are being handled by their usual caretaker. Increased levels of aggression, for example, with the associated risk of sustaining an injury from a kick or bite, should also be assessed in view of how the horse is being handled on a day-to-day basis.

In contrast, the study by Hartmann *et al.* (2012) investigated the risk factors associated with removing horses from a herd. The authors were able to identify that remaining stationary together with the target horse seemed to cause the most problematic situations. Other horses would approach the handler and the target horse, arguably out of curiosity or the need to maintain a cohesive group. However, especially for a human, being in close contact with several loose horses can be potentially dangerous, as the human might be caught out by sudden flight reactions or aggressive behaviors. The authors recommend, in particular, avoiding standing still with the target horse and exiting the field as quickly as possible, preferably with a helper to assist with the opening and closing of the field gate.

As already discussed in the previous sections, the most prevalent cause of rider injury is falling or being thrown off a horse. Clearly, a number of riders fall or are being thrown off as a direct result of their horses' spooking, making a mistake at or refusing an obstacle during jumping. Yet many more riders become unseated because of their horses' bucking, rearing, spinning around or shying, for seemingly no apparent reason. Casey (1999) suggested that the underlying cause for many equine behavioral problems may be pain. Owners who fail to keep up with regular dental maintenance might be confronted with their horses experiencing considerable pain in their mouths (Dixon *et al.* 2004), while careless or inexpert shoeing can lead to foot soreness (Balch *et al.* 1997). Unsuitable tack, including badly fitting saddles (de Cocq *et al.* 2004, 2006) or artificial riding aids, such as draw reins or running martingales that are used inexpertly (Rhodin *et al.* 2005), have all been shown to cause discomfort in the horse.

A survey-based study by Hockenhull and Creighton (2012) aimed to determine risk factors associated with different equipment and training methods used in horses displaying common behavioral problems. Dressage or working hunter saddles, for example, were associated with a decreased risk of slowing down or resistance problems, which may be due to greater freedom of movement in the shoulder. Unsurprisingly perhaps, regular checks of saddle fit by the owners were thought to reduce the risk of discomfort (e.g. bucking, resistance to turn, tripping, cantering on the wrong lead, refusal to move forward), possibly because regular checks are indicative of greater owner vigilance to initial symptoms of the horse not being well. Interestingly, horses that had last been seen by a farrier seven or more weeks earlier demonstrated a four-fold increase of displaying discomfort behavior. While published research relating to shoeing and equine performance is sparse, common industry guidelines suggest trimming and/or shoeing of feet every four to six weeks.

Findings also showed that the use of artificial training aids (e.g. whip, spurs, running martingale, standing martingale, running/draw reins, drop/flash noseband) increased the risk of horses displaying signs of discomfort, extreme conflict (i.e. bucking, rearing or bolting), refusal to slow or showing resistance and jumping issues (e.g. refusal, running, rushing at fences). The authors note that, because of the nature of the study, it is difficult to determine causal effect, i.e. whether artificial aids were used to deal with the consequences of problem behavior or whether artificial aids had caused the behavior in the first place. Subsequent research is needed to investigate these issues in more detail. However, the findings do demonstrate very clearly the potential link between pain, training approaches and so-called misbehavior. Once riders have to resort to artificial aids to exert more control over their horses, rider safety and equine welfare become a concern – especially if riding without such artificial aids is no longer possible. Riders therefore need to ask themselves, first of all, which kind of undesirable behaviors they are trying to control or even mask and then start looking for the cause of the problem. It goes without saying that riders' first port of call must be to eliminate any potential source of pain, again both from a safety and welfare point of view. The next step clearly involves addressing any deficits in training in order to avoid any source of accidents.

Don't hit the road, Jack!

While not the most common cause of equestrian related injuries (Silver and Lloyd Parry 1991), the thought of being involved in a road traffic-related accident makes many riders' blood run cold with fear. While relatively few riders end up actually being involved in a traffic accident, a significantly greater number experience 'near misses' (Chapman and Musselwhite 2011), which is likely to impact considerably on feelings of safety and levels of enjoyment while out hacking. Musselwhite *et al.* (2010) argued that, while out on the road, horse riders may be considered as similarly vulnerable as pedestrians or cyclists. They move at comparatively slower speeds, have little physical protection and often less manoeuvrability. Most importantly, perhaps, if involved in an accident, horses are also likely to panic, causing potentially even greater levels of injuries to those involved. In a paper investigating perceptions, attitudes and beliefs of equine-related road users, Chapman and Musselwhite (2011) stress the importance of assessing the behavior of all road users within the context of how they perceive risk and, more specifically, how much skill, ability and control they attribute to a user (Musselwhite *et al.* 2010). This means that drivers might make assumptions about the competence level of riders based on the age and gender of the rider, the type of gear that is worn and, potentially, the behavior of the horse. For example, they are likely to engage in more cautious driving when encountering a child on a pony, rather than when encountering an adult rider, riding on a relaxed horse at a walk. Chapman and Musselwhite (2011) were able to show that especially younger, less-experienced drivers believed riders to have a high amount of control over their horses. As a result, they engage in driving behavior that puts horse and rider at risk. While most drivers believed themselves to have sufficient skill to interact safely with horses on the road, in actual fact, they often lacked knowledge relating to the nature of the horse. Consequently, they were unable to perceive potential hazards on the road as dangerous and failed to adapt their driving behavior accordingly.

Overtaking of horse and rider quite often causes the most amount of strife between riders and drivers. While riders understandably become particularly concerned or even angry at drivers overtaking at high speeds or pulling in too soon, Chapman and Musselwhite (2011) found in their research that, once they had initiated an overtaking manoeuver, drivers' perceptions of vulnerability changed. They realized that, in case of any oncoming traffic, they would be in a highly dangerous position, making them wish to get back to the relative safety of 'their' side of the road as quickly as possible. In addition, drivers are also likely to be influenced by feelings of empathy towards the horse riders they encounter, depending on how much they feel they can identify with them (Tajfel and Turner 1986).

Lastly, aspects of emotional affect, such as levels of frustration through being held up (Fuller *et al.* 2008) or feeling angry by the – erroneous – idea that horse riding is a leisure pursuit and riders therefore have little right to mingle with other road users on their way to work. On the other hand, drivers who perceive horse riders as legitimate road users also behaved more considerately towards them (Chapman and Musselwhite 2011).

While it is likely that riding on the roads will remain a particularly hazardous activity for some time to come, precautionary action should be taken by riders in the meantime. High-visibility gear is a must, as is the appropriate safety attire. Chapman and Musselwhite (2011) suggest that riders using a whip sticking out at right angles to create space for themselves should make sure that even the end points are highly visible. The authors even recommend the development of new products to that effect. Furthermore, riders should also refrain from riding during busy times of day, both to decrease the frequency of coming into contact with cars but also in view of the effect that emotions such as frustration or anger might have on other drivers. But most importantly, perhaps, greater understanding and levels of empathy should be developed between different groups of road users. Even indirect involvement with horses, through friends and family, is likely to change drivers' attitudes and riders are encouraged to speak to friends and family as much as possible about their experiences with horses on the road to encourage greater understanding (Chapman and Musselwhite 2011).

The dangers of horse sports: comparing disciplines

Having discussed injury rates, types of injury and the modifying impact of appropriate safety equipment, aspects of equine management that might increase the risk of equestrian injuries, as well as the dangers of riding on the road, we now turn to the dangers of participating in different disciplines of equestrian sports. There can be no doubt that disciplines such as dressage, Western riding or endurance also carry inherent dangers, especially when they are performed on a young or inexperienced horse, by a young or inexperienced rider and/or under conditions that increase the risk of accidents, as discussed above. However, these types of disciplines might generally be considered somewhat safer, as they generally involve more controlled movements, with horse and rider not normally moving at either extreme speeds or leaving the ground in a jumping effort. In contrast, the discipline of polo involves the horse and rider moving at relatively high speeds, with the added risk of polo sticks being swung at great velocity, often in close proximity to other horse–rider combinations. In their study assessing injuries to polo players, Costa-Paz *et al.* (1999) classified most of the recorded injuries as major, providing evidence that polo might, indeed, be considered one of the more dangerous equestrian disciplines. Vaulting (i.e. the performance of gymnastic movements on a cantering horse) brings with it the obvious dangers of the vaulter falling off the horse or landing awkwardly. Rodeo, a discipline more commonly performed in the USA, Canada, Australia and New Zealand, has also recorded frequent injury rates, including in particular fractures, concussions and dislocations (e.g. Butterwick and Meeuwisse 2002; Meyers *et al.* 1990).

Showjumping: the sky's the limit

Equally, as evidenced regularly by even the most experienced of riders falling off, the discipline of showjumping might be considered one of the more dangerous activities, as the potential for rider and/or horse falls is considerable, either due to horse refusal or following a mistake that results in the horse landing in the middle of a fence or by being tripped by a flying pole. It is therefore particularly surprising that so little empirical evidence seems to exist relating to aspects of safety and performance in showjumping. At the same time, showjumping is a discipline that traditionally offers the greatest amount of prize money and enjoys considerable backing of well-known sponsors at shows and might thus be considered to have the necessary financial resources at its disposal. In one of the few studies on the topic, Stachurska *et al.* (2002) investigated the type of obstacles most problematic for show jumping horses and found that, at increasing height, more obstacles were knocked down but run-outs did not change significantly. Obstacles of two contrasting colours caused significantly fewer problems than uniformly coloured obstacles, with white fences causing the most faults. Perhaps not altogether surprisingly, the wall, a solid structure, which can appear rather imposing to the rider, caused the most faults, with a significant amount of run-outs. The authors highlight the issue that their results demonstrate not only the ability of horses to jump fences faultlessly but also riders' commitment to take their horses over the fences. It is therefore important to also consider attributes of rider psychology when investigating elements relating to horse–rider safety in showjumping and, indeed, other disciplines. Furthermore, from an even more practical perspective, one of the fundamental ways to decrease accidents in showjumping competitions and, indeed, in other equestrian disciplines, is to optimize external conditions, such as surfacing, fence design, maximum number of competitors permitted in the warm-up ring at any given time, appropriate parking conditions for trailers and lorries, and so on. Indeed, one of the only studies on the topic by Sasimowski *et al.* (1986) showed that showjumping course conditions varied considerably between shows, with ground firmness ranging from 1.7 MPa to 3.0 MPa and the distribution of uprights and oxers also varying significantly. While it may be argued that the nature of competitive sport demands an array of unforeseen challenges, the safety of horse and rider should be paramount. Future research should therefore aim to investigate in more detail those elements likely to impact on equestrian safety, in particular with regard to different disciplines.

Eventing: the 'triathlon' of equestrian sports

There can be no doubt that, of the equestrian disciplines that are gathered under the umbrella of the FEI, eventing is considered by far the most dangerous. In the period 1997–2008, a total of 37 deaths occurred in the cross-country phase (Havlik 2010), with an average of 5.59 per cent of falls (translating to one fall per 18 starters) in FEI-registered competitions (FEI 2012). Frequently referred to as the 'triathletes' of equestrian sports, eventing horse–rider combinations have to perform in the phases of dressage, showjumping and cross-country jumping. The cross-country phase is where most serious injuries are sustained, as horse and rider have to negotiate a course of several kilometres in length across natural terrain and between 12–20 (lowest level) and 30–40 (highest level) solid, natural-looking obstacles at speeds of up to 570 metres per minute – serious demands on both horse and rider.

Not surprisingly then, most of the injuries reported in the current literature were sustained when either the rider fell from the horse or horse and rider fell together. In the time period 2004–2011 and at FEI-approved events, an average of 95 per cent of falls occurred before, during or immediately after a fence, with only five per cent of falls occurring on the flat (FEI 2012). A study by Whitlock (1999) determined equestrian injuries in a sample of 16,940 horses competing in one-day eventing competitions ('horse trials') between 1992 and 1997. The author was able to demonstrate an injury rate of 1.1 per cent ($N = 193$), with two deaths when the horse fell on top of and crushed the rider. Injuries to the head predominated (31.1 per cent), followed by the shoulder girdle and upper limbs (20.7 per cent). Paix (1999) reported similar findings in a smaller study including 4,220 competitors: an injury incident rate of 0.88 per cent, with head and neck injuries the most common. Mirroring the interpretations from other authors (e.g. Bond *et al.* 1995), Whitlock argued that a more sophisticated helmet design reduced the severity of an injury. While all riders were wearing a body protector, none of the riders who sustained a shoulder injury was wearing a shoulder protector. Of those riders who fell and could have reasonably incurred a shoulder injury but were wearing shoulder protection, all were able to continue competing the next day. It should be noted that this particular study is already more than a decade old and both product development in equestrian sports as well as safety precautions regarding course and fence design continue to advance considerably. Indeed, both Whitlock's (1999) and Paix's (1999) findings send a clear message regarding the dangers of eventing. Despite an overall decrease of fall rates from 2004 to 2011 in all FEI-affiliated competitions bar 1* (FEI 2012), the inherent nature and associated risks of the sport have not really changed, with considerable danger to horse and rider. The dreaded 'rotational fall', whereby the horse cartwheels over the fence to, in many instances, land on top of the rider, continues to be the cause of serious rider injury in 22.63 per cent of all cases (FEI 2012). And even though the incidence rate of the rotational fall may be considered relatively low at 0.19 per cent (FEI 2012), it nevertheless poses a considerable risk for what is generally perceived to be a recreational activity. What is more, level of expertise does not seem to be moderating risk, as incidence rates of falls increase with progression through the levels: In 2011, 4.26% of 1* riders fell, yet almost three times as many 4* riders (11.82 per cent) parted company with their horses.

Is it possible then to identify some of the risk factors associated with falls at cross-country fences? A study by Stachurska *et al.* (2010) identified factors such as successive elements of combinations, narrow obstacles, brush type fences and fences with alternative routes across 1* through to 4* competitions to be affecting the frequency of faults made.

The distinction of different levels in the analysis of jumping faults also highlighted additional factors, such as that more inexperienced horses occurred more faults at upright fences, while at 3* and 4* level, more opposing spread fences seemed to be causing greater difficulties. In their discussion, Stachurska *et al.* (2010) highlight the fact that the equine visionary system and, in particular, the reduced binocular visual field might inhibit horses from perceiving fences accurately, for example in a combination of fences. Murray *et al.* (2005) identified the additional risk factors in one-day events of fences with a drop landing, fences with an approach from water, riders who knew that they were in the lead and those who received cross-country tuition. In two- and three-day events, however, the only factors associated with risk were the camber of the fence and participation in other sports. In a follow-up article, Murray *et al.* (2006) determined additional risk factors for incurring a fall, such as riders who retrospectively reported approaching the fence at speeds either too slow or too fast and who had already incurred a refusal at some point during the course.

Several conclusions might be drawn from the varied findings regarding risk factors in the cross-country phase of eventing. While it is, of course, possible to search for explanations behind the different risk factors, the lack of consistent patterns might also be considered an important indicator to the nature of risk factors in eventing. Considering that the sport of eventing is dependent on a myriad of horse and rider variables, combined with changing external circumstances of different events (e.g. characteristics of the terrain, types of fences and order of fences), it seems clear that additional research needs to be conducted to identify clearer patterns relating to falls and, by extension, rider injuries. However, the authors of the different studies also managed to identify a number of factors that might well be related to previously undetermined rider variables. The fact that riders who had previously incurred a refusal are more prone to fall later on in the course may be indicative of either the rider's riding ability or of psychological variables, such as anxiety or aggression, which might lead to different and ineffectual styles of riding. It seems clear that additional research is required to shed additional light on to risk factors associated with horse–rider falls.

In the meantime, event organizers and riders alike should do everything in their power to improve safety standards in eventing competitions. Ensuring appropriate footing and equipping fences with the 'frangible pin' system, whereby a solid obstacle gives way upon impact, are precautions that are implemented across most modern events. Equally, riders need to ensure that they continue to invest in the most up-to-date protective equipment, with the equine industry investing into research to continue to identify relevant risk factors.

Racing: the sport of kings

The press referred to the 2012 edition of the Grand National, the most famous National Hunt race in the world as 'Another National tragedy'. Only 15 horses from a field of 40 reached the finishing line, with two horses having to be put down after falling in the race (Delgado 2012). These kinds of statistics unfortunately speak for themselves, underlining the notion that racing is one of, if not the, most dangerous equestrian discipline. Nevertheless, racing remains one of the most popular and most lucrative activities around the world, with race attendance in the USA exceeding that of any other sporting event (Press *et al.* 1995). Undoubtedly, public popularity on the one hand and considerable risk to horses and jockeys on the other are forcing racing authorities to revise and improve their safety standards year after year. Such efforts must, of course, be considered fundamental in the ongoing attempt to protect the welfare of horses and jockeys.

The equestrian sport of horse racing may be broadly divided into 'flat racing' and 'jump racing', which, in turn, may include several different race formats. Flat racing is performed on closed grass or turf tracks and, as the name suggests, does not include jumps. Jump racing is divided into either hurdling or steeple chasing. Hurdles are fences with a solid base but consisting of brush and usually measuring up to 3.5 feet. Many of the best horses competing in hurdling will go on to compete in steeplechases, where they will have to jump brush-type fences of a minimum of 4.6 feet. Generally, only professional jockeys will ride in flat, hurdle or steeple races, while amateur jockeys participate in point-to-point races, which also include jumps but are held in open fields.

Whether it is the raw display of speed and power, the thrill of the chase or the addictive properties of betting that makes racing such an attractive sport is difficult to say. It is a fact, however, that for the jockeys (as well as for horses), it is an extremely dangerous pastime. A study by Waller *et al.* (2000) investigating jockey injuries in the USA revealed 606 injuries per 1,000 jockey years, while Rueda *et al.* (2010) found a fall rate of 115–140 falls per 1,000 rides for amateur jump riders and 51.0–85.3 falls per 1,000 rides for professional jump riders in races in Ireland, France and Britain for the racing seasons of 1999–2006. Irish, French and British professional flat racing jockeys fell decisively less often, with 2.68–4.43 falls per 1,000 rides. While not every fall automatically leads to an injury, flat racing was seen to produce the highest rates of injury per fall (344–439 injuries per 1,000 falls). Injury rates for professional jump racing were found to be between 100–180 per 1,000 falls. In a similar study comparing injury in professional racing in France from 1991 to 2001, with incidences in Great Britain between 1992 and 2001, McCrory *et al.* (2006) found similar results, with injury rates per fall in flat racing considerably higher than in jump racing (38.7–41.4 per cent compared with 12.9–18.0 per cent). Balendra *et al.* (2007) reported the frequency of falls for amateur jump jockeys to be nearly two to three times as high as for professional jump jockeys, meaning that amateurs also experience twice as many injuries. In essence, the empirical findings are concerning but not surprising. Considering their professional status and the associated number of horses that they are likely to ride, professional jockeys are prone to be more competent than their amateur counterparts. While not guaranteeing safety by any means, experience in horse racing seems to at least provide a moderating effect on injury rates – despite the rates of fatalities in professional horse racing still being above that in other sports (Turner *et al.* 2002). Indeed, a study by Hitchens *et al.* (2010) determined amateur or apprentice status of jockeys as a predictor of falls. Furthermore, the existence of obstacles in jump racing almost inevitably causes greater fall rates. However, the greater injury/fall rate in flat racing jockeys might stem from higher velocities displayed in flat racing.

It will come as no surprise to readers that the most common manner of sustaining an injury in racing was reported to be falls from a horse (Cowley *et al.* 2007; Waller *et al.* 2000), particularly in and around the starting gate or on the home stretch, as this is where tension and the determination to succeed and, subsequently, the willingness to take risks is highest (Waller *et al.* 2000).

Soft-tissue injuries tend to be the most frequent types of injuries, followed by fractures, concussions and dislocations (Balendra *et al.* 2007; McCrory *et al.* 2006). However, varying manners of injury reporting and diagnosis are likely to lead to slightly varying results, depending on country and specific racing discipline. Much like in other equestrian disciplines, the dangers of incurring head injuries remain relatively high. The high incidence of concussion (Balendra *et al.* 2007; Rueda *et al.* 2010; McCrory *et al.* 2006) is indicative of the nature of falls in racing. Considering that jockeys have to balance on their stirrups with their bodies crouched over, most falls are likely to be head first, increasing the risk of a head injury. Yet the improvement in head gear in recent years will have contributed to a substantial decrease in head injuries as well (Rueda *et al.* 2010).

The question that presents itself most strongly is whether accident and injury rates can be substantially curtailed. In their study on accident predictors, Hitchens *et al.* (2010) argue that, in addition to jockey experience, equine experience also seems to be an important factor. It is likely that, in a pressured environment such as racing, a young, inexperienced horse is more easily inclined to behave in a way that increases the risk to its jockey. As a preventive step, the authors suggest a restriction on young, inexperienced jockeys riding inexperienced horses, to avoid a potentially dramatic cumulative effect. Hitchens *et al.* (2010) also found greater incidences of falls on drier, faster tracks and in more tightly bunched fields. Higher velocities clearly leave fewer margins for error, while the restricted space of a tight group of horses and riders allows for hardly any room to manoeuver.

Much like in other equestrian disciplines, more attention needs to be paid to determining risk factors and developing appropriate strategies, involving regulatory and technological innovations on the one hand and paying attention to equine behavior as well as psychological and physiological parameters in the rider on the other.

Concluding thoughts

The current chapter has provided a comprehensive overview of injury rates and types of injuries common in equestrian sport, potential causal factors and, most importantly, preventative strategies. While there can be no doubt that, from a psychological point of view, riders should be as free from fear of injury as possible, a realistic understanding of the risk factors involved is likely to improve the safety and welfare of all concerned.

Efforts must be undertaken to further improve the safety aspects in all equestrian disciplines. In addition to injury occurrence, underlying factors such as level of competence (e.g. Whitlock *et al.* 1987; Paix 1999), equine fitness and behavior (e.g. Hawson *et al.* 2010) or fence design (Murray *et al.* 2004, 2005) must be investigated further.

Appropriate measures to safeguard and protect the rider need to be integrated more stringently into daily riding and training activities. As such, students of equine and equitation science must be aware of the latest developments in aspects relating to functionality of safety equipment on the one hand and appropriate training methods in line with equine behavior on the other. But above all, a good dose of common sense and the knowledge that horses cannot, and will not, adhere to safety implications out of their own accord are key requirements in improving safety in equestrian sports.

Chapter highlights

1. The combination of horses' size, strength, the fact that they have a 'mind of their own', their inherent unpredictability and the speed at which we frequently ride them, make equestrian sport one of the most dangerous activities that exists.

2. Despite the unpleasantness of being confronted with the real and serious dangers of someone's chosen activity, true understanding of why accidents and subsequent injuries occur should eventually lead to better prediction and avoidance of such injuries.

3. While there are a number of empirical studies investigating accidents and injuries in horse sport, the results will be influenced by the equestrian culture of the relevant country, as well as the type of data collection that was applied. Students of the topic therefore need to be careful with any direct comparisons of data.

4. While female riders tend to be overrepresented in injury statistics (as is the case in most other equine-related research), male riders' injuries are reported to be more severe. Future research needs to identify why this might be.

5. Some studies claim that as much as 25 per cent of all lethal sports-related injuries in children are related to equestrianism. Again, average injury incidence rates seem to be more frequent in girls than in boys.

6. The most common way of being injured is by falling from or being thrown off a horse, with being kicked lying in second. Being crushed, trodden on, bitten or dragged while leading the horse also featured as common causes for injuries.

7. Despite head injuries being the most common only a few decades ago, more recent findings indicate a decrease, a likely result of improved head gear. Nevertheless, the potential repercussions of head injuries are serious, evidenced by the tragic example of Courtney King-Dye. Current research reports upper and lower extremities as frequent sites of injury, followed by injuries to the torso. Even though not as frequent, the potential severity of spinal injuries makes them also important to consider.

8. While the career risk of injury is considerably higher for professional and advanced riders, beginners or novice riders, including children, face a more immediate risk of incurring an injury as they do not yet possess the relevant skill levels to deal with the sometimes unpredictable nature of horse sports.

9. Any initiative to improve safety measures in equestrian sports should therefore necessarily begin with a thorough understanding of equine ethology, principles of learning theory and the effects of management on equine behavior.

10. To avoid accidents or 'near-misses' on the road or in traffic, drivers must be made aware of the nature of horses, while riders need to appreciate the effect of emotions such as frustration or anger on driver behavior. Riders must note that they have the same rights and responsibilities as all other road users.

11. Eventing and both flat and jump racing are undoubtedly the most dangerous disciplines of equestrian sports, clearly because either jumps or great speeds are involved. However, to date relevant data relating to other 'dangerous' disciplines such as showjumping, polo or vaulting, are as yet sparse or missing.

6   Horse–human interactions

Art or science?

Introduction: the wonders of the horse

> 'Do you want to get up?' I asked him, not expecting a response. 'Up!'
>
> It was the first time I'd received a direct answer to a direct question. I bent down, scooped him up, and put him in the saddle. Immediately the flailing and shouting stopped. His grin was so wide it seemed to stretch off the sides of his face and into the air on either side.
>
> (Extract from *The Horse Boy* by Rupert Isaacson: 31)

It is the story of an incredible journey on horseback to the outer edges of Mongolia. More importantly, it is also the story of Rowan Isaacson, a small boy suffering from some of the most debilitating symptoms of autism: uncontrollable temper fits, agonizing anxiety attacks, the inability to connect with his environment and incontinence at the age of almost six. Shortly after Rowan is diagnosed at the age of two and a half, Rupert Isaacson, an avid horseman himself, notices a strange yet wonderful connection between his son and an old mare, Betsy, who belongs to one of Isaacson's neighbours. During the first ride on the mare, with Rowan perched in front of his father, the boy's speech becomes more lucid and he is able to engage in simple to-and-fro conversation.

An idea – and hope – is borne and, after a couple of years of planning, Isaacson takes his wife and son on an arduous trek on horseback through the steppe and mountains of Mongolia to see one of the most powerful shamans in the world. 'Ghoste' belongs to the reindeer people in Siberia. It is during those long days in and out of the saddle, surrounded by one of the truly wild natural habitats, that Rowan starts to show signs of real improvement. He is able to connect with others, starts to show imaginative thought and is even able to overcome some of his paralyzing episodes of fear. Having finally arrived at the camp of the reindeer people, Rowan undergoes a traditional healing ritual performed by Ghoste. Whether it is indeed the ritualistic healing or whether it is the gently rocking rhythm of the horses during the long journey across country that brings about what happens next, remains impossible to say. Nevertheless, the results are truly wondrous: only 30 hours after the visit to the shaman, Rowan is healed of his incontinence, his tantrums and his inability to connect with the world around him.

The horse – man's 'other' best friend! Even as long as 10,000 years ago, towards the end of the upper Palaeolithic period, the fortunes of man and horse were inextricably entwined. In those early days, horses were in all likelihood primarily hunted, much like other species of big game. After all, horsemeat has a high glycogen content, making it sweet and thus very attractive to hunting cultures (McMiken 1990). In all likelihood, early domestication of horses occurred in the Eurasian steppes (Anthony 1986) between 9000BC and 4000BC, when the domestication of other animals, such as dogs, goats, sheep, pigs and cattle was already (relatively speaking) commonplace.

Fast-forward to the more modern times of the late nineteenth/early twentieth century and horses had long since been embedded in the fabric of society, with national economies heavily dependent on horses to keep industries of agriculture, transport and warfare turning over (Crossman and Walsh 2011).[1] With the industrial revolution and ever more efficient mechanization, however, the use of horses in an industrial setting rapidly declined from the end of World War I onwards. It is a mark of the truly adaptable nature of *equus caballus* that a new niche was carved. The use of horses in leisure pursuits meant that, by the end of the twentieth century, horses were once again contributing considerably to the socioeconomic development of the Western world. In a nutshell, horses have played and undoubtedly will continue to play an important role in the cultural, social and economic development of modern civilization. But what is it that makes the connection between horses and humans so unique that, even once their utilitarian bonds were severed, they continue to forge ahead along the same continuous path? This chapter provides a general overview of different definitions of horse–human interaction and how these interactions may impact on humans and their potential benefits on physical and psychological health.

The benefits of owning an animal...

Intuitively, those of us who own horses or, indeed, any other type of pet or companion animal, might wish to conclude that being around an animal is good for you. At least, that is what animal lovers have fervently believed all along and early empirical evidence seems to be supporting their claims. Having to communicate non-verbally with a member of a different species is thought to have considerable benefits in counselling and therapeutic settings (e.g. hippotherapy, therapeutic riding, equine-assisted activities or equine-assisted therapy: Beck and Katcher 1996; Karol 2007; Quiroz Rothe *et al.* 2005), as well as a positive impact on health. Researchers hypothesize, for example, that pet ownership positively influences the psychosocial risk factors of coronary heart disease. More specifically, dog owners are likely to be more physically active as they will have to take their dog for a walk. They will also be more likely to engage with other dog owners or animal lovers in conversation, increasing social interactions, which, in turn, are likely to have a beneficial effect on their state of mind (Patronek and Glickman 1993). Studies by Friedmann and colleagues (Friedmann *et al.* 1980; Friedmann and Thomas 1995) also indicated that owners of pets (primarily dogs and cats) enjoyed increased survival rates after a coronary incident and had a decreased risk of cardiovascular disease (Allen *et al*. 2002; Anderson *et al*. 1992). They were also found to have slightly lower systolic blood pressures, plasma cholesterol and triglyceride values (Anderson *et al*. 1992), while this decrease in levels of physiological arousal was also associated with relaxation of the facial muscles, arguably resulting in a more relaxed appearance (Katcher *et al*. 1983).

When talking to their pets, people do so more slowly and in a more relaxed mode (Katcher and Beck 1986), in itself both an indicator of and a precursor to more relaxation. Elderly pet owners were also found to use their general practitioner services less frequently (Headey 1999; Headey and Grabka 2007) and experienced lower feelings of loneliness and depression (Garrity *et al*. 1989) than individuals without a furry friend. Furthermore, several research efforts focusing on the relationship between children and animals have found that children derive emotional support from their pets (e.g. Bryant 1985; Covert *et al*. 1985; Melson and Schwarz 1994) and tend to show greater levels of empathy (Ascione 1992; Bryant 1985; Melson *et al*. 1992). Yet there remain a number of studies that were unable to replicate these altogether positive findings on animal ownership, reporting instead no benefits of pet ownership to health or wellbeing (Clark Cline 2010; Koivulsilta and Ojanlatva 2006; McNicholas *et al*. 2005; Pachana *et al*. 2005; Parslow *et al*. 2005) or levels of empathy in children (Daly and Morton 2006).

Why might this be and where does it leave us? Firstly, studies investigating the impact of pet ownership on health and wellbeing are clearly not as clear-cut as people (in particular owners of pets) would like us to believe. Secondly, there may be other confounding factors, such as gender, marital status, overall status of health, level of education (Rijken and van Beek 2011) but also individual differences, such as personality traits, which may affect the impact that animal ownership has on people. In many ways, this raises more questions than it answers – which might be argued is always a good thing for an animal or equine scientist! But the most obvious question in the context of this book is, of course, to what extent these findings might be transferable to ownership of and involvement with horses.

The benefits of riding horses: lending a helping 'hoof'

While research investigating the impact of human–animal relationships focusing on companion animals and, in particular, dogs and cats, is generally more popular – undoubtedly because dogs and cats are somewhat easier and cheaper to acquire and care for than horses – an increasing number of studies have started to investigate the impact that riding, grooming or simply being around horses might have on people (e.g. Karol 2007; Hakanson *et al*. 2009; Haylock and Cantril 2006; McGee and Reese 2009; Porter-Wenzlaff 2007). The therapeutic benefits of riding horses were first openly acknowledged by the Greek physician Hippocrates almost 2,500 years ago (400BC), who is thought to have referred to horse riding as having a 'healing rhythm'. However, it was the sporting success of the Danish dressage rider Lis Hartel, who won Olympic silver in 1952 in Helsinki and 1956 in Stockholm, that seemed to have moved the potential health benefits of riding into the modern spotlight. At the age of 23, Hartel was struck down by polio, which resulted in her being paralyzed from the knee down. She continued to ride, however, only needing help to get on and off the horse, crediting much of her physical recovery to riding.

Since then, a number of studies have investigated the efficacy of riding on medical conditions in controlled settings, resulting in numerous positive findings for conditions such as cerebral palsy, Down's syndrome, spina bifida, sensory modulation disorder, language disorders, intellectual disabilities and visual impairments (e.g. Brenda *et al.* 2003; Biery and Kauffman 1989; Candler 2003; Dismuke 1984; Macauley and Gutierrez 2004; Lehrman and Ross 2001; Sterba *et al.* 2002; Winchester *et al.* 2002). More specifically, the physical benefits of inter-action with horses in a therapy context included, for example, improved speech and language abilities (Macauley and Gutierrez 2004); improved balance and gait (Haehl *et al.* 1999) and muscle symmetry (Benda *et al.* 2003), as well as psychosocial benefits such as improved self-concepts (Cawley *et al.* 1993) and behavior (Emory 1992).

While evidence for the therapeutic effects of horse–patient interaction is undoubtedly on the increase, we still know very little regarding the underlying processes of how and why horses have such a potent effect on people with disabil-ities. In addition, much of the terminology surrounding any kind of equine activity deemed beneficial beyond the level of sports and leisure riding can be very confusing, with the terms 'hippotherapy', 'equine-assisted therapy', 'equine-facilitated psychotherapy', 'equine-assisted activities' and 'therapeutic riding' sometimes being used interchangeably. We therefore look at each of these activ-ities in turn to help to crystallize their meaning, including some theoretical foundations for their efficacy.

Equine-assisted activities and therapeutic riding

To begin with, terms such as equine-assisted activities or therapeutic riding usually refer to activities that are not under the direct supervision of a qualified therapist. They primarily focus on the teaching of riding-related skills to people with learning disabilities or any other kind of physical or mental limitation. While these activities undoubtedly have positive effects on health and wellbeing that are likely to mirror those occurring during more structured equine therapy sessions (see below for more detail), the main focus remains on teaching how a human, the rider, can manage, work and ride a horse and, as a result, learn how to interact with it in a controlled and safe manner. At its most elementary level, the interac-tion with horses can teach particularly children but also adults to care for and look after another living being, teaching them, by extension, how to care for and look after themselves (Karol 2007).

Further to beneficial effects for children, the use of horses in adult settings has recently been on the increase. Humans mainly depend on verbal communications, whereas, according to van Dierendonck and Goodwin (2005), there is a greater dependency among horses on nonverbal communication expressed through body language because of the dangers associated with vocal communication in attracting the attention of predators. Such awareness on the part of the horse implies that any minute changes of body position, muscular tension, respiration and even heart rate from the rider are likely to be picked up and reacted upon by the horse (Keeling *et al.* 2009; Munsters *et al.* 2012; Wolframm and Micklewright 2009). The innate sensitivities of the horse are therefore thought to lend themselves to teaching skills associated with, for example, displaying confidence, emotional management and leadership skills. While many organizations and individuals promote and deliver 'management courses' with horses, based on anecdotal experience only, several scientific studies exist, investigating how social communication strategies between equids can be successfully used to improve interactions among humans (Rickards 2000). However, as the main focus to date of peer-reviewed research has been on equine-related therapies, the following passages will concentrate on those.

Hippotherapy

Hippotherapy, derived from the Greek *hippo*, meaning horse, is defined as a treatment strategy relying purely on the movement of the horse and might feature in a broader treatment plan of physical therapy, occupational therapy or speech therapy. It is therefore important to note that hippotherapy does not involve the teaching of riding-specific or general horse management skills and should be performed by a qualified therapist.

Especially in view of the many, many anecdotal reports detailing how horses can help people to overcome physical and mental ailments, it is perhaps not altogether surprising that a good number of empirical studies have been able to show a positive effect of hippotherapy. McGibbon *et al.* (2009), for example, was able to demonstrate the immediate improvement of muscle asymmetry in 47 children with spastic cerebral palsy following a ten-minute session of hippotherapy compared with ten minutes of barrel sitting. In the second part of the same study, a smaller sample of six children, also suffering from cerebral palsy, participated in a 12-week hippotherapy treatment programme and showed improvement across several functional domains. These findings mirrored those of Casady and Nichols-Larsen (2004), who were able to provide evidence of the beneficial effect of hippotherapy on the functional performance of ten children with cerebral palsy. Furthermore, in a longitudinal study of one year, three of four children with physical impairments and/or motor delays showed significant improvement (Murphy *et al.* 2008), supporting findings from other authors on the positive impact of hippotherapy on motor function (e.g. Benda *et al.* 2003; Lechner *et al.* 2003; Shurtleff *et al.* 2009). Furthermore, hippotherapy has been found to lead to significant improvement not only in children but also in adults. Silkwood-Sherer and Warmbier (2007) showed that, in patients suffering from multiple sclerosis, weekly hippotherapy sessions for 14 weeks showed significant improvements compared with control conditions. Similarly, Lechner *et al.* (2007) were able to demonstrate the significant benefits of hippotherapy on adult spasticity compared with three other control treatments.

Hippotherapy has also been found to be beneficial in developing psychological components, such as improvement in motivation to engage in daily activities, communication and social interaction in children with autism (Citterio 1997; Garrique *et al.* 1994; Leitao 2004; Taylor *et al.* 2009; Umbarger 2007) or on the perceived wellbeing in patients with spinal cord injury (Lechner *et al.* 2007). While it would be too early to unequivocally support the use of hippotherapy in all patients, scientific evidence at least seems to point towards it being a potentially highly beneficial complementary treatment option.

Equine-assisted therapy

Equine-assisted therapy (EAT) is a collective term for all types of equine activities that make use of the horse to achieve structured therapy aims. Different types of therapy, such as equine-assisted psychotherapy, might therefore be argued to be included under the heading of EAT. As EAT is also considered to be a form of therapy, it needs to be conducted under the supervision of a qualified therapist. But, rather than focusing on the movement of the horse *per se*, as in hippotherapy, EAT emphasizes the triad relationship of horse, patient and therapist. Håkanson *et al.* (2009) very succinctly describe the process as follows: 'EAT thereby alters the traditional patient role into a three-part relationship – rider, horse and therapist' (p. 44). To Karol (2007), the fact that horse–human communication relies primarily on nonverbal cues becomes an important trigger in the therapeutic process, which is then picked up and used by the accompanying therapist. Once the horse responds to the patient's attempts to interact, whether this takes place during grooming, while leading the horse or while in the saddle, the therapist can use this information to help patients to understand and to control their own bodies, with the ultimate aim of transferring those new-found skills into the 'outside world'. Patients who might have difficulties controlling their temper are likely to initially fail to get the horse to react the way that they wish. Once they learn how to calm themselves, both physically and mentally, horses are very likely to respond more favourably, providing immediate reinforcement to the patient (Karol 2007). In support of these notions, a number of studies have shown that the informal interaction with horses can help children to test and improve their self-management skills and emotional responses (Dyer 2000), physical awareness and motor coordination (Benda *et al.* 2003).

The science behind the art: theoretical underpinnings

While the scientific evidence is strong that different forms of equine-related therapies, in particular hippotherapy, seem to have beneficial effects, the rationale as to why this might be is, as yet, not entirely clear. In a review, Granados and Agis (2011) provide an outline of a number of theoretical concepts and frameworks explaining the beneficial effects of hippotherapy. Dynamic systems theory, is based on the assumption that the human body continuously acts on, interacts with and adapts to the three domains of its own body, the task executed and the environment. Development of an individual occurs as he or she tries to achieve stability within these three domains and the relevant emotional, cognitive and behavioral responses emerge (Lewis 2000), such as changes in postural control, arousal, motivation and rhythm (Granados and Agis 2011).

The theory of sensory integration takes a different approach, assuming that learning and behavior depend on the functional integration of sensory and motor capacities (Randall 2006), such as being able to react accordingly when perceiving a certain visual or auditory stimulus. When riding a horse, sensory experiences of touch, sight, smell and sound are stimulated, together with appropriate motor control, sense of balance and direction. Such innate integration is thought, in the long run, to have a positive effect on the holistic development of a child or adult patient. Supportive of this would be anecdotal accounts of many trained physiotherapists using hippotherapy, who claim that no other intervention is as effective at regulating muscle tone (Debuse *et al.* 2005).

Additional factors, such as the horse's higher core temperature and the natural rhythm of its gait, which has been shown to mimic human walking patterns (Uchiyama *et al.* 2011), are thought to aid in the loosening of muscles and encourage the repetition of rhythmic movements off the horse as well (Granados and Agis 2011).

However, it is important to emphasize that, while all of these theories seem intuitively plausible, much more empirical evidence is needed, especially as there are studies that show no significant improvements in health parameters while engaged with horses. When investigating the immediate effects of a hippotherapy session on temporal and spatial gait parameters in cerebral palsy patients, McGee and Reese (2009) were unable to find significant results. While there are many more studies reporting positive findings as opposed to no significant benefits of equine-related therapies, the likelihood for publication bias, i.e. the tendency of researchers to only publish positive results, is relatively strong in a field where committed practitioners might be highly motivated to provide support for their area of expertise. In a review on hippotherapy, Sterba (2007) comments that, while hippotherapy is likely to be efficacious in the rehabilitation of gross motor skills, additional studies with larger sample sizes and blinded assessments are needed to provide more conclusive evaluations.

Lastly, it should also be noted that equine-related activities or therapeutic pursuits might not be equally suited to all clients. Children or adults who suffer from conditions predisposing them towards injury more than others (such as fragile bones or epilepsy) or who might engage in activities detrimental to the welfare of the horse might need to participate in a different form of therapy with lower innate levels of risk.

An attempt at theory behind human–horse relationships: more science

Even if we accept, then, that the benefits of animal ownership in general and equine-related activities in particular may not always be objectively and universally quantifiable and apply to some people more than others, the fact remains that animals play – and have played – a major role in our lives. As such, they provide a considerable source of both emotional and physical support to their owners. Why else would all existing cultures keep pets, even though the preferred type of species varies (Beck and Meyers 1996), and spend considerable amounts of money on them (Serpell 2003)? The concept of the 'human–animal bond', quite clearly, is 'alive and well', despite – or perhaps because of – all its complexities and intricacies.

But what about the horse? Today, we are still able to see the evidence of both the practical and the symbolic significance of equines: many historical figures of military importance are depicted on horseback – on the one hand to show them 'in action' but on the other to symbolize them towering literally and figuratively over their subjects (Birke and Brandt 2009). Similarly, indigenous peoples, such as Native Americans or Mongols, are thought to have identified strongly with their horses, to the extent that they believed their fate to be intertwined with that of their mounts (Lawrence 1988). The image of the horse as a symbol of power and greatness is not limited to the past, nor does it belong to peoples populating more remote corners of the globe. It continues to feature strongly in modern life as evidenced, for example, by the use of horse-related imagery in modern advertising. Equally, and probably as potent a symbol, horses are also depicted as gentle, caring creatures that are able to invoke both psychological and physical healing in people.

Quite clearly then, the types of relationships that mankind has with horses are many and varied. Yet, to date, no unifying theory of the human–animal bond – let alone the bond between humans and horses – has been determined (Brown 2004), even though parallels have been drawn between animal–animal, human–human or human–object relationships (Kidd and Kidd 1987). More recently, considerable effort has been made to develop human–animal bond theories in their own right, such as aspects of social/psychological support (Collis and McNicholas 1998); the concept of self-psychology developed within a framework of psychoanalysis (Alper 1993; Wolf 1994); evolutionary psychology, in particular biophilia (Wilson 1984) and socioeconomic/sociocultural perspectives (Mullin 1999). Appreciating the theory-driven foundations for human–animal relationships in general and human–horse dyads in particular provides an important background to the understanding of the varying roles that horses might play in people's lives, the different motivations of equine enthusiasts for keeping horses and the kind of elements which might impact on the quality of horse–rider dyads. To understand and appreciate the full value of the different approaches to explaining horse–human bonds, these approaches are considered one by one for their individual merits in the following section.

However, before we proceed, a word of caution seems to be in order: many of the theoretical models developed to understand human–animal bonds are derived from existing models of human–human relationships. As such, there exists considerable danger in endowing animals with the same kind of physical and psychological attributes, skills and needs that humans possess. Such tendencies are generally referred to as anthropomorphism, as expressed by Kidd and Kidd (1987), 'the attribution of human mental and emotional capacities to animals, and the assumption that animals act from motives similar to those of humans.' (p. 143). Any student or scholar of human–animal interaction should therefore try to monitor closely their own inclinations to anthropomorphize.

Themes of horse ownership: what horses mean to people

In a review on sociocultural studies of human–animal relationships, Mullin (1999) highlights the multifaceted identities that animals kept as pets or companion animals have been endowed with in recent years: commodities, family members, companions, the embodiment of 'nature' but also, still, a source of food. While it clearly is not only citizens from Western societies that keep pets (e.g. Descola 1994), the social and economic conditions associated with middle and upper classes are likely to enable the emotional attachment with and investment in animals (Mullin 1999). In many ways, and even though many owners may be loath to admit to it, from a conceptual point of view, companion animals, including horses, are on many levels comparable to consumer goods. They are commodities that help construct identities. Time and again, the equine industry has seen plenty of evidence of how horses can – unwittingly – build identities, especially at the upper levels of competitive sports. Previously relatively unknown riders have shot to fame and recognition, with a myriad sponsors knocking on their door, because that one special horse helped them to win a European, World or Olympic medal. While it is clear that those riders had to have exceptional ability in the first place, it was that one horse which helped define them as being world class. Especially to professional riders and jockeys, who ride horses for a living, the relationship they have with their four-legged sport partners are necessarily based around the fulfilment of the immediate needs of the job. In many ways, these riders have no choice but to objectify their horses, almost out of necessity, to spare themselves from too much emotional trauma should, following another successful competition, yet another horse be sold off to the highest bidder, given to another rider or taken out of the sport altogether.

Quite clearly, such examples of riders at the top of their game are the exception rather than the rule and most equine enthusiasts will develop a relationship with their horses over a number of years. In a qualitative study on the nature of horse–human relationships, Keaveney (2008) outlines and develops some of the themes or motives that people may have when engaging in horse-related activities. Notions of friendship, love and even emotional support feature strongly, mirroring those experienced with other household animals. But, perhaps most importantly, interacting with horses appears to teach people about their own abilities and limitations, especially with regards to their own physicality, more than any other human–animal bond: 'riding a horse adds a level of physicality, intimacy and intensity unique from anything experienced with household-animal companions' (Keaveney 2008: 448). The fact that even the most subtle of body movements can create a response in the horse is thought to be the source of feeling 'one' with the horse. Another important theme focuses on the establishment of a working relationship on the way towards achieving a (sporting) goal. Keaveney notes that mutual trust and respect are core values for the participating riders involved in the study. Additional themes include bonding through adversity, whereby the bond between horse and rider would become stronger after having overcome a serious challenge together; a sense of spirituality, captured in what Keaveney summarizes as 'awe-inspiring power and beauty symbolizing sacredness of the horse' (p. 450) and shared flow (Csikszentmihalyi 1978), whereby horse owners would experience a feeling of deep concentration, resulting in loss of self-awareness and, at times, even transcendence. Keaveney summarizes the last two emerging themes as 'communitas', which describes the sense of camaraderie amongst fellow horse-owners that tends to negate pre-existing rules of social hierarchy, and life lessons, which focuses on how the interaction with horses can teach people skills that are transferable to 'real life'.

Despite Keaveney's work not being a theoretical construct, it nevertheless summarizes and examines the different themes that shape human–horse relationships in an empirical setting. As such, it also manages to reaffirm the tenets of love, care and companionship in the general animal–human bond, while also acknowledging that horse riding is an activity fraught with inherent risks. The combination of those almost contradictory notions makes for much of the fascination of the horse–human relationship.

The biophilia hypothesis: drawn to nature

The Austrian scientist, Konrad Lorenz, may easily be described as one of the founding fathers of modern ethology (the scientific study of animal behavior) and, in 1973, together with Karl von Frisch and Nikolaas Tinbergen, he received the Nobel Prize in Physiology or Medicine 'for their discoveries concerning organization and elicitation of individual and social behavior patterns' (Nobel Foundation 2013). His thoughts and ideas on human–animal relationships have paved the way for future generations of animal scientists. Even if, at times, Lorenz was criticized for excessive anthropomorphism, his musings in his book, *King Solomon's Ring*, from 1952, nevertheless give pause for thought: 'The wish to keep an animal usually arises from a longing for a bond with nature' (p. 57). This original idea that humanity's attraction to animals stems from an intrinsic need was followed up in the 1960s through more serious research into the human–animal bond (e.g. Heiman 1965). A couple of decades later, Edward O. Wilson (Kellert and Wilson 1993; Wilson 1984, 1993) was one of the first researchers to attempt to conceptualize the principles of the human–animal bond. His biophilia hypothesis suggests that mankind possesses a biologically based or innate predisposition to pay attention and/or be drawn to natural elements, such as animals or plants. In more simple terms, Wilson argued that humans are 'hard wired' to be drawn to nature, as this would increase their chances of locating and procuring sustenance and thus survive. These powerful and intrinsic attachments are thought to lead, in turn, to strong emotional connections between humans and animals that are beyond rationalization – examples of which those of us who deal with animals witness on an almost daily basis and of which the astounding story of the autistic boy, Rowan Isaacson, is another powerful illustration. As the theory of biophilia seems to provide an attractive explanation for why most humans seem inexorably drawn to animals, a number of researchers have embraced it in their work aimed at explaining human–animal relationships (i.e. Melson and Fine 2006; Ulrich 1993). While there are no studies explicitly focusing on the biophilia hypothesis to demystify horse–rider relationships, many of the apparent physical and psychological benefits of horse sports might arguably be explained through various aspects of the theory.

Yet, despite its intuitive appeal, several researchers have highlighted inconsistencies that question the validity of biophilia as a general theory for human–animal attraction (Beck and Katcher 2003; Lawrence 1993). First of all, the theory does not propose that humans are primarily concerned with the health and wellbeing of animals, as our innate attraction to them has been argued to stem from our need for sustenance. This, in turn, implies that our primary aim would be to kill and eat, rather than nurture, animals (Katcher and Wilkins 1993). Furthermore, it is difficult to test the application of the theory in its entirety, rather than focusing on a case-by-case approach. Even in those circumstances where biophilia might provide the most appropriate explanation, care must be taken to separate cultural determinants from innate, inborn ones.

Social support theory: I'll scratch your back if you scratch mine

Probably unbeknown to him, the English poet, John Donne, coined a phrase that has clearly stood the test of time. 'No man is an island' resonates as true today as it did at the end of the sixteenth century. Not surprisingly, the notion is in fact supported by a large body of research describing physical and mental health benefits of human companionship (e.g. Lynch 1977; Lynch *et al.* 2000). In essence, social support theory has derived and developed from the sociological concept of symbolic interactionism (Stewart 1989) and encompasses many different components of the way in which humans may be able to support one another through planned or involuntary interactions. A network of friends, support from neighbors, compassion and the proverbial shoulder to cry on are all examples of how personal relationships can go a long way towards meeting varying needs of individuals (Kawachi and Berkman 2000).

Essentially, social support can be broken down into several components, ranging from emotional esteem or instrumental support to levels of social integration and opportunities for nurturing and protection (Collis and McNicholas 1998). While the detailed mechanisms explaining why social support seems to have considerable health benefits still remain somewhat ambiguous (Serpell 2003), the principle advantages seem to involve social relationships being able to protect against or ameliorate the negative health effects of prolonged stress (Ader *et al.* 1995). Put simply, because humans can talk to one another, they are able to share their thoughts, feelings and interpretations. As a direct result, they are in a position to make sense of difficult situations or even receive vital assistance in solving a task. In return, this considerably improves people's ability to cope and decreases the perceived severity of a stressful situation.

Despite animals not being able to speak to their owners in the same way that humans do, they nevertheless seem to provide a form of social support that is in many ways comparable to that borne out of human relationships. In fact, many people consider their pet or companion animal to be a confidant, with whom they will share thoughts and secrets (Cain 1983; Katcher 1981). Research has been able to demonstrate that children are as likely to share sad, angry, happy or secret experiences with their pets as with their siblings (Covert *et al.* 1985). Serpell (2003) argues that the value of animals for the provision of social support hinges on them showing their owner that they love and care for them, even hold them in 'high esteem' (Serpell 2003: 89). However, the difficulty that presents itself here is, of course, that it is very difficult, if not impossible, to know the emotional and cognitive depth of an animal.

This is where behavioral parameters of the animal go a long way towards 'fuelling' owners' perceptions of how their animals 'feel' about them. In fact, animals that behave according to their owners' preferred behaviors were generally considered by those owners to make 'better' companions; i.e. their owners would grow more attached to them (Serpell 1996). Equally, research by Budge *et al.* (1998) showed that owners who perceived their animals to behave in similar ways to them experienced better overall mental health, enhanced feelings of wellbeing, less distress and generally fewer symptoms of ill health. In fact, Bonas *et al.* (2000) asked people to describe and evaluate their different types of social relationships, including those with their pets. It transpired that the quality of relationships that people had with their pets rivalled those they had with other humans. More specifically, dogs scored even higher than humans on the relationship components of 'reliable alliance', 'nurturance' and 'companionship', allowing for the conclusion that people do indeed value the potential for social support from their four-legged companions as much, if not more, than those from other humans.

Undoubtedly, this is at least in part due to the fact that animals often appear to provide unconditional support (Furman 1989). As they are unable to talk, animals also cannot criticize, mock or deceive their owners, leaving them in the belief that their pets hold them in the highest regard, no matter what they do. These principles might equally be applied to the human–horse relationship, which may be one of the reasons why, of late, horses have been used more frequently in therapeutic settings (see the section above). In an article on the therapeutic use of horses to help women to overcome the detrimental effects of domestic violence, Porter-Wenzlaff (2007) describes the process of developing trust and gaining support through the relationship with their equine partner as follows:

Over time, clients begin to look to the horse's behavior to understand their own and thus begin to recognize their feelings more readily, eventually recognizing increasingly subtle changes in their own emotions. As this process occurs, they enter into a deeper and more trusting relationship with the horse and themselves.

(Porter-Wenzlaff 2007: 533)

However, the fact that owners so readily evaluate their relationships with their animals in the same fashion as they do those between humans provides evidence that animal owners' thinking is heavily influenced by anthropomorphic notions. Owners attribute their animals with the same kind of cognitions, emotions, desires and motives as humans – which, in return, enables them to perceive their relationships with animals as supportive in the first place. In the context of social support theory as an explanation for human–animal bonds, anthropomorphism sounds not only understandable but downright necessary, as by imbuing animals with being capable of experiencing human feelings, such as love, admiration or jealousy, humans can derive physical and psychological benefits from their four-legged companions (Serpell 1996).

However, anthropomorphic means of perceiving, dealing with and managing animals has been shown to have serious welfare consequences, as animals are no longer considered with the needs of the particular species in mind. Human needs and desires are imposed upon them instead. Especially for horses, an anthropomorphic way of perceiving them might arguably be the source of many welfare concerns, including physical and psychological problems resulting from inappropriate housing, turnout, exercising and feeding practices or health conditions (see a review by Hausberger *et al.* 2008 for additional information).

Concepts of self-psychology: knowing me, knowing you

While evolutionary disposition and the need for social support might be argued to shed some light on the reasons why humans might feel attached to animals, they do not provide all the answer to why different people have different motives for keeping animals. The theory of self-psychology is grounded in psychoanalytical work and is used to assist the therapist in determining their patients' intrinsic needs and resulting relationship styles (Kohut 1984). The theory centres on the concepts of the 'self' and the 'self-object'. The self is thought to form the core of personality. It is made up of values, ideals, ambitions and abilities and is the source of self-esteem, wellbeing and cohesion (Wolf 1988). To maintain a healthy, 'whole' sense of self, individuals are dependent on certain responses from their environment. People, objects, experiences and ideals are all thought to provide feedback that either fuels or undermines a person's self. A self-object is therefore defined as an object, person or experience that is thought to 'evoke, maintain and give cohesion to the self' (Wolf 1988: 63). In line with Kohut's (1984) original definitions, there are three types of self-object functions that aim to create or ensure wholeness of the self:

1. Mirroring self-objects are thought to affirm, confirm and recognize the self in its grandness, goodness and entirety;
2. Idealizing self-objects sustain the self by providing the opportunity for the self to become part of an admired and/or respected self-object, that exudes calmness, confidence and power;
3. Alter-ego (or twinship) self-objects provide the experience of finding likeness in another's self.

(Wolf 1988: 55)

In view of the relationship that many people have with their animals, it hardly comes as a surprise that animals are thought to be able to provide varying degrees of self-object feedback. The theory of self-psychology seems to lend itself as a foundation for the closer examination of the human–animal bond (Brown 2004, 2007, 2011) and the motives that people might have for owning animals. For example, Alper (1993: 262) described how a pet dog functioned as a mirroring self-object to a child. The dog would seemingly listen to the girl's poetry readings and would respond to her questions as to whether 'he had liked it' by wagging its tail and jumping up and down. To the girl, the behavioral response of the dog would seem to be enthusiastically affirmative, which served to confirm her feelings and actions as meaningful. It is not difficult to come up with a number of similar examples depicting how the behavior of horses might be construed as affirmative of their owners as 'good' or even 'worthy' humans. Upon the owner setting foot on the yard, the horse whinnies in apparent greeting. In all likelihood, the horse is actually displaying a learned response to a treat that shortly follows the whinny. Yet, to the owner, the horse's whinny strikes them as a display of unconditional love and affection, regardless of any real or imagined imperfections, which, in turn, might render the horse a powerful mirroring self-object.

Alper also uses the example of a woman who shows her dog in judged competitions to highlight the role of animals as idealizing self objects: 'Showing her dog, an extension of herself, provided Hilary with an avenue for the development of her thwarted narcissism, channeling it into a form that was given public and familial approval.' (Alper 1993: 261). Alper argues that the dog's owner, Hilary, was able to identify with the achievements of her dog, which, in turn, would help bolster her own sense of self-worth. In an equestrian setting, the idealizing self-object seems particularly applicable. Many horse owners derive pleasure from showing or competing their horses. In fact, aesthetic appeal has been found to be one of the most important criteria when purchasing a horse (Górecka-Bruzda *et al.* 2011; Hennessy *et al.* 2008). Owning a horse that is acknowledged to be beautiful, either 'officially' in a competitive setting or even unofficially through comments by friends or acquaintances, will, according to the concept of self-psychology, bolster a horse owner's feelings of self-worth.

Finally, the concept of twinship self-objects describes how the self is sustained by feelings of oneness with another, by sharing a level of understanding and appreciation of one another that goes beyond mundane levels of interaction (Silverstein 1999). The concept of 'oneness' between horse and rider is, of course, one that features strongly in most equestrian pursuits. In her study, investigating different themes in horse–rider relationships, Keaveney (2008) quotes the participants as having a sense of being 'one with the horse' or 'When I am with my horse ... we are one in both heart and spirit' (p. 451). Anecdotally, most riders will describe a 'perfect ride' as one where the horse seems to be reacting to the mere thoughts of its rider and where the rider feels so in tune with the horse that no apparent effort is required. The concept of the twinship self-object, whereby the human experiences a feeling of complete understanding and 'wholeness' with another living being, therefore might be argued to provide another strong motive for the bond between horse and rider.

Despite there only being limited theoretical underpinnings to the horse–human relationship, the concepts outlined above seem to provide a valid starting point for developing an even greater understanding of how the bond between horses and humans may be defined. Most importantly, perhaps, self-psychology might also shed additional light on the development of anthropomorphic thoughts and behaviors in horse owners. Subsequent insights might be gained on how anthropomorphism might impact upon and colour human perceptions of the interaction with their horses. Just to reiterate, while an anthropomorphic interpretation of a horse's – or for that matter any animal's – behavior might be considered 'useful' to the human's psychological development (e.g. as outlined in social support theory or concepts of self-psychology), it might also lead to considerable welfare problems once horses' physical and psychological needs are treated within a human frame of reference. Quite clearly then, anyone engaging in interactions with horses should therefore remain aware of the implications of the horse's nature at all times.

Foundations for horse–rider quality: how to know when it's right

Further to any conceptual frameworks that allow social scientists to investigate and ultimately to understand horse–human relationships, horse enthusiasts quite often merely wish to know whether there are any common principles determining how well they are likely to get on with a particular horse. Put simply, people who are about to spend money on buying a horse want to be fairly certain that they end up with a horse they can enjoy. The most obvious aspect, and one that will be at the forefront of the minds of most riders or horse owners, is whether a horse might meet their expectations and fulfil their immediate or long-term goals and ambitions. Depending on whether the potential purchaser is an amateur rider, who keeps horses primarily for fun and a sense of personal achievement, or a professional earning a living from training horses or someone who considers horses an investment, the type of horse they are looking for is likely to vary considerably in terms of price, athletic ability, age and previous experience. Put more succinctly, the types of activities that horse owners wish to undertake with their horses will differ and thus affect the type of horse they choose. A horse that will be kept as a companion animal in a field at the back of the house and taken only for an occasional ride through the woods will need to possess very different physical and behavioral characteristics than one that was purchased to compete. Despite many studbooks nowadays aiming to breed anatomically correct sports horses that theoretically could be used in a number of equestrian disciplines, one might wish to argue that the increasing technical requirements in any sport mean that, to do well, horses need to meet very specific physical requirements.

Not surprisingly, therefore, breeding associations tend to value physical ability in their breeding stock above any other traits. A study by Koenen *et al.* (2004) investigated the breeding objectives of the major European studbooks and found that aspects relating to conformation, gait and sports performance were the primary selection criteria. However, it seems that, to many horse owners, especially those who keep their horses at least in part for the pleasure of riding, characteristics other than physical are as – if not more – important when choosing the 'right' kind of horse. In fact, a study by Górecka-Bruzda *et al.* (2011) surveying the opinions of 197 riders (of whom 78.8 per cent were female) showed that 'all of the riders desired tractable, healthy and unproblematic horses in terms of behavior and maintenance.' (p. 391). Similarly, Buckley *et al.* (2004) found that, in addition to equine size and ability, 59 per cent of Pony Club horse owners particularly valued temperament and suitability for their riders. According to Górecka-Bruzda *et al.* (2011), leisure riders in particular look for horses that are easy to handle and trained to a basic standard of obedience, rather than possessing outstanding dressage or jumping ability. The authors also note that leisure riders in particular would benefit from horses habituated to novel situations and comment that breeding associations might be well placed to pay more attention to aspects relating to equine personality, to safeguard rider safety and satisfaction (Górecka-Bruzda *et al.* 2011).

Even though a handful of European studbooks, most notably that of the Dutch warmblood (KWPN), have started to include equine temperament testing in their selection procedure, the equine industry still seems to be primarily motivated by performance and the idea of producing 'the next Olympic champion'. Not surprisingly then, Hennessy *et al.* (2008) were able to show that producers attached significantly more importance to gender, colour, pedigree details and performance records in horses than potential purchasers, who valued equine temperament and aesthetic appeal significantly more. On aspects relating to soundness, conformation and movement, producers and purchasers were found to agree.

Why is it then that, sometimes, even though objectively a horse might 'tick all the boxes' in terms of suitable temperament and physical ability, horse and rider still do not seem to be getting along?

As we have argued throughout this chapter, the relationship between humans and horses depends on a myriad of components, all inexorably interlinked. There can be no question that effective communication between horse and rider considerably depends on the rider's level of experience and skill, especially with a view of reacting to unforeseen movements or reactions from the horse (Visser *et al.* 2008). However, as we well know, not all riders are equally skilled nor do they have the inclination to be so, yet they still wish the interactions with their horses to be satisfying, harmonious and, perhaps most importantly, safe. In reality, however, many horse–rider combinations are often far from ideal, both from a performance and a communicative point of view (Hausberger *et al.* 2008; Hennessy *et al.* 2008). Many riders, for example, have horses that regularly engage in conflict or evasive behaviors, such as head tossing, head shaking or tail swishing (Kaiser *et al.* 2006; McGreevy and McLean 2005) or even, at its most extreme, bucking, rearing or backing up (de Cartier d'Yves and Ödberg 2005). A study by Visser *et al.* (2008) investigating the relationship between subjective and objective perceptions of horse–rider cooperation and equine behavior showed that frequent evasive behaviors by horses tended to influence riders' perception of cooperation negatively. Horses that were perceived to be attentive to the riders' aids, on the other hand, were having a positive influence on horse–rider cooperation scores. In essence, then, riders are likely to wish to engage in interactions with horses that show little evasive behavior and are attentive to their riders.

Yet there still remain horse–rider combinations deemed unsuitable, whereby communication between horses and riders does not proceed smoothly and either the horse or the combination becomes a danger to themselves or others. The principle of 'ethical equitation' stipulates that riders have a moral responsibility to deal with horses and must bear in mind their optimal welfare (McGreevy and McLean 2010b). Such responsibility should necessarily extend to determining the underlying factors that are conducive to harmonious horse–rider relationships. Considering the high level of injuries in equestrian sports and the increasing amounts of equine wastage from horses being deemed 'unrideable' or 'unmanageable', determining which types of horse and rider are best suited to each other seems particularly important.

The magic between riders and horses

Human personality traits are widely recognized to affect different aspects of life, such as relationships, employment preferences or recreational activities (Gattis *et al.* 2004). Some researchers have even gone as far as claiming that personality might affect the quality of interpersonal relationships (e.g. Asendorpf and Wilpers 1998; Baumeister and Leary 1995; Epstein and Baucom 2002; Karney and Bradbury 1995) and can predict relationship satisfaction (e.g. Bradbury and Fincham 1988). Yet while there can be little doubt that personality components play an important role in determining the quality of relationships, few studies have investigated how aspects relating to temperament, character and personality might impact on the interaction between horse and rider (Pretty 2000b; Visser *et al.* 2008).

Seeing that horses are reactive, rather than reflective, they are unlikely to demonstrate the same intricacies of personality traits as riders. Nevertheless, animals are thought to exhibit a number of different 'personalities'. Momozawa *et al.* (2003, 2005) were able to identify several traits, including anxiety, novelty seeking, understanding, trainability and affability, when asking caretakers to assess their equine charges with the help of questionnaires. Other researchers have reported dimensions such as flightiness, willingness to perform (Visser *et al.*

2001); fearfulness or gregariousness (Wolff *et al.* 1997) and six trait dimensions of dominance, anxiousness, excitability, protection, sociability and inquisitiveness (Lloyd *et al.* 2007, 2008). It must be noted that, at present, no unequivocal way of assessing equine personality has been determined (König van Borstel *et al.* 2011). It is reasonable to assume, however, that the varying forms of behavior displayed by horses are indicative of different types of personality. As a result, the quality of horse–rider interactions, much like relationships between humans, must at least in part also be subject to interactions between the different personality traits displayed by horses and riders (Hausberger *et al.* 2008).

For example, emotionality (neuroticism) in horses was generally correlated negatively to learning (Heird *et al.* 1986; LeScolan *et al.* 1997) and has also been linked to increased levels of arousal in riders (Wolframm and Micklewright 2010a). The question that presents itself, however, is whether certain personality traits in horses might in fact be desirable in different disciplines, regardless of the effect they might have on their riders. To that effect, Hausberger *et al.* (2004) demonstrated that show horses displayed greater levels of emotionality than leisure horses, while draught horses might be selected for low levels of excitability and anxiousness (Lloyd *et al.* 2008), and racing thoroughbreds for high levels of reactivity (McGreevy and Thomson 2006).

Yet, despite some evidence regarding the type of equine personality traits likely to be beneficial for different equestrian disciplines, we still know very little regarding the extent to which rider personality traits might interact best with which type of horse. In a large-scale study involving 2525 female riders, Wolframm and Meulenbroek (2012) investigated which equine and female rider personality components co-varied with the (rider-perceived) quality of horse–rider relationships. Findings did, in fact, indicate that co-variations of personality traits between horse and female riders differ depending on the perceived quality of the relationship. A number of weak correlations between perceived horse and rider personality constructs were found for horse–rider dyads perceived to be 'good', regardless of the length of the relationship, age or skill level of the rider. Horse–rider combinations perceived as 'mediocre' were defined through two correlations of horse and rider personality traits that were nearing significance. No correlations could be found for poor relationships.

More specifically, results showed that easily excitable, emotional riders also perceived the horses with which they had a good relationship to be highly emotionally reactive. Less sensitive riders, on the other hand, preferred horses that were calmer and more relaxed. Riders who considered themselves to be adventurous, risk taking and impulsive indicated that they had mediocre to good relationships with horses they found to be imaginative, clever and dominant. Possible explanations for this might be that riders who thrive on excitement prefer horses that demonstrate challenging behavior.

The rider personality trait of 'consideration', composed of accommodating, altruistic and dutiful, was found to correlate with the equine trait of 'gregariousness', i.e. affectionate, sociable and curious. A likely explanation might be that riders with a more accommodating, compromising mind-set prefer affectionate horses, while riders who are less willing to give way to others are likely to prefer horses that do not seek as much physical contact. Riders scoring higher on the construct 'leadership' and who thus perceived themselves to be more competent and assertive, thought their relationships most satisfying with horses they found to be 'intelligent' and 'willing (to work)'. Interestingly, the personality concept of 'willingness (to work)' was the only construct to show a main effect on overall quality of relationships. It is possible that this is one personality characteristic that riders unanimously value in their horses – a finding that is mirrored by the results from Górecka-Bruzda *et al.* (2011).

While the study of Wolframm and Meulenbroek (2012) provides an interesting starting point for identifying 'ideal' horse–rider combinations, the correlations found in the study were highly significant yet weak. While confounding variables such as age, level of skill, breed, horse gender and discipline were controlled for, there may have been additional aspects that influenced the results of the study and, indeed, any new or existing horse–rider partnerships. Previous positive or negative experience with horses, fine motor skill of the rider (which often is indicative of rider ability and goes beyond competitive level), changes in rider (or horse) mood, joint action characteristics or indeed talent of the horse, are likely to impact on the quality of current and future relationships riders have with their horses.

What is real? Powers of perception in horse–rider relationships

One of the key criticisms of most studies trying to assess horse–rider interactions, refers to the fact that people (i.e. riders) are asked to rate various aspects of themselves and of their horses. By its very definition, these types of assessments can never be considered to be entirely objective reflections but may also be influenced by other factors, such as previous experience, current mood states, aspects of social desirability, personal motives and more. Again, the study by Wolframm and Meulenbroek (2012) on horse–rider personality co-variants serves to highlight some of the issues associated with perception and reality. For example, participating riders considered mares to be less gregarious than either geldings or stallions. The question that needs to be asked is whether this is a true reflection of mare temperament or whether these findings might be informed by common 'hearsay' in the equine sector that mares are more difficult. Furthermore, high scores on the construct of equine willingness (to work) were perceived to be instrumental to 'good' horse–rider relationships. Firstly, this raises the fundamental question as to whether horses even possess the motivational capacity to be 'willing' to do their riders' bidding. It may simply be that these horses have been trained well enough to respond to the cues offered by their riders. Secondly, correlations are no indicators of cause and effect. Horse–rider relationships might be perceived to be good because horses appear to do as the riders ask or horses do as their riders ask because the relationship is good. Any future research investigating components of horse–rider relationships must bear these potential limitations in mind.

Finally, any assessment of horse–rider relationships by the rider is likely to reflect and be influenced by riders' own personality traits, their tendencies to interpret behavior of their horses in a certain way. Highly anxious riders, for example, might be quick to consider their own horse as anxious or easily stressed at the slightest over-reaction on the part of the horse. Riders, who by their very nature are more relaxed and level-headed in their outlook, might not pay much heed to their horses' temperamental outbursts. Riders might also be inclined to project either their own desires and hopes or their worries and fears on to their current or future horses. The perception of the quality of the relationship with their horse might therefore be coloured accordingly.

Lastly, personality shapes people's behavior, their actions and subsequent reactions. The interaction with and training of horses is achieved through the complex system of nonverbal communication, determined by the conventions and intrinsic dimensions of either species. The way that riders perceive the (equine) world around them, including their horses, will have a direct effect on how they behave towards their horses. This behavior, determined by individual psychological profiles, must result in a reaction, any reaction, on behalf of the horse, which, in turn, will be interpreted by the rider based on their own personal frame of reference. In short, the way that riders perceive their horses will determine how they react towards them and how the horse reacts towards them in return. Especially from a welfare perspective, with a view to avoiding that horses are labelled 'undesirable' and thereby possibly being condemned to the knacker's yard, riders should be encouraged to reflect on how their own behavior might affect perceptions of their horses. When tempted to 'label' a horse in a positive or, more importantly, a negative way, riders should first question whether that particular label might have arisen based on their own psychological profile rather than the horse's temperament or character.

Boys will be boys – and girls will love their horses

Despite equestrianism being one of the few sports where men and women compete against each other on equal terms, one of the most intriguing elements of modern horse–human relationships is the inherent dichotomy with regards to gender participation. Historically, equestrian pursuits were the domain of men, who depended on horses in warfare, transport and agriculture (Hedenborg and White 2012; Robinson 1999). However, in modern times, the majority of horse owners are female, with figures ranging from 70 per cent to 85 per cent (Hedenborg and White 2012; Meyers and Sterling 2000). The reason, which intuitively appeals and also supports much of what has been discussed in this chapter, is that looking after and dealing with horses plays to the feminine trait of care giving and legitimizes the feminization of equestrian sports (Hedenborg 2009). However, a different school of thought has emerged, which argues that becoming involved with horses enables girls to develop a whole new set of competencies revolving around feelings of competence and leadership (Plymoth 2012). Working in and being around a traditionally male-dominated environment, such as the stable yard, and managing animals that weigh half a ton has been argued to stimulate self-esteem (Traaen and Wang 2006), management qualities, bravery and leadership skills (Plymoth 2012). But rather than discarding one over the other theory, what might attract generations of girls and women to equestrian sports is the unique combination of being able to establish emotional relationships with the horse on the one hand (as previously discussed), while also being able to develop traditionally male qualities such as leadership and competence on the other.

And yet, despite horse-related activities apparently establishing themselves as the realm of women, at Olympic level, which might be considered the very top of equestrian sports, male competitors still tend to dominate the disciplines of showjumping and eventing. In their study on changes in female participation patterns in equestrian sports, Hedenborg and White (2012) are able to show that, from the inception of female Olympic participation in showjumping in 1956 and eventing in 1964 (the sport was initially deemed too dangerous to admit women), the male–female ratio of participation stoically stayed below the 0.5 mark. This means that more than twice as many male as female riders competed in the disciplines of showjumping and eventing. In the discipline of dressage at least, the tide started to turn in favour of greater female participation in 1972, with three times as many female dressage riders compared with male dressage riders competing in the Olympic Games of 1992 (Hedenborg and White 2012). Incidentally, since then, the trend seems to have moved towards a renewed surge of male dressage competitors, with only 1.4 times as many female riders compared with male riders at the 2012 Olympic Games in London.

Why is it then that, even though many more girls and women seem to ride, male riders still remain over-represented at the very top of equestrian competitions? Could it be that male riders tend to perform better in competition after all? While there is little formal evidence regarding performance outcomes between male and female riders, a study investigating the elite competitive performance of 810 showjumping riders competing at the 2008/09 FEI Rolex World Cup showed no significant differences between the sexes in final ranking or points achieved (Whitaker *et al.* 2012). Indeed, most riders would probably agree that physiological and morphological differences in men, which in other sports might be advantageous, do not result in being able to ride better. Men do however generally have superior levels of fitness, resulting in the delayed onset of muscular fatigue, which might arguably be beneficial during intensive training sessions or competitions (see Chapter 2 for more details). In any case more male riders make their way to the top than female riders. Research does seem to suggest that the psychological profile of male riders is better suited to coping under pressure and thus to competitive sports. Greater effect sizes of self-confidence for performance in men, as shown in a meta-analysis by Woodman and Hardy (2003) and more facilitative interpretation of pre-competitive levels of anxiety by male athletes (Williams and Perry 1998) only lend support to this notion, particularly as confidence and facilitative anxiety are considered the two most important qualities for success in sport (Hardy 1996a). Research by Meyers *et al.* (1997) seemed to provide additional evidence for these findings in an equestrian setting. They found that male riders showed higher anxiety management and lower mood disturbance scores, indicating that, even as they progress through the competitive levels, male riders might be better equipped to deal with the increasing pressure of more advanced competition. From a performance point of view, one conclusion might be that, in future, female riders should pay even more attention to developing relevant coping skills to keep up with their male counterparts even at the higher levels of competition. On the other hand, as we have seen in the sections above, the relationship with horses and their potential and actual benefit to their human owners, riders and handlers goes far beyond 'mere' sporting performance. Aspects of enjoyment, personal development and building human–horse bonds are surely equally as, if not more, fulfilling and are enough to keep striving for.

Concluding thoughts

The nature of human–animal relationships in general and human–horse bonds in particular is undoubtedly very special and sometimes nothing short of wondrous. The great variety of ways in which humans might be inclined to interact with their horses adds an additional dimension to an otherwise already overwhelming topic. This chapter has drawn together relevant research findings elucidating aspects such as the effect of horse–rider interactions on physical and psychological health and wellbeing, which personality traits might impact on the quality of horse–rider relationships, but also on the topic of gender in equestrian sports. What holds true in previous chapters is no different here: more research is required to develop an even greater understanding – and appreciation – of the wonderful and intriguing mysteries that constitute horse–rider relationships.

Chapter highlights

1. The history of horse–human interactions reaches all the way back towards the end of the upper Palaeolithic period, when man hunted horses for their sweet and highly palatable meat. Up until the end of World War I, horses were indispensable in keeping national economies from collapsing through their role in agriculture, transport and warfare. Towards the end of the 20th century, horses were primarily used for leisure pursuits but still considered valuable contributors to the socioeconomic development of the Western world.
2. Some evidence suggests that owning an animal has physical and psychological benefits, even though the extent of this might be confounded by demographic and personal factors.
3. Referring to the more- or less-structured activities on and around the horse aimed at improving aspects of physical or mental health, the terms hippotherapy, equine-assisted therapy, equine-facilitated psychotherapy, equine-assisted activities and therapeutic riding should not be used interchangeably.
4. While the evidence is strong that different forms of equine-related therapies seem to have beneficial effects, the rationale as to why this might be is, as

yet, not entirely clear. Dynamic systems theory and the theory of sensory integration attempt to provide some theoretical underpinnings for therapeutic benefits.

5. In addition to potential health benefits, there are a number of theoretical concepts attempting to explain man's attraction to animals in general and horses in particular, including the biophilia hypothesis, social support theory and self-psychology theory.

6. When trying to define human–horse relationships, riders should beware of anthropomorphizing their horses, i.e. endowing them with the same kind of mental and emotional capacities as they themselves possess.

7. The quality of relationships between horses and humans is thought to be influenced by aspects relating to intended purpose, physical ability, including conformation, gait and sports performance (which might be considered closely related to intended purpose), health, behavioral parameters and horse–rider personality traits.

8. Any relationship between horse and human is likely to be influenced by human perceptions, desires and expectations, which may lead to behavioral expressions, which, in turn might impact on equine behavior. Objective assessments of horse–human relationships are therefore difficult at best.

9. While, historically, equestrian pursuits were the domain of men, modern horse owners are predominantly female. One school of thought argues that looking after horses plays to the feminine trait of care giving. However, an opposing theory states that working in a previously male-dominated environment helps women to develop new 'masculine' competencies of leadership and feeling competent.

10. In modern top sports, the distribution of male and female competitors varies according to discipline. To date, men seem to dominate the Olympic disciplines of eventing and showjumping, with female competitors more frequently participating in dressage.

7 In conclusion

Quo vadis, equestrian science?

It is true that riding is a science; any science is based on principles, and doctrines are absolutely essential because anything really good and beautiful cannot be based on accident.

(Earl of Pembroke 1778)

Henry Herbert, the tenth Earl of Pembroke, was a Lieutenant General in the British Army and in his lifetime considered an authority on schooling and training cavalry horses. His book, *Military Equitation: Or A Method of Breaking Horses, and Teaching Soldiers to Ride*, published in 1761 with a fourth edition produced by 1793, quickly became the standard work throughout the British cavalry. In many ways, the content and sentiment of Pembroke's ideas as expressed so succinctly in the above quote are far from surprising, considering their periodic and societal context. Pembroke's work and life during the eighteenth century were in all likelihood heavily influenced by the Age of Enlightenment, during which time society was reformed using reason and knowledge advanced through scientific means of investigation. Nevertheless, many of the principles underpinning equestrian sports today are based heavily on tradition and conjecture, rather than systematic observation and measurement, followed by the formulation and experimental testing of hypotheses. Scientists aim for results to speak for themselves, trying not to let their own values and opinions influence their interpretations. Yet equestrian sports, and even the mere interaction with horses, is to this day prone to being considered as much a form of art as it is a scientific discipline. Many of the characteristics used to describe horses are not easily quantifiable. Concepts such 'presence', 'spirit', and of course 'beauty' inevitably lie in the eye of the beholder, meaning that personal experiences, opinions and emotions almost certainly will influence what people believe to be the correct way to manage and train their horses. Yet while people's right to their own opinions should not – and cannot – be called into question, there does seem to be more at stake here. Seeing that equestrian sports are based on the interaction with another sentient being, i.e. the horse, riders and horse owners are responsible for making sure they do everything in their power to ensure the welfare of the horses in their care. An important element must necessarily involve the scientific, that is the systematic and objective, investigation of the different elements that influence horse–rider performance. The rider or human handler obviously and inevitably plays an important part in determining the quality of any horse–rider interaction. Subsequently, scientific investigations must extend to what humans do, think and feel and how they act when engaged with horses.

It should have become clear throughout this book that, while the first steps have finally been taken to integrate scientific principles of investigation into equestrian sports, much work remains to be done. There still exist a myriad of areas that require thorough investigation by ambitious, innovative, yet also practically orientated equestrian scientists in the coming years. By tackling the many remaining questions within and surrounding equitation science in a holistic and innovative manner, empirical findings are likely to help ensure the safety as well as performance of horse–rider dyads. In fact, there can be no doubt that only an innovative, novel approach that is also solid in its scientific application can help push equitation science into the twenty-first century. In these last few pages, a number of rider-related topics are highlighted that may be of interest for future scientific investigation. It should be noted, however, that these ideas and suggestions are by no means exhaustive or exclusive. Primarily, they serve to stimulate the minds of future researchers to go out and examine the possibilities of equestrian sports with an open mind and a fresh eye.

Coordination dynamics between horse and rider: moving 'in sync'

One of the most important themes throughout this book is how current knowledge in other sports- or movement-related settings can help to advance science in equestrian sports. To come up with a satisfactory answer, the immediate approach must be to investigate existing principles and concepts from other scientific fields and apply those to horse–rider contexts. Especially in settings where successful coordination between movement parameters of two or more people may lead to performance enhancement, such as in partner or team sports, the possibilities resulting from the successful identification and definition of relevant parameters of motor synchronization are considerable. They range from the identification of future sporting talent, through to effective motor learning and optimizing performance. Indeed, experienced athletes have been found to react significantly more quickly and accurately to cues given by their co-actors, providing valuable support for the notion that motor synchronicity can foster optimal performance (Mann *et al.* 2007; Shim *et al.* 2005). While research studies have shown that optimal behavioral coupling or movement synchronicity may be considered a function of successful performance in human–human interactions (e.g. Miles *et al.* 2009, 2010), evidence regarding the existence of similar patterns in equestrian sports remains, to this day, largely anecdotal.

As discussed in Chapter 1, current research findings suggest that rider adaptation to and control of movement patterns of horses might be influenced by rider expertise (e.g. Lagarde *et al.* 2005; Peham *et al.* 1998, 2001; Schöllhorn *et al.* 2006). Yet little structural knowledge exists determining the underlying dynamic mechanisms of coordinative processes between horse and rider or the objective parameters necessary to define optimal horse–rider synchronicity (Lagarde *et al.* 2005). Studies investigating interpersonal coordination patterns show that the formation of coordinative structures or 'synergies', i.e. the temporary formation of neuromuscular elements that function as a unit, reduces the number of independent ways in which systems can move,[1] in joint action tasks. As such, effective synergies are able to provide stability against externally or intrinsically induced perturbations and/or fluctuations via reciprocal compensations (e.g. Bernstein 1967; Whiting *et al.* 1992). The question that presents itself is whether movement coordination in human–horse dyads might also be governed by relevant synergies. Furthermore, at what point might such synergies guard against external disturbances of movement, whilst still allowing for the flexibility necessary to deal with the sometimes unpredictable behavior patterns of the horse? An initial study by Lagarde *et al.* (2005) investigated phase–time differences for horse–rider movement in trot, while Wolframm *et al.* (2013) outlined several baseline parameters relating to horse–rider coordination dynamics across all three gaits (i.e. walk, trot (rising and sitting) and canter) and for different levels of expertise. Significant differences in a number of coordination parameters between horse and rider indicate that, independent of expertise, during canter, horse and rider move more harmoniously than in trot or walk, supporting anecdotal accounts that the canter is the easiest gait in which to sit. The coordination parameters measured included, for example, correlation coefficients between the vertical displacement of horse and rider, relative phase values (i.e. to what degree horse and rider are 'out of sync' while moving) and standard deviations of relative phase values (i.e. the degree of variation of synchronicity between horse and rider movement across several movement cycles).

As we have seen when discussing motor learning in riders, there exists a dearth of scientific evidence regarding the extent to which riders are able to coordinate their movement patterns to that of their horses and whether these abilities are innate or developed over time (e.g. Kang *et al.* 2010), which in and of itself is a field of research that requires future attention. Furthermore, while previous research identified a number of important aspects relating to the role of dispositional traits, levels of anxiety and mental skills in horse–rider performance (e.g. Wolframm and Meulenbroek 2012; Wolframm and Micklewright 2011a, 2011b), additional evidence is required on how psychological characteristics (for example, levels of empathy) might impact on the learning and retention of relevant equestrian motor skills and appropriate movement coordination patterns. Clearly, such knowledge would assist in the identification of equestrian talent, as well as determining relevant teaching and training methodologies to be used in the equestrian sector from grassroots through to advanced level.

Quantifying matters of the mind and body

But even beyond the – almost impossibly broad – field of biomechanical interactions between horse and rider, there are a number of elements where equestrian science must attempt to move beyond the traditional mindset of the equine sector, starting with the following: riders are athletes too! The implications of this somewhat obvious and rather simplistic statement are still commonly overlooked in a sporting environment that is primarily concerned with the performance of the four-legged athlete, the horse. More specifically, this means that many of the principles relating to athletic performance in other sports can and should be applied to riders as well. The body of sport science research is large and growing steadily, focusing on a myriad of topics. These range from sport physiological themes, such as the effect of optimal levels of physical fitness and strategic training programmes on performance to how mental skills, concentration, motivation or situation-induced mood and emotional states might make the difference between winning and also-ran (e.g. Weinberg and Gould 2010). A more systematic investigation of how these factors impact on rider performance on the one hand and their subsequent integration into rider training on the other will undoubtedly prove rather effective in achieving more consistent performances in riders at all levels. To that effect, both academically minded students and applied practitioners of equestrian sports should study the research methodologies commonly used in a more general sport science context and replicate those in equestrian settings.

In addition to what might be considered relatively 'straightforward' research which tries to determine the *direct* effects of mental attributes on only the rider, an equally, if not more important dimension is the investigation of how principles of rider psychology might indirectly influence the behavior of the horse and subsequent performance of the horse–rider dyad. While there can be little doubt that different mental states have an associated physiological effect, such as feelings of anxiety almost invariably causing muscular tension, any effects on the horse have not as yet been empirically validated or, indeed, determined. In many ways, this is not altogether surprising, as it is no easy task to first of all determine and then measure various psychological, physiological and psychophysiological parameters in the rider, while subsequently identifying associated equine responses. Relevant psychological parameters might range from semi-permanent traits and situation-induced mood, emotional or motivational states, to various coping and psychological skills, all of which are most frequently measured through questionnaires (e.g. Beauchamp and Whinton 2005; Meyers *et al.* 1997; Wolframm and Meulenbroek 2012; Wolframm and Micklewright 2011) or open, structured or semi-structured interviews (e.g. Pummell *et al.* 2008). While physiological measurements, such as heart rate and heart rate variability, are relatively straightforward and non-invasive to carry out, necessary care must be taken to interpret results correctly. Both heart rate and heart rate variability can be used to measure the physiological response to exercise but might also be indicators of the psychological attributes of stress and may thus also be used to determine psychophysiological effects (e.g. Visser *et al.* 2002; von Borell *et al.* 2007). In fact, a number of authors have already initiated this novel, yet vital line of inquiry and investigated the possible interactive effects between horse–rider heart rates during competition (Bridgeman *et al.* 2005), and under fear-inducing conditions for the rider (Keeling *et al.* 2009). Munsters *et al.* (2012) also investigated correlations between heart rate, heart rate variability, equine behavioral scores and horse–rider match during a challenging object test, while Peeters *et al.* (2013)

focused on levels of free cortisol in horse and rider before and following competition.

Despite the potential difficulties relating to the correct identification and measurement of what may be considered psychological distress in both horse and rider, or what might merely be indicative of the physiological reaction to exercise, future studies should try and establish relevant baseline parameters to draw more valid conclusions relating to the interactive effect of physiological and psychological elements in and between horse and rider.

Science in coaching = scientific coaching

Clearly though, on the route towards combining equine welfare, rider safety and horse–rider performance, it is not merely the rider but also the equestrian coach who has an important role to play. As previous chapters have shown, the 'eye on the ground' is a fundamental prerequisite in the development and maintenance of appropriate levels of motor control and psychological characteristics facilitative to optimal horse–rider performance. Coaching in equestrian sports not only supports the development of riding skills and ability but may also play a major role in preventing accidents and subsequent injuries to horse–rider combinations. It is therefore paramount that coaches, as well as riders, understand and are able to apply principles of learning theory in horses. Research by Warren-Smith and McGreevy (2008), investigating the knowledge of learning theory among accredited equestrian coaches in Australia, showed that only a relatively small minority of participants was able to explain correctly the use of positive reinforcement, negative reinforcement and punishment in horses. It seems particularly important that greater attention is paid to improve elements of equestrian coach education, focusing in particular on the scientific underpinnings of equine learning and, more importantly, how these may apply to daily horse training.

Furthermore, scientific means of measuring and monitoring horse and rider in training and competition can provide equestrian coaches with objective, in-depth data to be used to develop effective, tailor-made coaching trajectories. As indicated previously, empirical evidence relating to the specifics of equestrian coaching is, as yet, rather sparse. Most equestrian coaches still 'make do' with providing appropriate feedback and instructions based merely on what they are able to see of horse and rider at any given moment. Yet the inherent nature of equestrian sport dictates that horse–rider interactions are likely to be very complex and subtle, making them often very difficult to identify for someone watching from the ground. In other fields of investigation, including sports and professional skill development, considerable efforts are being devoted to the scientific, i.e. systematic, examination of different aspects of human performance and how any subsequent findings may be incorporated into effective coaching practices (e.g. Cossman 2012; Miles *et al.* 2012). A study by Hu *et al.* (2012) investigating the use of video-based coaching in operative surgeons serves as an excellent example of how modern technology can be used to effectively improve skill level in the learner. For the purpose of the study, operative surgeons of varying degrees of seniority were given the opportunity to go through a video recording of an operation they had performed together with a nominated coach (a very senior surgeon that participants knew and respected for his level of skill and experience). Qualitative findings showed high educational value of the practice, as video recordings were thought to support the reflective process that has long since been recognized as a prerequisite step in any skill development (Mezirow 1978). While the use of such video recordings therefore play an important role in the learner-centred and self-directed continuing professional development of surgeons, such techniques also lend themselves exceptionally well to equestrian coaching. As Hu *et al.* (2012) note, one of the most prominent assets of the use of video is that 'it allows one to view oneself in the third person and provides incontrovertible evidence to counteract the inaccuracies of one's memory.' (p. 120). More specifically, using post-training video sessions would allow, firstly, the systematic classification of behaviors displayed by the coach–rider–horse triad, something that is clearly fundamental to equestrian sports but that has, as yet, only been examined rather infrequently (Cumyn 2000; Maw 2012). From an applied point of view, the examination of video recordings also allows for an objective assessment and evaluation of both riding and coaching skills and techniques, which will ultimately lead to considerable improvement in performance.

Clearly, much is left to be gained in equestrian coaching, both from the point of view of the way in which systematic observation of effective coaching practice can help to improve precisely such practice and how the objective, direct measurement of rider parameters can assist in providing more appropriate feedback. Coaches and riders alike should work on the premise that the better they are able to reflect on, assess and evaluate rider skills and techniques, the greater the potential for improved welfare of the horse, increased safety for the rider and enhanced horse–rider performance.

Staying safe: the future of equestrian sports

The development of equestrian sports especially in the last few decades is really nothing short of astounding. While many horse lovers still engage in the activity of riding in their spare time and as a means of relaxation, most facets of equestrian sports have become exceedingly commercial. It is therefore not surprising that the equine breeding industry, working on the age-old business principle of supply and demand, have been working hard to produce horses that epitomize the perfect athlete. The modern sports horse is a far cry from its short-legged, shaggy-coated ancestor. Even compared with an Olympic medallist from 50 years ago (which, in the context of equine evolution can only be considered a mere blip), the current equine elite is more powerful yet lighter on its feet, more athletic with better paces. Despite what many riders put them through, most modern sports horses remain very trainable, adaptable and seemingly amenable to providing incredible feats of athleticism day in, day out. Still, no matter how much progress we make in breeding the 'ideal' sport horse, no matter how much time a day riders commit to their horses and their sport or, indeed, no matter how much we love and trust our four-legged partners, equestrian sports will always remain a relatively dangerous pastime, simply because we are dealing with an innately sensitive animal. The statistics as cited in Chapter 5 clearly speak for themselves: with the potential for injury greater than in traditionally high-risk sports such as automobile or motorcycle racing, football or skiing (Ball *et al.* 2007), equestrian sports are not for the faint of heart. While it is undoubtedly important to encourage greater understanding of the dangers involved, investigating and implementing relevant methods to help prevent accidents in the first place and, secondly, protecting athletes from incurring serious injuries must be paramount.

The emergence of equitation science as the 'objective, evidence-based understanding of the welfare of horses during training and competition' (ISES 2013) should clearly be considered as a vital step on the road towards these endeavours of preventing unnecessary accidents in equestrian sports. As McGreevy (2007) so aptly notes in his review 'The Advent of Equitation Science': 'inappropriate training practices can lead to conflict behaviors that jeopardise the safety of riders and handlers and can have a negative impact on the horse's welfare' (p. 495). By encouraging the understanding and correct application of the principles of learning theory and how they apply to equine training, the likelihood of the horse engaging in dangerous behaviors decreases considerably. Clearly then, the integration of learning theory into the arsenal of knowledge of all riders, handlers and horse trainers has to take absolute priority. Riders' appreciation of and sensitivity to timing need to be schooled to much the same extent as the horse needs to learn to respond to different riders' cues. It is here that the advancement of technologies and their use in equitation and equestrian science can offer much additional benefit. To date, a number of studies investigating elements important to equine welfare are making use of technological advances such as measuring pads to investigate pressure distribution in saddles (e.g. Byström *et al.* 2010; de Cocq *et al.* 2006; Kotschwar *et al.* 2010), rein tension gauges to determine the amount of tension applied during different movements (Clayton *et al.* 2003; Preuschoft *et al.* 1999; Warren-Smith *et al.* 2007), differences in rein tension on either rein, depending on equine laterality (Kuhnke *et al.* 2010) or associating different types of equine behaviors with differences in rein tension (Egenvall *et al.* 2012). Quite clearly, in addition to the obvious benefits regarding equine welfare, such technologies also lend themselves to providing objective feedback of rider behavior, which, in turn, may be used to improve aspects relating to safety and performance. While immediate practical advantages are apparent, especially if riders (and their coaches) are familiar with how to use and interpret obtained data, longer-term scientific studies investigating differences between different levels of rider expertise will help to develop greater understanding of what is effective, 'good' and safe riding, and precisely how effective, 'good' riders do what they do best. On that basis, riders and coaches would be able to develop coaching trajectories aimed specifically at the individual needs of horse and rider, while also gaining a better understanding of fundamental differences between, for example, grassroots and advanced riders. Such 'benchmarking' of optimal rider behavior at physiological, biomechanical and psychological level is likely also to improve equestrian coaching at a fundamental level and help to attain greater measures of safety in horse sports.

Beyond the thrill of riding

As has been shown throughout this book, the possible mental or physical health benefits of equestrian sports or merely being around horses are nothing short of astounding. At present, however, being involved with horses or even engaging in activities associated with riding seems to be viewed by many as a privilege, a luxury, and only accessible to a small section of the population. Yet many of the benefits that activities with horses can provide might also be transferred to populations other than those who have committed themselves wholeheartedly to a life with horses. Indeed, the application of the more general principles that are at play when humans become involved with horses and the use of novel research designs and set-ups might lead to astonishing findings that could be of benefit to a much wider target group. One example is a study by Hosaka *et al.* (2010), who investigated the effects of daily mechanical horseback riding on insulin sensitivity and resting metabolism in people with type-2 diabetes. After a three-month training programme, which included daily passive training sessions on the mechanical horse, patients showed significantly decreased serum immunoreactive insulin concentrations and increased resting metabolic heart rates. The findings by Hosaka *et al.* complement earlier studies by Kubota *et al.* (2006) or Shinomiya *et al.* (2002). While Shinomiya and colleagues were able to attest to the increase in muscular strength of the abdomen and back using horseback riding therapeutic equipment, Kuboa *et al.* (2006) were able to demonstrate an increase in glucose infusion rate and subsequent improvement in insulin sensitivity in a cohort of elderly patients suffering from type-2 diabetes, who exercised regularly on a mechanical horse. The authors argue that the increase in heart rate associated with mechanical horseback riding mirrors that found in walking or easy cycling and might thus be considered a valid alternative to other forms of mild exercise. Considering that geriatric patients suffering from symptoms associated with type-2 diabetes, such as diabetic neuropathy (e.g. damage to nerves in the body owing to high blood sugar levels), numb lower extremities and osteoporosis, might no longer be able to engage in more traditional forms of exercise, mechanical horseback riding might provide a real alternative.

But beyond the 'mere' physical benefits associated with riding horses, there exists another dimension to riding and engaging with horses that warrants further investigation. Scientific evidence shows that exposure to and exercising in natural places and environments can greatly enhance mental health (e.g. Barton and Pretty 2010; Pretty *et al.* 2005). In a meta-analysis, Barton and Pretty (2010) show that acute short-term exposure to exercise in 'green' (i.e. natural) settings, induces improved mood states and feelings of self-esteem. Indeed, most riders will readily acknowledge that riding usually has the welcome effect of lifting one's mood, even after a long, tiring day. However, while one of the ten studies included in Barton and Pretty's meta-analysis also included horse riding as an example of 'green exercise', empirical findings relating to horse riding as a mood enhancer are sparse at best. Future scientific studies should therefore endeavour to investigate exactly what the mood enhancing effects of horse-riding might be, to broaden the appeal of the sport to a wider array of people – which, after all, is something that all of those involved with horses continuously tend to try to do anyway!

Horses, humans and what it all means

As all of us involved in equestrian sports will be aware, much of the existing riding-related knowledge is based on 'gut feeling', hearsay and traditional teachings. None of these are, of course, by definition bad or wrong – but neither are they necessarily good or right. It has been the aim of this book to investigate aspects relating to the human, the rider, the handler, the coach, in short, the two-legged partners of the horse–human dyad, using empirical, scientific findings both from the ever-broadening field of equitation science and the related fields of sports science, psychology, medicine and more. Such an approach was, of course, driven primarily by necessity as the scientific literature for many rider- or human-related topics in the field of equitation science is still scarce. Nevertheless, this approach had many advantages, as it has allowed us to 'think outside the box', so to speak, and to investigate many of the important questions in equestrian sports in view of a much broader and deeper backdrop of knowledge. The inherent disadvantage of such an approach is nevertheless apparent: there is still much we do not yet know about how to interact with horses (in whatever capacity) in the most beneficial, productive, safe, morally sound and welfare-orientated way. I would therefore like to end this book with the same sentiment of encouragement that I already employed in the introduction: readers of this book, students of equitation science in the broadest sense of the word, are encouraged to look upon the world of equestrian sports with an open mind and a questioning attitude – and take another step towards a better future with our horses.

Notes

1 Motor control of the rider: On moving and being moved

1 Throughout his career, Eadweard Muybridge produced more than 100,000 high-speed photographs of both humans and animals.
2 Suggested readings on the topic include Back and Clayton (2000) or Clayton (2004).
3 Interested readers are encouraged to consult Rosenbaum (2010) for more detailed information.
4 Previous research (and anecdotal evidence) has also shown that humans are still able to complete certain motor tasks without any sensory input, albeit rather stiltedly (e.g. Lashley 1917; Marsden *et al.* 1984).
5 Also commonly referred to as visual search behavior.
6 The 'Spanish' Riding School of Vienna has included the 'Spanish' part of its name in reference to the predominantly white stallions, which, during the sixteenth century, originated from the Iberian Peninsula.
7 For a detailed outline of learning principles and their application in equestrian sports, please consult additional literature, e.g. McGreevy and McLean (2010).

2 Performance physiology and rider fitness: Riders are athletes too!

1 Interested readers are strongly encouraged to peruse additional works on sport and exercise physiology (e.g. Kenney *et al.* 2012; Sewell *et al.* 2012).
2 Owing to space restrictions, only a short overview of the specifics of the three metabolic pathways could be provided. Interested readers are once again advised to consult more in-depth reference works on sport and exercise physiology.
3 Readers should note that, owing to space constraints, only some of the various physiological parameters reported in the different studies are reported here. Interested readers and researchers are encouraged to consult the original studies for additional details.

3 Sport psychology in equestrian sport: Merely mind games?

1 For a more detailed analysis of empirically based principles of equine training, please consult additional literature, e.g. McGreevy and McLean (2010).
2 Readers who are interested in the topic are advised to consult the works of, for example, Ewen (2009) or John, Robins and Pervin (2008).
3 Elite riders were defined as currently competing or recently having competed at the top level in their respective equestrian discipline (grand prix in dressage, 1.60 metres in showjumping, three to four star competitions in eventing). Amateur riders were defined as currently competing or recently having competed at no higher than intermediate level, e.g. elementary to medium level in dressage, 1.10–1.20 metres in

showjumping, 1.0–1.10 metres in eventing. Leisure riders were defined as not competing or never having competed their horses. Non-riders were defined as never having ridden before or during the time of the study. They also did not take part in any other competitive sports.

4   For more information on the specifics of Lazarus' work on stress, please see his collected works.

5   Students interested in a detailed description of different mental skills and their applications are advised to consult sport psychology text books by, for example, Hanrahan and Andersen (2012) or Moran (2012).

4 Coaching riders: From a different perspective

1   Please note that, owing to space constraints, the current chapter does not cover the theoretical and practical underpinnings of the training of horses. The interested reader is advised to consult the extensive works of, for example, McGreevy and McLean.

2   The survey was distributed via social media and resulted in a response rate of N = 124 (female = 111; male = 9; unknown = 4). Participants' ages ranged between 19 and 70 years, with the largest percentage (29%) in the age group 31–40 years. Represented nationalities included Australia, Belgium, Canada, Germany, Ireland, New Zealand, Poland, Sweden, the Netherlands, UK, USA and others. Dressage coaching was represented the most with 41.1%, while combined dressage and show jumping coaching was carried out by 20.2% of participants, followed by eventing (11.3%), showjumping (4.8%), Western (4.8%), leisure (4%) and others (13.7%).

3   We refer here to the horse as a reactive animal that does not possess higher cognitive functions and is thus thought unable to 'reflect' on its own abilities. It is therefore thought to be unable to develop 'self-confidence' or suffer from a lack thereof.

6 Horse–human interactions: Art or science?

1   Historical accounts of the use and domestication of horses have been reported elsewhere in considerable detail (e.g. Crossman and Walsh 2011; McMiken 1990; Telegin 1986; Olsen 1988).

7 In conclusion: *Quo vadis*, equestrian science?

1   Referred to as 'degrees of freedom' in the field of human motor control.

References

Abraham, A. and Collins, D. (2011) Taking the next step: ways forward for coaching science, *Quest*, 63 (4), 366–84.

Abraham, A., Collins, D. and Martindale, R. (2006) The coaching schematic: validation through expert coach consensus, *Journal of Sports Sciences*, 24 (6), 549–64.

Abu-Zidan, F. M. and Rao, S. (2003) Factors affecting the severity of horse-related injuries, *Injury*, 34, 897–900.

Adams, J. A. (1971) A closed-loop theory of motor learning, *Journal of Motor Behavior*, 3, 111–150.

Ader, R., Cohen, N. and Felten, D. (1995) Psychoneuroimmunology: interactions between the nervous system and the immune system, *Lancet*, 345 (8942), 99–103.

Alfredson, H., Hedberg, G., Bergstrom, E., Nordstrom, P. and Lorentzon, R. (1998) High thigh muscle strength but not bone mass in young horseback-riding females, *Calcified Tissue International*, 62, 497–501.

Allen, K., Blascovich, J. and Mendes, W. B. (2002) Cardiovascular reactivity and the presence of pets, friends, and spouses: the truth about cats and dogs, *Psychosomatic Medicine*, 64, 727–39.

Allport, G. W. (1937) *Personality – A Psychological Interpretation*, New York: Henry Holt and Company.

Alper, L. S. (1993) The child–pet bond, in A. Goldberg (ed.) *The Widening Scope of Self Psychology: Progress in Self Psychology*, Hillsdale, NJ: Analytic Press.

Ames, C. (1992) Classroom, goal structures, and student motivation, *Journal of Educational Psychology*, 84, 261–74.

Anderson, A., Knowles, Z. and Gilbourne, D. (2004) Reflective practice for applied sport psychologists: a review of concepts, models, practical implications and thoughts on dissemination, *The Sport Psychologist*, 18, 188–201.

Anderson, J. R. (2000) *Learning and Memory: An Integrated Approach*, 2nd edn. Hoboken, NJ: John Wiley.

Anderson, W., Reid, P. and Jennings, G. L. (1992) Pet ownership and risk factors for cardiovascular disease, *Medical Journal of Australia*, 157, 298–301.

Ansorge, C. J. and Scheer, J. K. (1988) International bias detected in judging gymnastic competition at the 1984 Olympic Games, *Research Quarterly for Exercise and Sport*, 59, 103–7.

Ansorge, C. J., Scheer, J. K., Laub, J. and Howard, J. (1978) Bias in judging women's gymnastics induced by expectations of within-team order, *Research Quarterly for Exercise and Sport*, 49, 399–405.

Anthony, D. W. (1986) The 'Kurgan Culture' Indo-European origins and the domestication of the horse: a reconsideration, *Current Anthropology*, 27, 291–313.

Anthony, W. A. and Liberman, R. P. (1986) The practice of psychiatric rehabilitation: historical, conceptual, and research base, *Schizophrenia Bulletin*, 12 (4), 543–59.

Arts, F. J. and Kuipers, H. (1994) The relation between power output, oxygen uptake and heart rate in male athletes, *International Journal of Sports Medicine*, 15 (5), 228–31.

Ascione, F. R. (1992) Enhancing children's attitudes about the humane treatment of animals: Generalization to human-directed empathy, *Anthrozoös*, 5, 176–91.

Asendorpf, J. B. and Wilpers, S. (1998) Personality effects on social relationships, *Journal of Personality and Social Psychology*, 74, 1531–44.

Atkeson, C. G. (1989) Learning arm kinematics and dynamics, *Annual Review of Neuroscience*, 3, 171–6.

Austin, N. P. and Rogers, L. J. (2007) Asymmetry of flight and escape turning responses in horses, *Laterality*, 12 (5), 464–74.

Azevedo, L. F., Perlingeiro, P. S., Brum, P. C., Braga, A. M. W., Negrão, C. E. and de Matos, L. D. N. J. (2011) Exercise intensity optimization for men with high cardiorespiratory fitness, *Journal of Sports Sciences*, 29 (6), 555–61.

Back, W. and Clayton, H. (2000) *Equine Locomotion*, London: W. B. Saunders.

Balch, O. K., Butler, D. and Collier, M. A. (1997) Balancing the normal foot: hoof preparation, shoe fit and shoe modification in the performance horse, *Equine Veterinary Education*, 9 (3), 143–54.

Balendra G., Turner M., McCrory P. and Halley W. (2007) Injuries in amateur horse racing (point to point racing) in Great Britain and Ireland during 1993–2006, *British Journal of Sports Medicine*, 41, 162–6.

Ball, C. G., Ball, J. E., Kirkpatrick, A. W. and Mulloy, R. H. (2007) Equestrian injuries: incidence, injury patterns, and risk factors for 10 years of major traumatic injuries, *American Journal of Surgery*, 193, 636–40.

Bandura, A. (1977a) Self-efficacy: toward a unifying theory of behavioral change. *Psychological Review*, 84 (2), 191–215.

Bandura, A. (1977b) *Social Learning Theory*, New York: General Learning Press.

Bandura, A. (1977c) *Self-efficacy: The Exercise of Control*, New York: Freeman.

Bandura, A. (1986) *Social Foundations of Thought and Action: A Social Cognitive Theory*, Upper Saddle River, NJ: Prentice-Hall.

Barber, H., Sukhi, H. and White, S. (1999) The influence of parent-coaches on participation motivation and competitive anxiety in youth sport participants, *Journal of Sport Behavior*, 22 (2), 162–79.

Barber, H. M. (1973) Horseplay: survey of accidents with horses, *British Medical Journal*, 3, 532.

Barelds, D. P. H. and Dijkstra, P. (2007) Relations between different types of jealousy and self and partner perceptions of relationship quality, *Clinical Psychology and Psychotherapy*, 14, 176–88.

Barrey, E. (2008) Biomechanics of locomotion in the athletic horse, in K. W. Hincliff, A. J. Kaneps, R. J. Geor, *Equine Exercise Physiology: The Science of Exercise in the Athletic Horse*, London: Saunders Elsevier, pp. 143–68.

Barstow, T. J. and Mole, P. A. (1987) Simulation of pulmonary oxygen uptake during exercise in humans, *Journal of Applied Physiology*, 63, 2253–61.

Barstow, T. J., Scremin, A. M., Mutton, D. L., Kunkel, C. F., Cagle, T. G. and Whipp, B. J. (1996) Changes in gas exchange kinetics with training in patients with spinal cord injury, *Medicine and Science in Sports and Exercise*, 28 (10), 1221–28.

Barton, J. and Pretty, J. (2010) What is the best dose of nature and green exercise for improving mental health? a multi-study analysis, *Environmental Science and Technology*, 44, 3947–55.

Baumeister, R. F. and Leary, M. R. (1995) The need to belong: desire for interpersonal attachments as a fundamental human motivation, *Psychological Bulletin*, 117, 497–529.

Beauchamp, M. W. and Whinton, L. C. (2005) Self-efficacy and other-efficacy in dyadic performance: riding as one in equestrian eventing, *Journal of Sport and Exercise Psychology*, 27, 245–52.

Beaulieu, P., Ottoz, H., Grange, C., Thomas, J. and Bensch, C. (1995) Blood lactate levels of decathletes during competition, *British Journal of Sports Medicine*, 29 (2), 80–4.

Beck, A. M. and Katcher, A. H. (1996) *Between Pets and People: the Importance of Animal Companionship*, rev. edn. West Lafayette: Purdue University Press.

Beck, A. M. and Katcher, A. H. (2003) Future directions in human–animal bond research, *American Behavioral Scientist*, 47 (1), 79–93.

Beck, A. M. and Meyers, N. M. (1996) Health enhancement and companion animal ownership, *Annual Review of Public Health*, 17, 247–57.

Becker, A. J. (2009) It's not what they do, it's how they do it: athlete experiences of great coaching, *International Journal of Sports Science and Coaching*, 4 (1), 93–119.

Beedie, C. J., Terry, P. C. and Lane, A. M. (2000) The profile of mood states and athletic performance: two meta-analyses, *Journal of Applied Sport Psychology*, 12, 49–68.

Belock, B., Kaiser, L. J., Lavagnino, M. and Clayton, H. M. (2012) Comparison of pressure distribution under a conventional saddle and a treeless saddle at sitting trot, *Veterinary Journal*, 193, 87–91.

Benda, W., McGibbon, N. H. and Grant, K. L. (2003) Improvements in muscle symmetry in children with cerebral palsy after equine-assisted therapy (hippotherapy), *Journal of Alternative and Complementary Medicine*, 9 (6), 817–25.

Bergerud, A. T. (1975) The reproductive season of Newfoundland caribou, *Canadian Journal of Zoology*, 53, 1213–21.

Berliner, D. C. (1988) Implications of studies of expertise in pedagogy for teacher education and evaluation, in *New Directions for Teacher Assessment. Proceedings of the ETS Invitational Conference (49th, New York, October 29, 1988)*, Princeton, NJ: Educational Testing Service, pp. 39–68.

Bernstein, N. (1967) *The Coordination and Regulation of Movement*, London: Pergamon Press.

Bertollo, M., Saltarelli, B. and Robazza, C. (2009) Mental preparation strategies of elite modern pentathletes, *Psychology of Sport and Exercise*, 10 (2), 244–54.

Biery, M. J. and Kauffman, N. (1989) The effects of therapeutic horseback riding on balance, *Adapted Physical Activity Quarterly*, 6, 221–29.

Birke, L. and Brandt, K. (2009) Mutual corporeality: gender and human/horse relationships, *Women's Studies International Forum*, 32 (3): 189–97.

Birke, L., Hockenhull, J., Creighton, E., Pinno, L., Mee, J. and Mills, D. (2011) Horses' responses to variation in human approach, *Applied Animal Behavior Science*, 134 (1), 56–63.

Bixby-Hammett, D. M. (1992) Pediatric equestrian injuries, *Pediatrics*, 89, 1173–6.

Bixby-Hammett, D. M. and Brooks, W. H. (1989) Neurologic injuries in equestrian sports, in B.D. Jordan, P. Tsairis, R. F. Warren (eds), *Sports Neurology*, Rockville, MD: Aspen, pp. 229–34.

Black, D. R., Larkin, L. J., Coster, D. C., Leverenz, L. J. and Abood, D. A. (2003) Physiological screening test for eating disorders/disordered eating among female collegiate athletes, *Journal of Athletic Training*, 38 (4), 268–97.

Blakeslee, M. L. and Goff, D. M. (2007) The effects of a mental strategies training package on equestrians, *The Sport Psychologist*, 21, 288–301.

Bloom, B. S. (ed.) (1985) *Developing Talent in Young People*, New York: Ballantine.

Bloom, G. A. and Stevens, D. E. (2002) Case study: A team building mental skills training program with an intercollegiate equestrian team, *Athletic Insight: The Online Journal of Sport Psychology*, 4 (1). Available online at www.Athleticinsight.com/Vol4Iss1/EquestrianTeamBuilding.htm (accessed on 20 September 2011).

Bloom, G. A., Salmela, J. H. and Schinke, R. J. (1995) Expert coaches views on the training of developing coaches, In R. Vanfraechem-Raway and Y. Vanden Auweele (eds) *Proceedings of the Ninth European Congress on Sport*, Brussels: Free University of Brussels, pp. 401–8.

Boen, F., Auweele Y. V., Claesa, E., Feysb, J. and De Cuyp, B. (2006) The impact of open feedback on conformity among judges in rope skipping, *Psychology of Sport and Exercise*, 7, 77–590.

Boesch, C. and Tomasello, M. (1998) Chimpanzee and human cultures, *Current Anthropology*, 39 (5), 591–614.

Bonas, S., McNicholas, J. and Collis, G. M. (2000) Pets in the network of family relationships: an empirical study, in A. L. Podberscek, E. S. Paul and J. A. Serpell (eds), *Companion Animals and Us: Exploring the Relationships Between People and Pets*, Cambridge: Cambridge University Press, pp. 209–36.

Bond, G. R., Christoph, R. A. and Rodgers, B. M. (1995) Pediatric equestrian injuries: assessing the impact of helmet use, *Pediatrics*, 95, 487–9.

Borg, G. (1982) Psychophysical bases of perceived exertion, *Medicine and Science in Sports and Exercise*, 14 (5), 377–81.

Borman, W. C. (1975) Effect of instruction to avoid halo error on reliability and validity of performance evaluation rating, *Journal of Applied Psychology*, 60, 556–60.

Bowes, I. and Jones, R. L. (2006) Working at the edge of chaos: understanding coaching as a complex, interpersonal system, *The Sport Psychologist*, 20 (2), 235–45.

Bradbury, T. (2001) Athletes doing it for themselves: self-coaching strategies of New Zealand Olympians, *Journal of Excellence*, 3, 55–66.

Bradbury, T. N. and Fincham, F. D. (1988) Individual difference variables in close relationships: a contextual model of marriage as an integrative framework, *Journal of Personality and Social Psychology*, 54, 713–21.

Brandt, K. (2004) A language of their own: an interactionist approach to human–horse communication, *Society and Animals*, 12 (4), 299–316.

Brenda, W., McGibbon, N. H., Grant, K. and Davis, M. (2003) Improvement in muscle symmetry in children with cerebral palsy after equine–assisted therapy (hippotherapy), *Journal of Alternative and Complementary Medicine*, 9, 817–21.

Bridgeman, D. J., Pretty, G. M. and Tribe, A. (2005) *Exploring heart rate as an indicator of synchronization between dressage horse and rider at training and competition*, Paper presented at the ISSP 11th World Congress of Sport Psychology, Sydney, Australia.

Brown, B. R. and Butterfield, S. A. (1992) Coaches: a missing link in the health care system, *American Journal of Diseases of Children*, 146, 211–17.

Brown, S. E. (2004) The human–animal bond and self-psychology: toward a new understanding, *Society and Animals*, 12, 67–86.

Brown, S. E. (2007) Companion animals as self-objects, *Anthrozoös*, 20 (4), 329–43.

Brown, S. E. (2011) Theoretical concepts from self-psychology applied to animal hoarding, *Society and Animals*, 19 (2), 175–93.

Bruner, M. W., Erickson, K., Wilson, B. and Côté, J. (2010) An appraisal of athlete development models through citation network analysis, *Psychology of Sport and Exercise*, 11 (2), 133–139.

Bryant, B. K. (1985) The neighbourhood walk: sources of support in middle childhood, *Monographs of the Society for Research in Child Development*, 50 (3), 1–122.

Buckley, P, Dunn, A. and More, S. (2004) Owners' perceptions of health and performance in pony club horses in Australia, *Preventative Veterinary Medicine*, 63, 121–32.

Buckley, S. M., Chalmers, D. J. and Langley, J. D. (1993) Injuries due to falls from horses, *Australian Journal of Public Health*, 17, 269–71.

Budge, R. C., Spicer, J., Jones, B. and St. George, R. (1998) Health correlates of compatibility and attachment in human–companion animal relationships, *Society and Animals*, 6, 219–34.

Burton, D. and Naylor, S. (1997) Is anxiety really facilitative? Reaction to the myth that cognitive anxiety always impairs sport performance, *Journal of Applied Sport Psychology*, 9, 295–302.

Buss, D. M. (1991) Conflict in married couples: personality predictors of anger and upset, *Journal of Personality*, 59, 663–88.

Butterwick, D. J. and Meeuwisse, W. H. (2002) Effect of experience on rodeo injury, *Clinical Journal of Sport Medicine*, 12 (1), 30–5.

Byström, A., Rhodin, M., von Peinen, K., Weishaupt, M. A. and Roepstorff, L. (2009) Basic kinematics of the saddle and rider in high-level dressage horses trotting on a treadmill, *Equine Veterinary Journal*, 41, 280–84.

Byström, A., Stalfelt, A., Egenvall, A., von Peinen, K., Morgan, K. and Roepstorff, L. (2010) Influence of girth strap placement and panel flocking material on the saddle pressure pattern during riding of horses, *Equine Veterinary Journal, Special Issue: Proceedings of the 8th International Conference on Equine Exercise Physiology*, 42 (38), 502–9.

Cain, A. (1983) A study of pets in the family system, in A. H. Katcher and A. M. Beck (eds), *New Perspectives on Our Lives with Companion Animals*, Philadelphia, PA: University of Pennsylvania Press, pp. 71–81.

Callow, N. and Waters, A. (2005) The effect of kinaesthetic imagery on the sport confidence of flat-race jockeys, *Psychology of Sport and Exercise*, 6, 443–59.

Callow, N., Hardy, L. and Hall, C. R. (2001) The effect of a motivational general-mastery imagery intervention on the sport confidence of four high level junior badminton players, *Research Quarterly for Sport and Exercise Psychology*, 72, 389–400.

Cañal-Bruland, R. and van der Kamp, J. (2009) Action goals influence action-specific perception, *Psychonomic Bulletin and Review*, 16, 1100–5.

Candler, C. (2003) Sensory integration and therapeutic riding at summer camp: occupational performance outcomes, *Physical and Occupational Therapy in Pediatrics*, 23 (3), 51–64.

Cannon, W. B. (1929) Organization for physiological homeostasis, *Physiological Review*, 9, 399–431.

Carver, C. S. and Scheier, M. F. (1986) Functional and dysfunctional responses to anxiety: the interaction between expectancies and self-focused attention, in R. Schwarzer (ed.), *Self-Related Cognitions in Anxiety and Motivation*, Hillsdale, NJ: Erlbaum, pp. 111–41.

Casaburi, R., Barstow, T. J., Robinson, T. and Wasserman, K. (1989) Influence of work rate on ventilatory and gas exchange kinetics, *Journal of Applied Physiology*, 67, 547–55.

Casady, R. L. and Nichols-Larsen, D. S. (2004) The effect of hippotherapy on ten children with cerebral palsy, *Pediatric Physical Therapy*, 16 (3), 165–72.

Casey, R. A. (1999) Recognising the importance of pain in the diagnosis of equine behavior problems, in P. A. Harris, G. Gomarsall, H. P. B. Davidson and R. Green (eds), *Proceedings of the British Equine Veterinary Association Specialist Meeting on Nutrition and Behavior*, Newmarket: Equine Veterinary Journal Ltd, pp. 25–8.

Causey, K. B. and Bjorklund, D. F. (2011) The evolution of cognition, in V. Swami (ed.), *Evolutionary Psychology: A Critical Introduction*, London: Wiley-Blackwell.

Cawley, R., Cawley, D. and Retter, K. (1994) Therapeutic horseback riding and self-concept in adolescents with special educational needs, *Anthrozoös*, 7 (2), 129–34.

Ceroni, D., de Rosa, V., de Coulon, G. and Kaelin, A. (2007) The importance of proper shoe gear and safety stirrups in the prevention of equestrian foot injuries, *Journal of Foot and Ankle Surgery*, 46, 32–9.

Cerretelli, P. and Samaja, M. (2003) Acid-base balance at exercise in normoxia and in chronic hypoxia. Revisiting the 'lactate paradox', *European Journal of Applied Physiology*, 90, 431–48.

Chapman, C. and Musselwhite, C. B. A. (2011) Equine road user safety: public attitudes, understandings and beliefs from a quantitative study in the United Kingdom, *Accident Analysis and Prevention*, 43, 2173–81.

Chelladurai, P. (1984) Discrepancy between preferences and perceptions of leadership behavior and satisfaction of athletes in varying sports, *Journal of Sport Psychology*, 6, 27–41.

Chelladurai, P. (1990) Leadership in sports: a review, *International Journal of Sport Psychology*, 21, 328–54.

Cheng, W. K., Hardy, L. and Markland, D. (2008) Toward a three-dimensional conceptualization of performance anxiety: rationale and initial measurement development, *Psychology of Sport and Exercise*, 10 (2), 271–8.

Chitnavis, J. P., Gibbons, C. L., Hirigoyen, M., Parry, J. L. and Simpson, A. H. (1996) Accidents with horses: what has changed in 20 years? *Injury*, 27, 103–5.

Christensen, J. W., Rundgren, M. and Olsson, K. (2006) Training methods for horses: habituation to a frightening stimulus, *Equine Veterinary Journal*, 38, 439–43.

Citterio, D. (1997) Autism and horses: intervention strategy from the point of view of a science of movement, in *Proceedings of the 9th International Therapeutic Riding Congress, Denver, Colorado*, Denver: North American Riding for the Handicapped Association, p. 211.

Clark Cline, K. M. (2010) Psychological effects of dog ownership: role strain, role enhancement, and depression, *Journal of Social Psychology*, 150 (2), 117–31.

Clausius, R. (1850) Über die bewegende Kraft der Wärme und die Gesetze, welche sich daraus für die Wärmelehre selbst ableiten lassen, *Annalen der Physik und Chemie*, 155 (3), 368–94.

Claxton, D. B. (1988) A systematic observation of more and less successful high school tennis coaches, *Journal of Teaching in Physical Education*, 7, 302–10.

Clayton, H. M. (2004) *The Dynamic Horse. A Biomechanical Guide to Equine Movement and Performance*, Mason, MI: Sport Horse Publications.

Clayton, H. M., Singleton, W. H., Lanovaz, J. L. and Cloud, G. L. (2003) Measurement of rein tension during horseback riding using strain gage transducers, *Experimental Techniques*, 27, 34–6.

Clayton, H. M., Singleton, W. H., Lanovaz, J. L. and Cloud, G. L. (2005) Strain gauge measurement of rein tension during riding: a pilot study, *Equine and Comparative Exercise Physiology*, 2 (3), 203–5.

Clitsome, T. and Kostrubala, T. (1977) A psychological study of 100 marathoners using the Meyers-Briggs type indicator and demographic data, *Annals of the New York Academy of Sciences*, 301, 1010–19.

Coatsworth, J. D. and Conroy, D. E. (2007) Youth sport as a component of afterschool programs, *New Directions for Youth Development*, 115, 57–74.

Collins, J. and Richmond, S. (1994) Hard-wired central pattern generators for quadrupedal locomotion, *Biological Cybernetics*, 71, 375–85.

Collis, G. M. and McNicholas, J. (1998) A theoretical basis for health benefits of pet ownership; Attachment versus psychological support, in C. C. Wilson and D. C. Turner (eds), *Companion Animals in Human Health*, Thousand Oaks, CA: Sage, pp. 105–22.

Compas, B. E. (1987) Coping with stress during childhood and adolescence, *Psychological Bulletin*, 101, 393–403.

Coopersmith, S. (1967) *The Antecedents of Self-esteem*, San Francisco. CA: W. H. Freeman and Co.

Cossman, P. H. (2012) Video-coaching as biofeedback tool to improve gated treatments: possibilities and limitations, *Zeitschrift für Medizinische Physik*, 22 (3) 224–30.

Costa, P. T. and McCrae, R. R. (1992) *Revised NEO Personality Inventory (NEO PI–R) and NEO Five–Factor Inventory (NEO FFI) Professional Manual*, Odessa, FL: Psychological Assessment Resources.

Costa-Paz, M., Aponte-Tinao, L. and Muscolo, D. L. (1999) Injuries to polo riders: a prospective evaluation, *Sports Medicine*, 33, 329–32.

Côté, J. (1999) The influence of the family in the development of talent in sport, *The Sport Psychologist*, 13, 395–417.

Côté, J. and Hay, J. (2002) Children's involvement in sport: a developmental perspective, in J. M. Silva and D. E. Stevens (eds), *Psychological Foundations of Sport*, Boston, MA: Allyn and Bacon, pp. 484–502.

Côté, J., Salmela, J. H., Trudel, P., Baria, A. and Russell, S. (1995a) The coaching model: a grounded assessment of expert gymnastic coaches' knowledge, *Journal of Sport and Exercise Psychology*, 17, 1–17.

Côté, J., Salmela, J. H. and Russell, S. (1995b) The knowledge of high-performance gymnastic coaches: competition and training considerations, *The Sport Psychologist*, 9, 76–95.

Cotugna, N., Snider, S. and Windish, J. (2011) Nutritional assessment of horse-racing athletes, *Journal of Community Health*, 36 (2), 261.

Covert, A. M., Whiren, A. P., Keith, J. and Nelson, C. (1985) Pets, early adolescents and families, *Marriage and Family Review*, 8, 95–108.

Cowley, S., Bowman, B. and Lawrance, M. (2007) Injuries in the Victorian thoroughbred racing industry, *British Journal of Sports Medicine*, 41 (10), 639–43.

Craven, J. A. (2008) Paediatric and adolescent horse-related injuries: does the mechanism of injury justify a trauma response? *Emergency Medicine Australasia*, 20, 357–62.

Creighton, E. (2007) Equine learning behavior: limits of ability and ability limits of trainers, *Behavioral Processes*, 76, 43–4.

Crossman, G. K. and Walsh, R. (2011) The Changing Role of the Horse: From Beast of Burden to Partner in Sport and Recreation, *International Journal of Sport and Society*, 2 (2), 95–110.

Csikszentmihalyi, M. (1978) Attention and the holistic approach to behavior, in K. S. Pope and Jerome L. Singer (eds), *The Stream of Consciousness: Scientific Investigation Into the Flow of Experience*, New York: Plenum, pp. 335–56.

Cuenca, A. G., Wiggins, A., Chen, M. K., Kays, D. W., Islam, S. and Beierle, E. A. (2009) Equestrian injuries in children, *Journal of Pediatric Surgery*, 44, 148–50.

Cumming, S. P., Smoll, F. L., Smith, R. E. and Grossbard, J. R. (2007) Is winning everything? The relative contributions of motivational climate and won–lost percentage in youth sports, *Journal of Applied Sport Psychology*, 19 (3), 322–36.

Cumyn, L. (2000) *Communication Processes in Dressage Coaching*, unpublished master thesis. University of Ottawa, Canada.

Curtis, B., Smith, R. E. and Smoll, F. L. (1979) Scrutinizing the skipper: a study of leadership behaviors in the dugout, *Journal of Applied Psychology*, 64, 391–400.

Dalin, G. and Jeffcott, L. B. (1994) Biomechanics, gait, and conformation, in D. R. Hodgson and R. J. Rose (eds), *The Athletic Horse: Principles and Practice of Equine Sports Medicine*, Philadelphia, PA: Saunders, pp. 27–48.

Daly, B. and Morton, L. L. (2006) An investigation of human–animal interactions and empathy as related to pet preference, ownership, attachment, and attitudes in children, *Anthrozoös*, 19 (2), 113–27.

David, J., Green, P., Martin, R. and Suls, J. (1997) Differential roles of neuroticism, extraversion and event desirability on mood in daily life: an integrative model of top-down and bottom-up influences, *Journal of Personality and Social Psychology*, 73, 149–59.

Davies, C. T., Di Prampero, P. E. and Cerretelli, P. (1972) Kinetics of the cardiac output and respiratory gas exchange during exercise and recovery, *Journal of Applied Physiology*, 32, 618–25.

de Barros Souza, F., Pacheco, M. T. T., Ingrid Brasil Strottmann, I. B., Teixeira, C. G. P., Fortes, C. E. A., Lyon, J. P., Moreira, L. M. and Os'orio, R. A. L. (2008) Metabolic and cardiorespiratory parameter analysis of young female adults during horseback riding at a walking gait, *Isokinetics and Exercise Science*, 16, 263–7.

de Cartier d'Yves, A. and Ödberg, O. F. (2005) A preliminary study on the relation between subjectively assessing dressage performances and objective welfare parameters, in P. D. McGreevy, A. N. McLean, A. K. Warren-Smith, D. Goodwin, and Waran, N. (eds), *Proceedings of the First International Equitation Science Symposium, Friday 26th and Saturday 27th August 2005, Australian Equine Behavior Centre, Melbourne, Australia*, Melbourne: Australian Equine Behavior Centre, pp. 89–110. Available online at http://eprints.soton.ac.uk/63517/1/proceedings05.pdf (accessed 13 March 2013).

de Cocq, P., Back, W. and van Weeren, R. (2004) Effects of a girth, a saddle and weight on the movements of the horse, *Equine Veterinary Journal*, 36 (8), 758–63.

de Cocq, P., van Weeren, R. and Back, W. (2006) Saddle pressure measuring: validity, reliability and power to discriminate between different saddle fits, *Veterinary Journal*, 172 (2), 265–73.

de Cocq, P., Clayton, H. M., Terada, K., Muller, M. and van Leeuwen, J. L. (2009a) Usability of normal force distribution measurements to evaluate asymmetrical loading of the back of the horse and different rider positions on a standing horse, *Veterinary Journal*, 181, 266–73.

de Cocq, P., Prinsen, H., Springer, N. C. N., van Weeren, P. R., Schreuder, M., Muller, M. and van Leeuwen, J. L. (2009b) The effect of rising and sitting trot on back movements and head-neck position of the horse, *Equine Veterinary Journal*, 41 (5), 423–7.

de Cocq, P., Duncker, A. M., Clayton, H. M., Bobbert, M. F., Muller, M. and van Leeuwen, J. L. (2010) Vertical forces on the horse's back in sitting and rising trot, *Journal of Biomechanics*, 43, 627–31.

Debuse, D., Chandler, C. and Gibb, C. (2005) An exploration of German and British physiotherapists' views on the effects of hippotherapy and their measurement, *Physiotherapy Theory and Practice*, 21 (1), 51–77.

Deci, E. L. and Ryan, R. M. (1985) *Intrinsic Motivation and Self-determination in Human Behavior*, New York: Plenum.

Deci, E. L. and Ryan, R. M. (1991) A motivational approach to self: integration in personality, in R. Dienstbier (ed.), *Nebraska Symposium on Motivation*, Perspectives on

Motivation, Vol. 38, Lincoln, NE: University of Nebraska Press, pp. 237–88.

Deci, E. L. and Ryan, R. M. (2000) The 'what' and 'why' of goal pursuits: human needs and the self-determination of behavior, *Psychological Inquiry*, 11, 227–68.

Deiber, M.-P., Wise, S. P., Honda, M., Catalan, M. J., Grafman, J. and Hallett, M. (1997) Frontal and parietal networks for conditional motor-learning: a positron emission tomography study, *Journal of Neurophysiology*, 78, 977–91.

Delgado, M. (2012) Another National tragedy: Despite public outcry after last year's carnage at Aintree, two more horses die at notorious jump – including the Gold Cup winner. *Daily Mail*, 14 April, updated 18 May. Available online at www.dailymail.co.uk/news/article-2129727/Grand-National-2012-horse-deaths-notorious-Aintree-jump-included-Gold-Cup-winner.html#ixzz2HeIjfEBE (accessed 11 January 2012).

Descola, P. (1994) *In the Society of Nature: A Native Ecology in Amazonia*, Cambridge: Cambridge University Press.

Devienne, M. F. and Guezennec, C. Y. (2000) Energy expenditure of horse riding, *European Journal of Applied Physiology*, 82 (5–6), 499–503.

DiMenna, F. J. and Jones, A. M. (2009) 'Linear' versus 'Nonlinear' O2 responses to exercise: reshaping traditional beliefs, *Journal of Exercise Science and Fitness*, 7, 67–84.

Dismuke, R. P. (1984) Rehabilitative horseback riding for children with language disorder, in R. K. Anderson, B. L. Hart and L. A. Hart (eds), *The Pet Connection: Its Influence on Our Health and Quality of Life*, Minneapolis: Censhare, pp. 131–40.

Dixon, P. M., Andrew, R., Brannon, H., Burgess, R. Gibson, A., Little, J. C., Orange, B., Ross, L., Rudolph, T. and Shaw, D. J. (2004) Survey of the provision of prophylactic dental care for horses in Great Britain and Ireland between 1999 and 2002, *Veterinary Record*, 155 (22), 693–8.

Dolan, E., Crabtree, N., McGoldrick, A., Ashley, D. T., McCaffrey, N. and Warrington, G. D. (2012) Weight regulation and bone mass: a comparison between professional jockeys, elite amateur boxers, and age, gender and BMI matched controls, *Journal of Bone and Mineral Metabolism*, 30 (2), 164–70.

Douglas, J.-L., Price, M. and Peters, D. M. (2012) A systematic review of physical, physiological demands and biomechanical performance in equestrian athletes, *Comparative Exercise Physiology*, 8 (1), 53–62.

Duda, J. L. and Whitehead, J. (1998) Measurement of goal perspectives in the physical domain, in J. L. Duda (ed.), *Advances in Sport and Exercise Psychology Measurement*, Morgantown, WV: Fitness Information Technology, pp. 21–48.

Dugdale, J. R. and Eklund, R. C. (2002) Do not pay attention to the umpires: thought suppression and task-relevant focusing strategies, *Journal of Sport and Exercise Psychology*, 24 (1), 306–19.

Dweck, C. S. (1986) Motivational processes affecting learning, *American Psychologist*, 41, 1040–1048.

Dwyer, J. and Bybee, R. (1983) Heart rate indices of the anaerobic threshold, *Medicine and Science in Sports and Exercise*, 15, 72–6.

Dyer, D. A. (2000) *Every Child's Dream: Horses Helping Kids Grow Up, A Parent's Guide*, Blacksburg, VA: Advantage ReSource.

Edmonds, S. (2012) Big Ben rings in Dujardin dressage win, *Reuters*, 9 August. Available online at www.reuters.com/london-olympics-2012/articles/equestrian/opens-individual/2012/08/09/big-ben-rings-dujardin-dressage-win (accessed 23 December 2012).

Egenvall, A., Eisersiö, M. and Roepstorff, L. (2012) Pilot study of behavior responses in young riding horses using 2 methods of making transitions from trot to walk, *Journal of Veterinary Behavior: Clinical Applications and Research*, 7 (3), 157–68.

Egloff, B. and Gruhn, A. J. (1996) Personality and endurance sports, *Personality and Individual Differences*, 21 (2), 223–9.

Ekberg, J., Timpka, T., Ramel, H. and Valter, L. (2011) Injury rates and risk-factors associated with eventing: a total cohort study of injury events among adult Swedish eventing athletes, *International Journal of Injury Control and Safety Promotion*, 18 (4), 261–7.

Elferink-Gemser, M. T., Jordet, G., Coelho-E-Silva, M. J. and Visscher, C. (2011) The marvels of elite sports: how to get there? *British Journal of Sports Medicine*, 45, 683–4.

Elliot, A. J. and Church, M. A. (1997) A hierarchical model of approach and avoidance achievement motivation, *Journal of Personality and Social Psychology*, 72, 218–32.

Emory, D. (1992) Effects of therapeutic horsemanship on the self–concepts and behavior of asocial adolescents, unpublished dissertation, University of Maine, *Dissertation Abstracts International*, DAI–B 53/05, 561.

Endler, N. S., Edwards, J. M. and Vitelli, R. (1991) *Multidimensional Anxiety Scales (EMAS), Manual*, Los Angeles, CA: Western Psychological Services.

Epstein, J. (1989) Family structures and student motivation: a developmental perspective, in C. Ames and R. Ames (eds), *Research on Motivation in Education*, Vol. 3, New York: Academic Press, pp. 259–95.

Epstein, N. B. and Baucom, D. H. (2002) *Enhanced Cognitive-Behavioral Therapy for Couples: A Contextual Approach*, Washington, DC: American Psychological Association.

Erickson, K. A., Côté, J., Hollenstein, T. and Deakin, J. (2011) Examining coach athlete interactions using state space grids: an observational analysis in competitive youth sport, *Psychology of Sport and Exercise*, 12, 645–54.

Ericsson, K. A. and Charness, N. (1994) Expert performance: its structure and acquisition, *American Psychologist*, 49 (8), 725–47.

Ericsson, K. A., Krampe, R. and Tesch-Roemer, C. (1993) The role of deliberate practice in the acquisition of expert performance, *Psychological Review*, 100, 363–406.

Evans, D. and McGreevy, P. (2011) An investigation of racing performance and whip use by jockeys in thoroughbred races, *PLoS One*, 6 (1), 1–5, e15622. doi: 10.1371/journal.pone.0015622.

Ewen, R. B. (2009) *An Introduction to Theories of Personality*, 7th edn. London: Psychology Press.

Eysenck, H. J. (1967) *The Biological Basis of Personality*, London: Transaction Publishers.

Eysenck, M. W. and Calvo, M. G. (1992) Anxiety and performance: the processing efficiency theory, *Cognition and Emotion*, 6, 409–34.

Eysenck, S. B. and Zuckerman, M. (1978) The relationship between sensation seeking and Eysenck's dimensions of personality, *British Journal of Psychology*, 69, 483–7.

Faria, E. W., Parker, D. L. and Faria, I. E. (2005) The science of cycling: physiology and training, part 1, *Sports Medicine*, 35 (4), 285–312.

FEI (2011) *Dressage Rules*, Lausanne: Fédération Equestre Internationale. Available online at www.fei.org/disciplines/dressage/rules (accessed 13 March 2013).

FEI (2012) *FEI Eventing Risk Management Programme Reports 204–2011*, Fédération Equestre Internationale. Available online at www.fei.org/disciplines/eventing/risk-management (accessed 13 March 2013).

Fenwick, I. and Chatterjee, S. (1981) Perception, preference, and patriotism: an exploratory analysis of the 1980 Winter Olympics, *The American Statistician*, 35, 170–173.

Findlay, L. C. and Ste-Marie, D. M. (2004) A reputation bias in figure skating judging, *Journal of Sport and Exercise Psychology*, 26, 154–66.

Firth, J. (1985) Equestrian injuries, in R. C. Schneider, J. C. Kennedy and M. I. Plant (eds), *Sports Injuries, Mechanisms, Prevention and Treatment*, Baltimore, MD: Williams and Wilkins, pp. 431–39.

Fitts, P. M. (1964) Perceptual-motor skill learning, in A. W. Melton (ed.), *Categories of Human Learning*, New York: Academic Press, pp. 243–85.

Folkman, S. and Lazarus, R. (1985) If it changes it must be a process, *Journal of Personality and Social Behavior*, 48, 150–70.

Folkman, S., Lazarus, R., Gruen, R. J. and De Longis, A. (1986) Stress processes and depressive symptomatology, *Journal of Abnormal Psychology*, 95, 107–13.

Franklin, B. A., Hodgson, J. and Buskirk, E. R. (1980) Relationship between percent maximal O2 uptake and percent maximal heart rate in women. *Research Quarterly for Exercise and Sport*, 51, 616–24.

Fraser, A. F. (2010) *The Behavior and Welfare of the Horse*, Cambridge: CAB International.

Fraser-Thomas, J. and Côté, J. (2009) Understanding adolescents' positive and negative developmental experiences in sport, *The Sport Psychologist*, 23, 3–23.

Friedmann, E. and Thomas, S. A. (1995) Pet ownership, social support and one year survival among post-myocardial infarction patients in the cardiac arrhythmia suppression trial (CAST), *American Journal of Cardiology*, 76, 1213–17.

Friedmann, E., Katcher, A. H., Lynch, J. J. and Thomas, S. A. (1980) Animal companions and one year survival of patients after discharge from a coronary care unit, *Public Health Reports*, 95 (4), 307–12.

Fritts, H. W. and Cournand, A. (1958) The application of the Fick principle to the measurement of pulmonary blood flow, *Proceedings of the National Academy of Sciences of the United States of America*, 44 (10), 1079–87.

Frühwirth, B., Peham, C., Scheidl, M. and Schobesberger, H. (2004) Evaluation of pressure distribution under an English saddle at walk, trot and canter, *Equine Veterinary Journal*, 36, 754–7.

Fuller, R., Hanningan, B., Bates, H., Gormley, M., Stradling, S., Broughton, P., Kinnear, N. and O'Dolan, C. (2008) *Road Safety Research Report 94. Understanding Inappropriate Speed, a Qualitative Analysis*, London: Department for Transport.

Funder, D. C. (2006) Towards a resolution of the personality triad: persons, situations, and behaviors, *Journal of Research in Personality*, 40, 21–34.

Fureix, C., Menguy, H. and Hausberger, M. (2010) Partners with bad temper: reject or cure? a study of chronic pain and aggression in horses, *PLoS ONE*, 5 (8), e12434, doi: 10.1371/journal.pone.0012434.

Furman, W. (1989) The development of children's social networks, in D. Belle (ed.), *Children's Social Networks and Social Support*, New York: Wiley, pp. 151–72.

Furnham, A. (1981) Personality and activity preferences, *British Journal of Social Psychology*, 20, 57–68.

Galvin, B. (1998) *A Guide to Mentoring Sports Coaches*, Leeds: National Coaching Foundation.

Garlinghouse, S. E., Bray, R. E., Cogger, E. A. and Wickler, S. J. (1999) The influence of body measurements and condition score on performance results during the 1998 Tevis Cup, in *Proceedings of the 16th Equine Nutrition and Physiology Society Symposium*, Champaign, IL: Equine Science Society, pp. 398–402.

Garrique, R., Moutiez, G. and Galland, H. (1994) The use of games on horses to improve communication with autistic subjects, in P. Eaton, K. Gibbons and H. Crispin-Morrall (eds), *8th International Therapeutic Riding Congress: The Complete Papers. Proceedings of the 8th International Therapeutic Riding Congress, Hamilton, New Zealand, January 17–20, 1994*. Levin: National Training Resource Centre, pp. 245–8.

Garrity, T. F., Stallones, L., Marx, M. B. and Johnson, T. P. (1989) Pet ownership and attachment as supportive factors in the health of the elderly, *Anthrozoös*, 3 (1), 35–44.

Gattis, K. S., Berns, S., Simpson, L. E. and Christensen, A. (2004) Birds of a feather or strange birds? Ties among personality dimensions, similarity, and marital quality, *Journal of Family Therapy*, 18 (4), 564–74.

Gaudreau, P. and Blondin, J. P. (2004) Different athletes cope differently during a sport competition: a cluster analysis of coping, *Personality and Individual Differences*, 36, 1865–77.

Gautier, C. H. and Cook, E. W. (1997) Relationship between startle and cardiovascular reactivity, *Psychophysiology*, 34 (1), 87–96.

Gearity, B. T. and Murray, M. A. (2011) Athletes' experiences of the psychological effects of poor coaching, *Psychology of Sport and Exercise*, 12 (3), 213–21.

Ghaye, T. (2008) *Putting Reflection at the Heart of Good Practice: The User Guide*, London: Reflective Learning-UK.

Ghaye, T. and Ghaye, K. (1998), *Teaching and Learning through Critical Reflective Practice*, London: D. Fulton Publishers.

Ghosh, A., Di Scala, C., Drew, C., Lessin, M. and Feins, N. (2000) Horse-related injuries in pediatric patients, *Journal of Pediatric Surgery*, 35, 1766–70.

Gilbert, W. and Côté, J. (2003) *Tracing the Developmental Process of Successful Coaches*, Paper Presented at the Meeting of the Canadian Society for Psychomotor Learning and Sport Psychology, Hamilton, Ontario, Canada.

Goldberg, L. R. (1993) The structure of phenotypic personality traits, *The American Psychologist*, 48, 26–34.

Gomá I Freixanet, M. (1991) Personality profile of subjects in engaged in high physical risk sports, *Personality and Individual Differences*, 12 (10), 1087–93.

Gómez Álvarez, C. B., Rhodin, M., Bobbert, M. F., Meyer, H., Weishaupt, M. A., Johnston, C. and van Weeren, P. R. (2006) The effect of different head and neck positions on the thoracolumbar kinematics in the unridden horse, *Equine Veterinary Journal*, Suppl. 36, 445–51.

Górecka-Bruzda, A., Chruszczewski, M., Jaworski, Z., Golonka, M., Jezierski, T., Długosz, B. and Pieszka, M. (2011) Looking for an ideal horse: rider preferences, *Anthrozoös*, 24 (4), 379–92.

Gottlieb, M., Essén-Gustavsson, B., Lindholm, A. and Persson, S. G. (1988) Circulatory and muscle metabolic responses to draught work compared to increasing trotting velocities, *Equine Veterinary Journal*, 20, 430–4.

Gould, D. and Carson, S. (2008) Life skills development through sport: current status and future directions, *International Review of Sport and Exercise Psychology*, 1 (1), 58–78.

Gould, D., Petlichkoff, L., Simons, J. and Vevera, M. (1987) Relationship between competitive state anxiety inventory-2 subscale scores and pistol shooting performance, *Journal of Sport Psychology*, 9, 33–42.

Gould, D., Eklund, R. C. and Jackson, S. A. (1993a) Coping strategies used by U.S. Olympic wrestlers, *Research Quarterly for Exercise and Sport*, 64, 83–93.

Gould, D., Finch, L. M. and Jackson, S. A. (1993b) Coping strategies used by national champion figure skaters, *Research Quarterly for Exercise and Sport*, 64 (4), 453–68.

Gould, D., Dieffenbach, K. and Moffett, A. (2002) Psychological characteristics and their development in Olympic champions, *Journal of Applied Sport Psychology*, 14 (3), 172–204.

Granados, A. C. and Agis, I. F. (2011) Why children with special needs feel better with hippotherapy sessions: a conceptual review, *Journal of Alternative and Complementary Medicine*, 17 (3) 191–7.

Graybiel, A., Jokl, E. and Trapp, C. (1955) Russian studies of vision in relation to physical activity, *Research Quarterly*, 26, 480–5.

Graziano, M. S. A. and Cooke, D. F. (2006) Parieto-frontal interactions, personal space, and defensive behavior, *Neuropsychologia*, 44, 845–59.

Greenspan, M. J. and Feltz, D. L. (1989) Psychological intervention with athletes in competitive situations, *The Sport Psychologist*, 12, 40–51.

Greve, L. and Dyson, S. (2012) The horse-saddle-rider interaction, *Veterinary Journal*, Nov 20. pii: S1090-0233(12)00455-8. doi: 10.1016/j.tvjl.2012.10.020 [Epub ahead of print].

Guba, E. and Lincoln, Y. (2005) Paradigmatic controversies, contradictions, and emerging confluences, in N. Denzin and Y. Lincoln (eds), *The Sage Handbook of Qualitative Research*, 3rd edn. Thousand Oaks: Sage, pp. 183–216.

Gutiérrez Rincón, J. A., Vives Turcó, J., Muro Martínez, I. and Casas Vaqué, I. (1992) A comparative study of the metabolic effort expended by horse riders during a jumping competition, *British Journal of Sport Medicine*, 26 (1), 33–5.

Haehl, V., Giuliani, C. and Lewis, C. (1999) The influence of hippotherapy on the kinematics and functional performance of two children with cerebral palsy, *Pediatric Physical Therapy*, 11, 89–101.

Hakanson, M., Möller, M., Lindström, I. and Mattsson, B. (2009) The horse as the healer. A study of riding in patients with back pain, *Journal of Bodywork and Movement Therapies*, 13, 43–52.

Hall, C., Buckolz, E. and Fishburne, G. (1989) Searching for a relationship between imagery ability and memory of movements, *Memory and Cognition*, 14, 469–77.

Hall, C., Liley, C., Murphy, J. and Crundall, D. (2009) The relationship between visual memory and rider expertise in a show-jumping context, *Veterinary Journal*, 181 (1), 29–33.

Halliburton, A. L. and Weiss, M. R. (2002) Sources of competence information and perceived motivational climate among adolescent female gymnasts varying in skill level, *Journal of Sport and Exercise Psychology*, 24, 396–419.

Halsband, U. (2006) Motorisches Lernen, in S. Gauggel and M. Herrmann (eds), *Handbuch der Neuro- und Biopsychologie*, Göttingen: Hogrefe.

Halsband, U. and Lange, R. K. (2006) Motor learning in man: a review of functional and clinical studies, *Journal of Physiology*, 99, 414–24.

Hancock, D. J., Rymal, A. M. and Ste-Marie, D. M. (2011) A triadic comparison of the use of observational learning amongst team sport athletes, coaches, and officials, *Psychology of Sport and Exercise*, 12, 236–41.

Hanin, Y. L. (1997) Emotions and athletic performance: individual zones of optimal functioning model, *European Yearbook of Sport Psychology*, 1, 29–72.

Hanin, Y. L. (2000) Individual zones of optimal functioning (IZOF) model: Emotion–performance relationships in sport, in Y. L. Hanin (ed.), *Emotions in Sport*, Champaign, IL: Human Kinetics, pp. 303–13.

Hanrahan, S. and Andersen, M. (2012) *Handbook of Applied Sport Psychology: A Comprehensive Guide for Students and Practitioners*, Abingdon: Routledge.

Hanton, S. and Jones, G. (1999) The effects of a multimodal intervention program on performers ii: training the butterflies to fly in formation, *The Sport Psychologist*, 13, 22–41.

Hanton, S., Mellalieu, S. D. and Hall, R. (2004a) Self-confidence and anxiety interpretation: a qualitative investigation, *Psychology of Sport and Exercise*, 5, 477–95.

Hanton, S., Thomas, O. and Maynard, I. (2004b) Competitive anxiety responses in the week leading up to competition: the role of intensity, direction and frequency dimensions, *Psychology of Sport and Exercise*, 3, 169–81.

Hardy, L. (1996a) A test of catastrophe models of anxiety and sports performance against multidimensional theory models using the method of dynamic differences, *Anxiety, Stress and Coping: An International Journal*, 9, 69–86.

Hardy, L. (1996b) Testing the predictions of the cusp catastrophe model of anxiety and performance, *The Sport Psychologist*, 10, 140–56.

Hardy, L. and Parfitt, G. (1991) A catastrophe model of anxiety and performance, *British Journal of Psychology*, 82, 163–78.

Harter, S. (1999) *The Construction of the Self: A Developmental Perspective*, New York: Guilford Press.

Hartmann, E., Söndergaard, E. and Keeling, L. (2012) Identifying potential risk situations for humans when removing horses from groups, *Applied Animal Behavior Science*, 136, 37–43.

Harwood, C., Spray, C. M. and Keegan, R. (2008) Achievement goal theories in sport, in T. S. Horn (ed.), *Advances in Sport Psychology*, 3rd edn. Champaign, IL: Human Kinetics, pp. 157–85.

Hatzigeorgiadis, A., Theodorakis, N. and Zourbanos, N. (2004) Self-talk in the swimming pool: the effects of self-talk on thought content and performance on water-polo tasks, *Journal of Applied Sport Psychology*, 16 (2), 138–50.

Hausberger, M. and Muller, C. (2002) A brief note on some possible factors involved in the reactions of horses to humans, *Applied Animal Behavior Science*, 76, 339–44.

Hausberger, M., Bruderer, C., Le Scolan, N. and Pierre, J. (2004) Interplay between environmental and genetics factors in temperament/personality traits in horses (Equus caballus), *Journal of Comparative Psychology*, 118, 434–46.

Hausberger, M., Roche, H., Henry, S. and Visser, E.K. (2008) A review of the human–horse relationship, *Applied Animal Behavior Science*, 109, 1–24.

Hausberger, M., Gautier, E., Biquand, V., Lunel, C. and Jégo, P. (2009) Could work be a source of behavioral disorders? A study in horses, *PLoS ONE*, 4 (10), e7625. doi: 10.1371/journal.pone.0007625.

Havlik, H. S. (2010) Equestrian sport-related injuries: a review of current literature, *Current Sports Medicine Reports*, 9 (5), 299–302.

Hawson, L. A., McLean, A. N. and McGreevy, P. D. (2010) The roles of equine ethology and applied learning theory in horse-related human injuries, *Journal of Veterinary Behavior*, 5, 324–38.

Hawson, L. A., Oddie, C., McLean, A. N. and McGreevy, P. D. (2011) Is safety valued in the Australian pony market? *Journal of Veterinary Behavior*, 6, 254–60.

Haylock, P. J. and Cantril, C. A. (2006) Healing with horses: fostering recovery from cancer with horses as therapists, *Explore: The Journal of Science and Healing*, 2 (3), 264–8.

Headey, B. (1999) Health benefits and health cost savings due to pets: preliminary estimates from an Australian national survey, *Social Indicators Research*, 47, 233–43.

Headey, B. and Grabka, M. M. (2007) Pets and human health in Germany and Australia: national longitudinal results, *Social Indicators Research*, 80, 297–311.

Hecimovich, M. (2004) Sport specialization in youth: a literature review, *Journal of the American Chiropractic Association*, 41 (4), 32–41.

Hedenborg, S. (2009) Unknown soldiers and very pretty ladies: challenges to the social order of sports in Post-War Sweden, *Sport in History*, 29 (4), 601–20.

Hedenborg, S. and White, M. (2012) Changes and variations in patterns of gender relations in equestrian sports during the second half of the twentieth century, *Sport in Society*, 15 (3), 302–19.

Heiman, M. (1965) The relationship between man and dog, *Psychoanalytic Quarterly*, 25, 568–85.

Heird, J. C., Whitaker, D. D., Bell, R. W., Ramsey, C. B. and Lokey, C. E. (1986) The effects of handling at different ages on the subsequent learning ability of 2-year-old horses, *Applied Animal Behavior Science*, 15, 15–25.

Heleski, C. R., Shelle, A. C., Nielsen, B. D. and Zanella, A. J. (2002) Influence of housing on weanling horse behavior and subsequent welfare, *Applied Animal Behavior Science*, 78, 291–302.

Heleski, C. R., McGreevy, P. D., Kaiser, L. J., Lavagnino, M., Tans, E., Bello, N. and Clayton, H. M. (2009) Effects on behavior and rein tension on horses ridden with or without martingales and rein inserts, *Veterinary Journal*, 181, 56–62.

Hennessy, K. D., Quinn, K. M. and Murphy, J. (2008) Producer or purchaser: different expectations may lead to equine wastage and welfare concerns, *Journal of Applied Animal Welfare Science*, 11 (3), 232–5.

Hill, A. V. and Lupton, L. (1923) Muscular exercise, lactic acid and the supply and utilization of oxygen, *Quarterly Journal of Medicine*, 16, 135–71.

Hitchens, P., Blizzard, L., Jones, G., Day, L. and Fell, J. (2011) Are physiological attributes of jockeys predictors of falls? A pilot study, *BMJ Open*, 1, e000142. doi: 10.1136/bmjopen-2011-000142.

Hitchens, P. L., Blizzard, C. L., Jones, G., Day, L. and Fell, J. (2010) Predictors of race-day jockey falls in flat racing in Australia, *Occupational and Environmental Medicine*, 67, 693–8.

Hobbs, G. D., Yealy, D. M. and Rivas, J. (1994) Equestrian injuries: a 5-year review, *Journal of Emergency Medicine*, 12, 143–5.

Hockenhull, J. and Creighton, E. (2012) Equipment and training risk factors associated with ridden behavior problems in UK leisure horses, *Applied Animal Behavior Science*, 137 (1–2), 36–42.

Holt, N. H. and Hogg, J. M. (2002) Perceptions of stress and coping during preparations for the 1999 women's soccer world cup finals, *The Sport Psychologist*, 16 (3), 251–71.

Horn, T. S. (1985) Coaches' feedback and changes in children's perceptions of their physical competence, *Journal of Educational Psychology*, 77, 174–86.

Horn, T. S. (2008) Coaching effectiveness in the sport domain, in T. S. Horn (ed.), *Advances in Sport Psychology*, Champaign, IL: Human Kinetics, pp. 239–67.

Hosaka, Y., Nagasaki, M., Bajotto, G., Shinomiya, Y., Ozawa, T. and Sato, Y. (2010) Effects of daily mechanical horseback riding on insulin sensitivity and resting metabolism in middle-aged type 2 diabetes mellitus patients, *Nagoya Journal of Medical Science*, 72, 129–37.

Howley, E. T. (2001) Type of activity: resistance, aerobic and leisure versus occupational physical activity, *Medicine and Science in Sports and Exercise*, 33 (6 Supplement), S364–S369.

Hu, Y., Peyre, S. E., Arriaga, A. F., Osteen, R. T., Corso, K. A., Weiser, T. G., Swanson, R. S., Ashley, S. W., Raut, C. P., Zinner, M. J., Gawande, A. A. and Greenberg, C. C.

(2012) Postgame analysis: using video-based coaching for continuous professional development, *Journal of the American College of Surgeons*, 214 (1), 115–24.

Hughes, C., Lee, S. and Chesterfield, G. (2009) Innovation in sports coaching: the implementation of reflective cards, *Reflective Practice: International and Multidisciplinary Perspectives*, 10 (3), 367–84.

Hurmuzlu, Y. and Basdogan, C. (1994) On the measurement of dynamic stability of human locomotion, *Journal of Biomechanical Engineering*, 116 (1), 30–6.

Iba, K., Wada, T., Kawaguchi, S., Fujisaki, T., Yamashita, T. and Ishii, S. (2001) Horse related injuries in a thoroughbred stabling area in Japan, *Archives of Orthopaedic and Trauma Surgery*, 121, 501–4.

Immes, B. (1993) *Reitsport im Subjektiven und Sozialen Kontext*, Unpublished PhD dissertation. Ruhr Universität Bochum, Germany.

Isaacson, R. (2009) *The Horse Boy*, Boston, MA: Little Brown.

ISES (2013) Welcome! International Society for Equitation Science. Available online at www.equitationscience.com (accessed 5 October 2012).

Jackson, B., Dimmock, J. A., Gucciardi, D. F. and Grove, J. R. (2011) Personality traits and relationship perceptions in coach–athlete dyads: Do opposites really attract? *Psychology of Sport and Exercise*, 12, 222–30.

Jacobson, E. (1938) *Progressive Relaxation*, Chicago, IL: University of Chicago.

Jagodzinski, T. and DeMuri, G.P. (2005) Horse-related injuries in children: a review, *Wisconsin Medical Journal*, 104, 50–4.

Jeffcott, L. B., Holmes, M. A. and Townsend, H. G. G. (1999) Validity of saddle pressure measurements using force-sensing array technology: preliminary studies, *Veterinary Journal*, 158, 113–19.

Jerome, G. J. and Williams, J. M. (2000) Intensity and interpretation of competitive state anxiety: relationship to performance and repressive coping, *Journal of Applied Sport Psychology*, 12, 236–50.

John, O. P., Robins, R. W. and Pervin, L. A. (eds) (2008) *Handbook of Personality – Theory and Research*, 3rd edn. New York: The Guilford Press.

Johnson, J. J. M., Hrycaiko, D. W. and Hallas, J. M. (2004) Self-talk and female youth soccer performance, *The Sport Psychologist*, 18, 44–59.

Jones, J. G. (1995) More than just a game: research developments and issues in competitive anxiety in sport, *British Journal of Psychology*, 86, 449–78.

Jones, J. G. and Cale, A. (1989) Pre-competition temporal patterning of anxiety and self–confidence in males and females, *Journal of Sport Behavior*, 12, 183–95.

Jones, J. G. and Hanton, S. (2001) Pre-competitive feeling states and directional anxiety interpretations, *Journal of Sports Sciences*, 19, 385–95.

Jones, J. G. and Swain, A. B. J. (1995) Predispositions to experience debilitating and facilitative anxiety in elite and non-elite performers, *The Sport Psychologist*, 9, 202–12.

Jones, J. G., Swain, A. B. J. and Hardy, L. (1993) Intensity and direction dimensions of competitive state anxiety and relationships with performance. *Journal of Sports Sciences*, 11, 525–32.

Jones, J. G., Hanton, S. and Swain, A. B. J. (1994) Intensity and interpretation of anxiety symptoms in elite and non-elite sports performers, *Personality and Individual Differences*, 17, 657–63.

Jones, M. V. (2003) Controlling emotions in sport, *The Sport Psychologist*, 17, 471–86.

Jones, R. L. and Wallace, M. (2005) Another bad day at the training ground: coping with ambiguity in the coaching context, *Sport, Education and Society*, 10 (1), 119–34.

Jones, R. L., Armour, K. and Potrac, P. (2003) Constructing expert knowledge: a case study of a top-level professional soccer coach, *Sport, Education and Society*, 8 (2), 213–29.

Jonge, F. H. and van den Bos, R. (eds) (2005) *The Human–Animal Relationship: Forever and a Day*, Assen: Royal van Gorcum, pp. 65–81.

Jowett, S. (2007) Interdependence analysis and the 3þ1Cs in the coach–athlete relationship, in S. Jowett and D. Lavallee (eds), *Social Psychology in Sport*, Champaign, IL: Human Kinetics, pp. 15–27.

Jowett, S. and Cockerill, I. M. (2003) Olympic medalists' perspective of the athlete–coach relationship, *Psychology of Sport and Exercise*, 4, 313–31.

Jueptner, M., Stephan, K. M., Frith, C. D., Brooks, D. J., Frackowiak, R. S. J. and Passingham, R. E. (1997) Anatomy of motor learning. I. Frontal cortex and attention to action, *Journal of Neurophysiology*, 77, 1313–24.

Kaiser, L., Heleski, C. R., Siegford, J. M. and Smith, K. A. (2006) Stress-related behaviors among horses used in a therapeutic riding program, *Journal of the American Veterinary Medical Association*, 228 (1), 39–45.

Kang, O.-D., Ryu, Y.-C., Ryew, C.-C., Oh, W.-Y., Lee, C.-E. and Kang, M.-S. (2010) Comparative analyses of rider position according to skill levels during walk and trot in Jeju horse, *Human Movement Science*, 29, 956–63.

Kantak, S. S. and Winstein, C. J. (2012) Learning-performance distinction and memory processes for motorskills: a focused review and perspective, *Behavioral Brain Research*, 228 (1), 219–31.

Karney, B. R. and Bradbury, T. N. (1995) The longitudinal course of marital quality and stability: a review of theory, method, and research, *Psychological Bulletin*, 118, 3–34.

Karol, J. (2007) Applying a traditional individual psychotherapy model to equine-facilitated psychotherapy (EFP): theory and method, *Clinical Child Psychology and Psychiatry*, 12, 77–89.

Katcher, A. and Wilkins, G. (1993) Dialogue with animals: its nature and culture, in S. R. Kellert and E. O. Wilson (eds), *The Biophilia Hypothesis*, Washington, DC: Island Press.

Katcher, A. H. (1981) Interactions between people and their companion animals: form and function, in B. Fogel (ed.), *Interrelations Between People and Companion Animals*, Springfield, IL: Charles C. Thomas, pp. 41–67.

Katcher, A. H. and Beck, A. M. (1986) Dialogue with animals, *Transactions and Studies of the College of Physicians of Philadelphia*, 8 (2), 105–12.

Katcher, A. H., Friedmann, E., Beck, A. M. and Lynch, J. J. (1983) Looking, talking, and blood pressure: the physiological consequences of interaction with the living environment, in A. H. Katcher and A. M. Beck (eds), *New Perspectives on Our Lives with Companion Animals*, Philadelphia: University of Pennsylvania Press, pp. 351–59.

Kawachi, I. and Berkman, L. (2000) Social cohesion, social capital, and health, in L. F. Berkman and I. Kawachi (eds), *Social Epidemiology*, Oxford: Oxford University Press, pp. 174–90.

Keaveney, S. M. (2008) Equines and their human companions, *Journal of Business Research*, 61, 444–54.

Keegan, R. J., Harwood, C. G., Spray, C. M. and Lavallee, D. E. (2009) A qualitative investigation exploring the motivational climate in early-career sports participants: coach, parent and peer influences on sport motivation, *Psychology of Sport and Exercise*, 10, 361–72.

Keele, S. W. (1968) Movement control in skilled motor performance, *Psychological Bulletin*, 70 (6), 387–403.

Keeling, L. J., Jonare, L. and Lanneborn, L. (2009) Investigating horse–human interactions: the effect of a nervous human, *Veterinary Journal*, 181 (1), 70–1.

Kellert, S. R. and Wilson, E. O. (1993) *The Biophilia Hypothesis*, Washington, DC: Island Press.

Kenney, W. L., Wilmore, J. and Costill, D. (2012) *Physiology of Sport and Exercise*, 5th edn. Champaign, IL: Human Kinetics.

Kerr, J. H. (1991) Arousal-seeking in risk sport participants, *Personal Differences*, 12 (6), 613–16.

Kidd, A. H. and Kidd, R. M. (1987) Seeking a theory of the human/companion animal bond, *Anthrozoös*, 1 (3), 140–57.

Kidd, A. H., Kelley, H. T. and Kidd. B. M. (1983) Personality characteristics of horse, turtle, snake, and bird owners, *Psychological Reports*, 52, 719–29.

Kidman, L. (2001) *Developing Decision Makers: An Empowerment Approach to Coaching*, Christchurch: Innovative Print Communications.

Kirk, D. (2005) Physical education, youth sport and lifelong participation: the importance of early learning experiences, *European Physical Education Review*, 11, 239–55.

Kiss, K., Swatek, P., Lénárt, I., Mayr, J., Schmidt, B., Pintér, A. and Höllwarth, M. E. (2008) Analysis of horse-related injuries in children, *Pediatric Surgery International*, 24, 1165–9.

Knapp, B. (1967) *Skill in Sport: The Attainment of Proficiency*, Abingdon: Routledge & Kegan Paul.

Knowles, Z., Tyler, G., Gilbourne, D. and Eubank, M. (2006) Reflecting on reflection: exploring the practice of sports coaching graduates, *Reflective Practice*, 7, 163–79.

Koenen, E. P. C., Aldridge L. I. and Philipsson, J. (2004) An overview of breeding objectives for warmblood sport horses, *Livestock Production Science*, 88 (1–2), 77–84.

König von Borstel, U., Pasing, S. and Gauly, M. (2011) Towards a more objective assessment of equine personality using behavioral and physiological observations from performance test training, *Applied Animal Behavior Science*, 136 (4), 277–85.

Kohut, H. (1984) *How Does Analysis Cure?* Chicago, IL: University of Chicago Press.

Koivulsilta, L. K. and Ojanlatva, A. (2006) To have or not to have a pet for better health, *PLoS ONE*, 1 (1), e109. doi: 10.1371/journal.pone.0000109.

Kotschwar, A. B., Baltacis, A. and Peham, C. (2010) The effects of different saddle pads on forces and pressure distribution beneath a fitting saddle, *Equine Veterinary Journal*, 42, 114–18.

Kubota, M., Nagasaki, M., Tokudome, M., Shinomiya, Y., Ozawa, T. and Sato, T. (2006) Mechanical horseback riding improves insulin sensitivity in elder diabetic patients, *Diabetes Research and Clinical Practice*, 71, 124–30.

Kuhnke, S., Dumbell, L., Gauly, M., Johnson, J. L., McDonald, K. and König von Borstel, U. (2010) A comparison of rein tension of the rider's dominant and nondominant hand and the influence of the horse's laterality, *Comparative Exercise Physiology*, 7, 57–63.

Lagarde, J., Peham, C., Licka, T. and Kelso, J. A. S. (2005) Coordination dynamics of the horse–rider system, *Journal of Motor Behavior*, 37 (6), 418–24.

Land, M. F. and Tatler, B. W. (2009) *Looking and Acting: Vision and Eye Movements in Natural Behavior*, Oxford: Oxford University Press.

Landin, D. (1994) The role of verbal cues in skill learning, *Quest*, 46, 299–313.

Lane, A. M. and Terry, P. C. (2000) The nature of mood: development of a conceptual model with a focus on depression, *Journal of Applied Sport Psychology*, 12, 16–33.

Lashley, K. S. (1917) The accuracy of movement in the absence of excitation from the moving organ, *American Journal of Physiology*, 43, 169–94.

Latimer, J. and Birke, L. (2009) Natural Relations: horses, knowledge and technology, *Sociological Review*, 57 (1), 1–27.

Laurent, M., Dinh Phung, R. and Ripoll, H. (1989) What visual information is used by riders in jumping? *Human Movement Science*, 8, 481–501.

Lawrence, E. A. (1988) Horses in society, *Anthrozoös*, 1(4), 223–31.

Lawrence, E. A. (1993) The sacred bee, the filthy pig, and the bat out of hell: animal symbolism as cognitive biophilia, in S. R. Kellert and E. O. Wilson (eds), *The Biophilia Hypothesis*, Washington, DC: Island Press, pp. 301–41.

Lawrence, G. and Kingston, K. (2008) Skill acquisition for coaches, in R. Jones, M. Hughes and K. Kingston (eds), *An Introduction to Sports Coaching: From Science and Theory to Practice*, Abingdon: Routledge, pp. 28–39.

Lazarus, R. S. (1991) *Emotion and Adaptation*, Oxford: Oxford University Press.

Lazarus, R. S. (2000) How emotions influence performance in competitive sports, *The Sport Psychologist*, 14, 229–52.

Lazarus, R. S. and Folkman, S. (1984) *Stress, Appraisal and Coping*, New York: Springer.

Leary, M. R. and Baumeister, R. F. (2000) The nature and function of self-esteem: sociometer theory, in M. P. Zanna (ed.), *Advances in Experimental Social Psychology*, Vol. 32, San Diego: Academic Press, pp. 1–62.

Lechner, H. E., Feldhaus, S., Gudmundsen, L., Hegemann, D., Michel, D., Zach, G. A. and Knecht, H. (2003) The short-term effect of hippotherapy in patients with spinal cord injury, *Spinal Cord*, 41, 502–5.

Lechner, H. E., Kakebeeke, T. H., Hegemann, D. and Baumberger, M. (2007) The effect of hippotherapy on spasticity and on mental well-being of persons with spinal cord injury, *Archives of Physical Medical Rehabilitation*, 88 (10), 1241–8.

Lee, K. H. and Steenberg, L. J. (2008) Equine-related facial fractures, *International Journal of Oral and Maxillofacial Surgery*, 37 (11), 990–1002.

Lehrman, J. and Ross, D. B. (2001) Therapeutic riding for a student with multiple disabilities and visual impairment: a case study, *Journal of Visual Impairment and Blindness*, 92 (2), 108–9.

Leitao, L. (2004) Therapeutic relations: an exploratory study of psycho-educational riding and autism, *Analise Psicologica*, 22 (2), 335–54.

LeScolan, N., Hausberger, M. and Wolff, A. (1997) Stability over situations in temperamental traits of horses as revealed by experimental and scoring approaches, *Behavioral Processes*, 41, 257–66.

Lesimple, C., Fureix, C., LeScolan, N., Richard-Yris, M. and Hausberger M. (2011) Housing conditions and breed are associated with emotionality and cognitive abilities in riding school horses, *Applied Animal Behavior Science*, 129, 92–9.

Lewczuk, D., Sloniewski, K. and Reklewski, Z. (2006) Repeatability of the horse's jumping parameters with and without the rider, *Livestock Science*, 99, 125–30.

Lewis, M. D. (2000) The promise of dynamic systems approaches for an integrated account of human development, *Child Development*, 71, 36–43.

Lloyd, A. S., Martin, J. E., Bornett-Gauci, H. L. I. and Wilkinson, R. G. (2007) Evaluation of a novel method of horse personality assessment: rater-agreement and links to behavior, *Applied Animal Behavior Science*, 105, 205–22.

Lloyd, A. S., Martin, J. E., Bornett-Gauci, H. L. I. and Wilkinson, R. G. (2008) Horse personality: variation between breeds, *Applied Animal Behavior Science*, 112, 269–383.

Lloyd, R. G. (1987) Riding and other equestrian injuries: considerable severity, *British Journal of Sports Medicine*, 21 (1), 22–4.

Locke, E. A. and Latham, G. P. (1985) The application of goal setting to sports, *Journal of Sport Psychology*, 12, 205–22.

Loder, R. T. (2008) The demographics of equestrian-related injuries in the United States: injury patterns, orthopedic specific injuries and avenues for injury prevention, *Journal of Trauma*, 65, 447–60.

Lorenz, K. and Huxley, J. (2002) *King Solomon's Ring*, 2nd edn. Abingdon: Routledge.

Lovett, T., Hodson-Tole, E. and Nankervis, K. (2004) A preliminary investigation of rider position during walk, trot and canter, *Equine and Comparative Exercise Physiology*, 2 (2), 71–6.

Lucas, M., Day, L. and Fritschi, L. (2009) Injuries to Australian veterinarians working with horses, *Veterinary Record*, 164, 207–9.

Lyle, J. (2002) *Sports Coaching Concepts: A Framework for Coaches' Behavior*, Abingdon: Routledge.

Lynch, J. J. (1977) *The Broken Heart: Medical Consequences of Loneliness*, New York: Basic Books.

Lynch, J. J., Davey Smith, G., Kaplan, G. A. and House, J. S. (2000) Income inequality and mortality: importance to health of individual income, psychosocial environment, or material conditions, *British Medical Journal*, 320, 1204–1220.

McArdle, S. and Duda, J. K. (2002) Implications of the motivational climate in youth sports, in F. L. Smoll and R. E. Smith (eds), *Children and Youth in Sport: A Biopsychosocial Perspective*, Dubuque, IA: Kendall/Hunt, pp. 409–34.

Macauley, B. L. and Gutierrez, K. M. (2004) The effectiveness of hippotherapy for children with language-learning disabilities, *Communication Disorders Quarterly*, 25, 205–17.

McCall, C. (1989) The effect of body condition of horses on discrimination learning abilities, *Applied Animal Behavior Science*, 22, 327–34.

McCall, C. (1990) A review of learning behavior in horses and its application in horse training, *Journal of Animal Science*, 68, 75–81.

McCrae, R. and Costa, P. (1997) Personality trait structures as a human universal, *American Psychologist*, 52, 509–16.

McCrory, P., Turner, M., LeMasson, B., Bodere, C. and Allemandou, A. (2006) An analysis of injuries resulting from professional horse racing in France during 1991–2001: a comparison with injuries resulting from professional horse racing in Great Britain during 1992–2001, *British Journal of Sports Medicine*, 40, 614–18.

McGee, M. C. and Reese, N. B. (2009) Immediate effects of a hippotherapy session on gait parameters in children with spastic cerebral palsy, *Pediatric Physical Therapy*, 21 (2), 212–18.

McGibbon, N. H., Benda, W., Duncan, B. R. and Silkwood-Sherer, D. (2009) Immediate and long-term effects of hippotherapy on symmetry of adductor muscle activity and functional ability in children with spastic cerebral palsy, *Archives of Physical Medicine and Rehabilitation*, 90 (6), 966–74.

McGibbon, V. and Haehl, N. (2002) Conceptual framework for hippotherapy: is it useful to practice of physical therapy. [PowerPoint slides]. Available online at www.pediatricapta.org/pass/pubs/CSM%2002%20Haehl.ppt (accessed 4 August 2012).

McGreevy, P. and McLean, A. (2010a) *Equitation Science*, Oxford: John Wiley and Sons Ltd.

McGreevy, P. and Ralston, L. (2012) The distribution of whipping of Australian Thoroughbred racehorses in the penultimate 200 m of races is influenced by jockeys' experience, *Journal of Veterinary Behavior: Clinical Applications and Research*, 7 (3), 186–90.

McGreevy, P. D. (2007) The advent of equitation science, *Veterinary Journal*, 174, 492–500.

McGreevy, P. D. and Boakes, R. A. (2006) *Carrots and Sticks: Principles of Animal Training*, Cambridge: Cambridge University Press.

McGreevy, P. D. and McLean, A. (2005) Behavioral problems with the ridden horse, in D. S. Mills and S. M. McDonnell (eds), *The Domestic Horse: The Origins, Development, and Management of its Behavior*, Cambridge: Cambridge University Press, pp. 196–211.

McGreevy, P. D. and McLean, A. N. (2007) Roles of learning theory and ethology in equitation. *Journal of Veterinary Behavior: Clinical Applications and Research*, 2, 108–18.

McGreevy, P. D. and McLean, A. N. (2010b) Ethical equitation: Capping the price horses pay for human glory, *Journal of Veterinary Behavior: Clinical Applications and Research*, 5, 203–9.

McGreevy, P. D. and Thomson, P. C. (2006) Differences in motor laterality between breeds of performance horse, *Applied Animal Behavior Science*, 99, 183–90.

McGreevy, P. D., Hahn, C. N. and McLean, A. N. (2004) *Equine Behavior: A Guide for Veterinarians and Equine Scientists*, Philadelphia, PA: W. B. Saunders.

McGreevy, P. D., Oddie, C., Burton, F. L. and McLean, A. N. (2009) The horse–human dyad: can we align horse training and handling activities with the equid social ethogram? *Veterinary Journal*, 181, 12–18.

McLean, A. N. (2008) Overshadowing: a silver lining to a dark cloud in horse training, *Journal of Applied Welfare Science*, 11, 236–48.

McLean, A. N. and McGreevy, P. D. (2004) *Equine Behavior: A Guide for Veterinarians and Equine Scientists*, Edinburgh: W.B. Saunders.

McLean, A. N. and McGreevy, P. D. (2010) Horse-training techniques that defy the principles of learning theory, *Journal of Veterinary Behavior: clinical applications and research*, 187–95.

McLean, D. A. (1992) Analysis of physical demands of rugby, *Journal of Sports and Sciences*, 10, 285–96.

McMiken, D. F. (1990) Ancient origins of horsemanship. *Equine Veterinary Journal*, 22, 73–8.

Macnab, A. C. and Cadman, R. E. (1996) Demographics of alpine skiing and snowboarding injury: lessons for prevention programs, *Injury Prevention*, 2, 286–9.

McNicholas, J., Gilby, A., Rennie, A., Ahmedzai, S., Dono, J. and Ormerod, E. (2005) Pet ownership and human health: a brief review of evidence and issues, *British Medical Journal*, 331, 1252–4.

Mageau, G. A. and Vallerand, R. J. (2003) The coach athlete relationship: a motivational model, *Journal of Sports Sciences*, 21, 883–904.

Magyar, T. M. and Feltz, D. L. (2003) The influence of dispositional and situational tendencies on adolescent girls' sport confidence sources, *Psychology of Sport and Exercise*, 4, 175–90.

Mahoney, M. J. and Avener, M. S. (1977) Psychology of the elite athlete: an explanatory study, *Cognitive Therapy and Research*, 1, 135–41.

Malim, T. and Birch, A. (1989) Social Psychology, New York: International Textbook Company Ltd.

Mamassis, G. and Doganis, G. (2004) The effects of a mental training program on juniors pre-competitive anxiety, self–confidence, and tennis performance, *Journal of Applied Sport Psychology*, 16, 118–37.

Mann, D. T., Williams, A. M., Ward, P. and Janelle, C. M. (2007) Perceptual-cognitive expertise in sport: A meta-analysis, *Journal of Sport and Exercise Psychology*, 29 (4), 457–78.

Marr, D. (1982) *Vision. A Computational Investigation into the Human Representation and Processing of Visual Information*, New York: W. H. Freeman.

Marsden, C. D., Rothwell, J. C. and Dell, B. L. (1984) The use of peripheral feedback in the control of movement, *Trends in the Neurosciences*, 7, 253–7.

Martens, R. (1997) *Successful Coaching*, Champaign, IL: Human Kinetics.

Maw, S. J. (2012) *Pedagogical Effectiveness of the Equestrian Syllabi in England and Western Australia*, unpublished doctoral dissertation, Murdoch University, Perth, Western Australia.

Mayberry, J. C., Pearson, T. E., Wiger, K. J., Diggs, B. S. and Mullins, R. J. (2007) Equestrian injury prevention efforts need more attention to novice riders, *Journal of Trauma*, 62 (3), 735–9.

Mellalieu, S. D., Hanton, S. and Jones, G. (2003) Emotional labelling and competitive anxiety in preparation and competition, *The Sport Psychologist*, 17, 157–74.

Melson, G. F. and Fine, A. H. (2006) Animals in the lives of children, in A. H. Fine (ed.), *Animal-Assisted Therapy: Theoretical Foundations and Guidelines for Practice*, 2nd edn, San Diego: Academic Press, pp. 207–26.

Melson, G. F. and Schwarz, R. (1994) Pets as social supports for families for young children, Paper presented at the annual meeting of the Delta Society, New York.

Melson, G. F., Peet, S. and Sparks, C. (1992) Children's attachment to their pets: links to socioemotional development, *Children's Environments Quarterly*, 8, 55–65.

Meyers, M. C. (2006) Effect of equitation training on health and physical fitness of college females, *European Journal of Applied Physiology*, 98, 177–84.

Meyers, M. C. and Sterling, J. C. (2000) Physical, hematological, and exercise response of collegiate female equestrian athletes, *Journal of Sports Medicine and Physical Fitness*, 40 (2), 131–8.

Meyers, M. C., Elledge, J. R., Sterling, J. C. and Tolson, H. (1990) Injuries in intercollegiate rodeo athletes, *American Journal of Sports Medicine*, 18, 87–91.

Meyers, M. C., Bourgeois, A. E., LeUnes, A. and Murray, N. G. (1997) Mood and psychological skills of elite and sub-elite equestrian athletes, *Journal of Sport Behavior*, 22, 399–409.

Meyners, E. (2004) *Effective Teaching and Riding: Exploring Balance and Motion*, Huson, MT: Goals Unlimited Press.

Mezirow, J. (1978) Perspective transformation, *Adult Education*, 28, 100–10.

Miles, H. C., Pop, S. R., Watt, S. J., Lawrence, G. P. and John, N. W. (2012) A review of virtual environments for training in ball sports, *Computers and Graphics*, 36 (6), 714–26.

Miles, L. K., Nind, L. K. and Macrae, C. N. (2009) The rhythm of rapport: interpersonal synchronicity and social perception, *Journal of Experimental Social Psychology*, 45 (3), 585–9.

Miles, L. K., Griffiths, J. L., Richardson, M. J. and Macreae, C. N. (2010) Too late to coordinate: contextual influences on behavioral synchrony, *European Journal of Social Psychology*, 40, 52–60.

Mischel, W. (1968) *Personality and Assessment*, New York: Wiley.

Mischel, W. (1976) *Introduction to Personality*, New York: Holg, Rinehart and Winston.

Mischel, W. (1977) The interaction of person and situations, in D. Magnusson and N. S. Endler (eds), *Personality at the Crossroads – Current Issues in Interactional Psychology*, Hillsdale: Erlbaum, pp. 333–52.

Model, R. L. (1983) *Coaching Behaviors of Non-Winning High School Football Coaches in Arizona*, Unpublished doctoral dissertation, Arizona State University, Tempe.

Momozawa, Y., Onon, T., Sato, F., Kikusui, T., Takeuchi, Y., Mori, Y. and Kusunose, R. (2003) Assessment of equine temperament by a questionnaire survey to caretakers and evaluation of its reliability by simultaneous behavior tests, *Applied Animal Behavior Science*, 91, 321–35.

Momozawa, Y., Kusunose, R., Kikusui., T., Takeuchi, Y. and Mori, Y. (2005) Assessment of equine temperament questionnaire by comparing factor structure between two separate surveys, *Applied Animal Behavior Science*, 92, 77–84.

Moormann, P. P. (1994) *Figure Skating Performance*, unpublished doctoral dissertation, Leiden University, The Netherlands.

Moran, A. (2012) *Sport and Exercise Psychology – A Critical Introduction*, Abingdon: Routledge.

Moran, A., Byrne, A. and McGlade, N. (2002) The effects of anxiety and strategic planning on visual search behavior, *Journal of Sports Sciences*, 20 (3), 225–36.

Moss, P. S., Wan, A. and Whitlock, M. R. (2002) A changing pattern of injuries to horse riders, *Emergency Medical Journal*, 19, 412–14.

Mullin, M. H. (1999) Mirrors and windows: sociocultural studies of human–animal relationships, *Annual Review of Anthropology*, 28, 201–24.

Munsters, C. B. M., Visser, K. E. K., Van den Broek, J. and Sloet van Oldruitenborgh-Oosterbaan, M. M. (2012) The influence of challenging objects and horse–rider matching on heart rate, heart rate variability and behavioral score in riding horses, *Veterinary Journal*, Insert 192, 75–80.

Murphy, D., Kahn-D'Angelo, L. and Gleason, J. (2008) The effect of hippotherapy on functional outcomes for children with disabilities: a pilot study, *Pediatric Physical Therapy*, 20, 264–70.

Murphy, M. and Arkins, S. (2007) Equine learning behavior, *Behavioral Processes*, 76, 1–13.

Murphy, M. and Martin, K. A. (2002) The use of imagery in sport, in T. S. Horn (ed.), *Advances in Sport Psychology*, 2nd edn. Champaign, IL: Human Kinetics.

Murray, J. K., Singer, E. R., Morgan, K. L., Proudman, C. J. and French, N. P. (2005) Risk factors for cross-country horse falls at one-day events and two-/three-day events, *Veterinary Journal*, 170 (3), 318–24.

Murray, J. K., Singer, E. R., Morgan, K. L., Proudman, C. J. and French, N. P. (2006) The risk of a horse-and-rider partnership falling on the cross-country phase of eventing competitions, *Equine Veterinary Journal*, 38 (2), 158–63.

Murray, J. K., Singer, E. R., Saxby, F. and French, N. P. (2004) Factors influencing risk of injury to horses falling during evening, *Veterinary Record*, 154, 207–8.

Musselwhite, C. B. A., Avineri, E., Fulcher, E. and Susilo, Y. O. (2010) *Understanding Public Attitudes to Road-user Safety: Literature Review, Final Report*. Road Safety Research Report No. 112, London: Department for Transport.

Nicholls, J. (1984) Conceptions of ability and achievement motivation, in R. Ames and C. Ames (eds), *Research on Motivation in Education: Vol. I. Student Motivation*, New York: Academic Press, pp. 39–73.

Nicholls, J. (1989) *The Competitive Ethos and Democratic Education*. Cambridge, MA: Harvard University Press.

Nielsen, B., Kubica, R., Bonnesen, A., Rasmussen, I. B., Stoklosa, J. and Wilk, B. (1981) Physical work capacity after dehydration and hyperthermia, *Scandinavian Journal of Sports Science*, 3, 2–10.

Nobel Foundation (2013) The Nobel Prize in Physiology or Medicine 1973: Karl von Frisch, Konrad Lorenz, Nikolaas Tinbergen. Nobelprize.org, 13 March. Available online at www.nobelprize.org/nobel_prizes/medicine/laureates/1973 (accessed 13 March 2013).

Oliver, E. J., Hardy, J. and Markland, D. M. (2010) Exploring elite coaches' views of athletes' practice behaviors, *Psychology of Sport and Exercise*, 11, 433–43.

Olsen, S. L. (1988) Big game hunting in the Upper Palaeolithic in Europe, American Association for the Advancement of Science, 154th National Meeting, Boston.

Pachana, N. A., Ford, J. H., Andrew, B. and Dobson, A. J. (2005) Relations between companion animals and self-reported health in older women: cause, effect or artefact? *International Journal of Behavioral Medicine*, 12, 103–10.

Paillard, J. (1982) The contribution of peripheral and central vision to visually guided reaching, in D. J. Ingle, M. A. Goodale and R. Mansfield (eds), *Advances in the Analysis of Visual Behavior*, Cambridge, MA: The MIT Press.

Paix, B. (1999) Rider injury rates and emergency medical services at equestrian events, *British Journal of Sports Medicine*, 33, 46–48.

Parfitt, G., Hardy, L. and Pates, J. (1995) Somatic anxiety and physiological arousal: Their effects upon a high anaerobic, low memory demand task, *International Journal of Sport Psychology*, 26 (2), 196–213.

Parslow, D. M., Morris, R. G., Fleminger, S., Rahman, Q., Abrahams, S. and Recce, M. (2005) Allocentric spatial memory in humans with hippocampal lesions, *Acta Psychologica*, 118, 123–47.

Patmore, A. (1986) *Sportsmen under Stress*, London: Stanley Paul.

Patronek, G. J. and Glickman, L. T. (1993) Pet ownership protects against the risks and consequences of coronary heart disease, *Medical Hypotheses*, 40 (4), 245–9.

Peeters, M., Closson, C., Beckers, J. and Vandenheede, M. (2013) Rider and horse salivary cortisol levels during competition and impact on performance, *Journal of Equine Veterinary Science*, 33 (3), 155–60.

Peham, C., Kapaun, M., Licka ,T. and Scheidl, M. (1998) Motion pattern consistency of the rider–horse system, in H. J. Riehle and M. M. Vieten (eds), *16 International Symposium on Biomechanics in Sports*, ISBS Conference Proceedings Archive. Available online at https://ojs.ub.uni-konstanz.de/cpa/article/view/1641 (accessed 14 March 2013).

Peham, C., Licka, T., Kapaun, M. and Scheidl, M. (2001) A new method to quantify harmony of the horse–rider system in dressage, *Sports Engineering*, 4 (2), 95–101.

Peham, C., Licka, T., Schobesberger, H. and Meschan, E. (2004) Influence of the rider on the variability of the equine gait, *Human Movement Science*, 23 (5), 663–71.

Peham, C., Hofmann, A, Molsner, J., Borkenhagen, B., Kuhnke, S. and Baltacis, A. (2008) Forces acting on the horse's back and the stability of the rider in sitting and rising trot – a comparison, *Pferdeheilkunde*, 24, 337–42.

Peham, C., Kotschwar, A.B., Borkenhagen, B., Kuhnke, S., Molsner, J. and Baltacis, A. (2010) A comparison of forces acting on the horse's back and the stability of the rider's seat in different positions at the trot, *Veterinary Journal*, 184, 56–9.

Piaget, J., Inhelder, J. and Inhelder, B. (1969) *The Psychology of the Child*, New York: Basic Books.

Platzer, H., Snelling, J. and Blake, D. (1997) Promoting reflective practitioners in nursing: a review of theoretical models and research into the use of diaries and journals to facilitate reflection, Teaching in Higher Education, 2 (2), 103–21.

Plessner, H. (1999) Expectation biases in gymnastics judging, Journal of Sport and Exercise Psychology, 21, 131–44.

Plessner, H. and Haar, T. (2006) Sports performance judgments from a social cognition perspective, *Psychology of Sport and Exercise*, 7, 555–75.

Plymoth, B. (2012) Gender in equestrian sports: an issue of difference and equality, *Sport in Society*, 15 (3), 335–48.

Porter-Wenzlaff, L. (2007) Finding their voice: developing emotional. cognitive, and behavioral congruence in female abuse survivors through equine facilitated therapy, *Nursing*, 3 (5), 529–34.

Potrac, P., Jones, R. and Armour, K. (2002) It's all about getting respect: the coaching behaviors of an expert English soccer coach, *Sport, Education and Society*, 7, 183–202.

Pounder, D. J. (1984) The grave yawns for the horseman, *Medical Journal of Australia*, 411, 611–14.

Powell, D. M., Bennett-Wimbush, K., Peeples, A. and Duthie, M. (2008) Evaluation of indicators of weight-carrying ability of light riding horses, *Journal of Equine Veterinary Science*, 28 (1), 28–33.

Powers, P. N. R. and Kavanagh, A. M. (2005) Effect of rider experience on the jumping kinematics of riding horses, *Equine and Comparative Exercise Physiology*, 2 (4), 263–326.

Prapavessis, H. (2000) The POMS and sports performance: a review, *Journal of Applied Sport Psychology*, 12, 34–48.

Press, J. M., Davis, P. D., Wiesner, S. L., Heinemann, A., Semick, P. and Addison, R. G. (1995) The national jockey injury study: an analysis of injuries to professional horse-racing jockeys, *Clinical Journal of Sport Medicine*, 5, 236–40.

Pretty, G. (2000a) Consulting with the horse and rider team: challenges for the sport psychologist, in G. Tenenbaum (ed.), *The Practice of Sport and Exercise Psychology: International Perspectives*, Morgantown, VW: Fitness Information Technology.

Pretty, G. H. (2000b) Understanding the enmeshment in equine and human relationships: how riders think about the horse in their attributions of performance success, *Australian Journal of Psychology*, Supplement 107.

Pretty, J., Peacock, J., Sellens, M. and Griffin, M. (2005) The mental and physical health outcomes of green exercise, *International Journal of Environmental Health Research*, 15 (5), 319–37.

Preuschoft, H., Falaturi, P. and Lesch, C. (1995) The influences of riders on their horses, *Tierärztliche Umschau*, 50, 511–21.

Preuschoft, H., Witte, H., Recknagel, S., Bar, H., Lesch, C. and Wuthrich, M. (1999) The effects of various head-gears on horses, *Deutsche Tierärztliche Wochenschrift*, 106, 169–75.

Pummell, E. K. L., Harwood, C. G. and Lavallee, D. (2008) Jumping to the next level: examining the within-career transition of adolescent event riders. *Psychology of Sport and Exercise*, 9, 427–47.

Quiroz Rothe, E., Vega, B. J., Torres, R. M., Soler, S. M. C. and Pazos, R. M. M. (2005) From kids and horses: equine facilitated psychotherapy for children, *International Journal of Clinical and Health Psychology*, 5 (2), 373–83.

Randall, M. (2006) *Sensory Integration*. Pre-conference Workshop, Special Needs, Learning Support Committee, Newsletter, The Hague, February 2006.

Regan, P. J., Roberts, J. O., Feldberg, L. and Roberts, A. H. N. (1991) Hand injuries from leading horses. *Injury*, 22 (2), 124–26.

Rhodin, M., Johnston, C., Roethlisberger Holm, K., Wennerstrand, J. and Drevemo, S. (2005) The influence of head and neck position on kinematics of the back in riding horses at the walk and trot, *Equine Veterinary Journal*, 37 (1), 7–11.

Rickards, T. (2000) Trust-based leadership: creative lessons from intelligent horsemanship, *Creativity and Innovation Management*, 9 (4), 259–66.

Rijken, M. and Beek, S. (2011) About cats and dogs…reconsidering the relationship between pet ownership and health related outcomes in community-dwelling elderly, *Social Indicators Research*, 102 (3), 373–88.

Rivera, E., Benjamin, S., Nielsen, B., Shelle, J. and Zanella, A. J. (2002) Behavioral and physiological responses of horses to initial training: the comparison between pastured versus stalled horses, *Applied Animal Behavior Science*, 78 (2–4), 235–52.

Robergs, R. A. and Landwehr, R. (2002) The surprising history of the 'HR$_{max}$ = 220–age' equation, *Journal of Exercise Physiology*, 5 (2), 1–10. Available online at http://www.cyclingfusion.com/pdf/220-Age-Origins-Problems.pdf (accessed 14 March 2013).

Roberts, G. C. (2001) Understanding the dynamics of motivation in physical activity: the influence of achievement goals on motivational process, in G. C. Roberts (ed.), *Advances in Motivation in Sport and Exercise*, Champaign, IL: Human Kinetics, pp. 1–50.

Roberts, M., Shearman, J. and Marlin, D. (2010) A comparison of the metabolic cost of the three phases of the one-day event in female collegiate riders, *Comparative Exercise Physiology*, 6 (3), 129–35.

Robinson, I. H. (1999) The human–horse relationship: how much do we know? *Equine Veterinary Journal*, Supplement 28, 42–5.

Rodin, J., Silberstein, L. and Striegel-Moore, R. (1985) Women and weight: a normative discontent, in T. B. Sondereregger (ed.), *Psychology and Gender*, Lincoln: University of Nebraska Press, pp. 267–307.

Roe J. P., Taylor T. K., Edmunds I. A., Cumming R. G., Ruff S. J., Plunkett-Cole M. D., Mikk M. and Jones R. F. (2003) Spinal and spinal cord injuries in horse riding: the New South Wales experience 1976–1996, *ANZ Journal of Surgery*, 73, 331–4.

Rosenbaum, D. A. (2010) *Human Motor Control*, London: Academic Press.

Rosenberg, M. (1965) *Society and the Adolescent Self-image*, Princeton, NJ: Princeton University Press.

Rosenberg, M. (1979) *Conceiving the Self*, New York: Basic Books.

Rueda, M. A., Cui, L. and Gilchrist, M. D. (2011) Finite element modelling of equestrian helmet impacts exposes the need to address rotational kinematics in future helmet designs, *Computer Methods in Biomechanics and Biomedical Engineering*, 14 (12), 1021–31.

Rueda, M. A., Halley, W. L. and Gilchrist, M. D. (2010) Fall and injury incidence rates of jockeys while racing in Ireland, France and Britain, *Injury*, 41, 533–9.

Rundell, K. W. (1996) Differences between treadmill running and treadmill roller skiing, *Journal of Strength and Conditioning Research*, 10, 167–72.

Sage, G. H. (1989) Becoming a high school coach: from playing sports to coaching, *Research Quarterly for Exercise and Sport*, 60 (1), 81–92.

Salmela, J. (1994) Tracing the roots of expert coaches: searching for inspiration, *Coaches Report*, 1, 9–11.

Salmoni A. W., Schmidt R. A. and Walter C. B. (1984) Knowledge of results and motor learning: a review and critical appraisal, *Psychological Bulletin*, 95 (3), 355–86.

Salthouse, T. A. (1985) Anticipatory processing in transcription typing, *Journal of Applied Psychology*, 70, 264–71.

Salthouse, T. A. (1986) Perceptual, cognitive, and motoric aspects of transcription typing, *Psychological Bulletin*, 99, 303–19.

Sasimowski, E., Pietrzak, S. and Lecewicz, W. (1986) Zmienność niektórych pozaregulaminowych warunków, w jakich odbywaj si oficjalne konkursy skoków przez przeszkody, *Annual UMCS EE*, 4, 148–56.

Saslow, C. A. (2002) Understanding the perceptual world of horses, *Applied Animal Behavior Science*, 78, 209–24.

Scanlon, J. M. and Chernomas, W. M. (1997) Developing the reflective teacher, *Journal of Advanced Nursing*, 25 (5), 1138–43.

Schantz, R., Randall-Fox, E., Hutchinson, W., Tyden, A. and Astrand, P. O. (1983) Muscle fibre type distribution, muscle cross-sectional area and maximal voluntary strength in humans, *Acta Physiologica Scandinavica*, 117 (2), 219–26.

Scheer, J. K. and Ansorge, C. J. (1979) Influence due to expectations: a function of internal–external locus of control, *Journal of Sport Psychology*, 1, 53–8.

Scheer, J. K. and Ansorge, C. J. (1980) Expectations in judging, *International Gymnast*, 22, TS1–TS2.

Scheer, J. K., Ansorge, C. J. and Howard, J. (1983) Judging bias by viewing contrived videotapes: a function of selected psychological variables, *Journal of Sport Psychology*, 5, 427–37.

Schils, S. J., Greer, N. L., Stoner, L. J. and Kobluk, C. N. (1993) Kinematic analysis of the equestrian walk, posting trot and sitting trot, *Human Movement Science*, 12, 693–712.

Schinke, R. J., Bloom, G. A. and Salmela, J. H. (1995) The evolution of elite Canadian basketball coaches, *Avante*, 1, 48–62.

Schinke, R. J., Draper, S. P. and Salmela, J. H. (1997) A conceptualization of team building in performance sport as a season-long process, *Avante*, 3 (2), 57–72.

Schmidt, R. A. (1975) A schema theory of discrete motor skill learning, *Psychological Review*, 82 (4), 225–60.

Schmidt, R. A. (1988) *Motor Control and Learning: A Behavioral Emphasis*, Champaign, IL: Human Kinetics.

Schmidt, R.A. and Lee, T.D. (2011) *Motor Control and Learning: A Behavioral Emphasis*, 5th edn. Champaign, IL: Human Kinetics.

Schöllhorn, W. I., Peham, C., Licka, T. and Scheidl, M. (2006) A pattern recognition approach for the quantification of horse and rider interactions, *Equine Veterinary Journal*, Supplement 68 (36), 400–5.

Schön, D. A. (1983) *The Reflective Practitioner: How Professionals Think in Action*, New York: Basic Books.

Schön, D. A. (1987) *Educating the Reflective Practitioner*. San Francisco: Jossey-Bass.

Seefeldt, V., Clark, M. A. and Brown, E. W. (eds) (2001) *Program for Athletic Coaches' Education*, 3rd edn. Traverse City, MI: Cooper Publishing.

Selfhout, M., Denissen, J., Branje, S. and Meeus, W. (2009) In the eye of the beholder: perceived, actual, and peer-rated similarity in personality, communication, and friendship intensity during the acquaintanceship process, *Journal of Personality and Social Psychology*, 96 (6), 1152–65.

Seltzer, R. and Glass, W. (1991) International politics and judging in Olympic skating events: 1968–1988, *Journal of Sport Behavior*, 14, 189–200.

Selye, H. (1956) *The Stress of Life*, New York: McGraw-Hill.

Serpell, J. (2003) Anthropomorphism and anthropomorphic selection – beyond the 'cute response', *Society and Animals*, 11 (1), 83–100.

Serpell, J. A. (1996) Evidence for an association between pet behavior and owner attachment levels, *Applied Animal Behavior Science*, 47, 49–60.

Sewell, D., Watkins, P. and Griffin, M. (2012) *Sport and Exercise Science, An Introduction*, 2nd edn. Abingdon: Routledge.

Shadmehr, R. and Holcomb, H. H. (1997) Neural correlates of motor memory consolidation, *Science*, 277, 821–5.

Shea, J. B. and Morgan, R. L. (1979) Contextual interference effects on the acquisition, retention, and transfer of a motor skill, *Journal of Experimental Psychology: Learning, Memory and Cognition*, 5, 179–87.

Sheldon, K. M., Ryan, R. M., Rawsthorne, L. and Ilardi, B. (1997) Trait self and true self: cross–role variation in the big five traits and its relations with authenticity and subjective well-being, *Journal of Personality and Social Psychology*, 73, 1380–93.

Shim, J., Carlton, L. G., Chow, J. W. and Chae, W. (2005) The use of anticipatory visual cues by highly skilled tennis players, *Journal of Motor Behavior*, 37, 164–75.

Shinomiya, Y., Wang, S., Ishida, K. and Kimura, T. (2002) Development and muscle strength training evaluation for horseback riding therapeutic equipment, *Journal of Robotics and Mechatronics*, 14, (6), 597–603.

Shurtleff, T. L., Standeven, J. W. and Engsberg, J. R. (2009) Changes in dynamic trunk/head stability and functional reach after hippotherapy, *Archives of Physical Medicine and Rehabilitation*, 90 (7), 1185–95.

Silkwood-Sherer, D. and Warmbier, H. (2007) Effects of hippotherapy on postural stability, in persons with multiple sclerosis: a pilot study, *Journal of Neurology and Physical Therapy*, 31 (2), 77–84.

Silver, J. R. (2002) Spinal injuries resulting from horse riding accidents, *Spinal Cord*, 40, 264–71.

Silver, J. R. and Lloyd Parry, J. M. (1991) Hazards of horse-riding as a popular sport, *British Journal of Sport Medicine*, 25 (2), 105–10.

Silverstein, M. (1999) *Self-Psychology and Diagnostic Assessment: Identifying Selfobject Functions through Psychological Testing*, Abingdon: Routledge.

Skinner, E. A., Edge, K., Altman, J. and Sherwood, H. (2003) Searching for the structure of coping: a review and critique of category systems for classifying ways of coping, *Psychological Bulletin*, 129, 216–69.

Smartt, P. and Chalmers, D. (2009) A new look at horse–related sport and recreational injury in New Zealand, *Journal of Science and Medicine in Sport*, 12 (3), 376–382.

Smink, F. R., van Hoeken, D. and Hoek, H. W. (2012) Epidemiology of eating disorders: incidence, prevalence and mortality rates, *Current Psychiatry Reports*, 14 (4), 406–14.

Smith, R. E. and Smoll, F. L. (1990) Self-esteem and children's reactions to youth sport coaching behaviors: a field study of self-enhancement processes, *Developmental Psychology*, 26, 987–93.

Smith, R. E. and Smoll, F. L. (1996) The coach as a focus of research and intervention in youth sports, in F. L. Smoll and R. E. Smith (eds), *Children and Youth in Sport. A Biopsychosocial Perspective*, Dubuque, IA: Brown and Benchmark, pp. 125–41.

Smith, R. E. and Smoll, F. L. (2005) Assessing psychosocial outcomes in coach training programs, in D. Hackfort, J.L. Duda, and R. Lidor (eds), *Handbook of Research in Applied Sport and Exercise Psychology: International Perspectives*, Morgantown, WV: Fitness Information Technology, pp. 293–316.

Smith, R. E., Smoll, F. L. and Hunt, E. (1977) A system for the behavioral assessment of athletic coaches, *Research Quarterly*, 48, 401–7.

Smith, R. E., Smoll, F. L. and Curtis, B. (1979) Coach effectiveness training: a cognitive behavioral approach to enhancing relationship skills in youth sport coaches, *Journal of Sport Psychology*, 1, 59–75.

Smith, R. E., Smoll, F. L. and Cumming, S. P. (2007) Effects of a motivational climate intervention for coaches on young athletes' sport performance Anxiety, *Journal of Sport and Exercise Psychology*, 29, 39–59.

Smith, R. E., Shoda, Y., Cumming, S. P. and Smoll, F. L. (2009) Behavioral signatures at the ballpark: intraindividual consistency of adults' situation-behavior patterns and their interpersonal consequences, *Journal of Research in Personality*, 43 (2), 187–95.

Smoll, F. L. and Smith, R. E. (2006) Conducting sport psychology training programs for coaches: Cognitive-behavioral principles and techniques, in J. M. Williams (ed.), *Applied Sport Psychology: Personal Growth to Peak Performance*, 5th edn. Boston, MA: McGraw-Hill, pp. 458–80.

Smoll, F. L., Smith, R. E., Barnett, N. P. and Everett, J. J. (1993) Enhancement of children's self-esteem through social support training for youth sport coaches, *Journal of Applied Psychology*, 78, 602–10.

Smoll, F. L., Smith, R. E. and Cumming, S. P. (2007) Coaching behaviors, motivational climate, and young athletes' sport experiences, in C. Goncalves, M. Coelho e Silva, L. Adelino and R.M. Malina, (eds), *Sport and Education*, Coimbra, Portugal: Coimbra University Press, pp. 165–76.

Sorli, J. M. (2000) Equestrian injuries: a five year review of hospital admissions in British Columbia, Canada, *Injury Prevention*, 6, 59–61.

Spielberger, C. D. (1988) *Manual for the State-Trait Anger Expression Inventory*, Odessa, FL: Psychological Assessment Resources.

Stachurska, A., Pięta, M. and Nesteruk, E. (2002) Which obstacles are most problematic for jumping horses? *Applied Animal Behavior Science*, 77, 197–207.

Stachurska, A., Pięta, M., Phaff Ussing, A., Kaproń, A. and Kwiencińska, N. (2010) Difficulty of cross-country obstacles for horses competing in three day events, *Applied Animal Behavior Science*, 123, 101–7.

Stallings, L. M. (1973) *Motor Skills: Development and Learning*, Boston, MA: WCB/McGraw-Hill.

Stefani, R. (1998) Predicting outcomes, in J. Bennett (ed.), *Statistics in Sport*, London: Arnold, pp. 249–75.

Stein, J., Bloom, G. A. and Sabiston, C. M. (2012) Influence of perceived coach feedback on athletes' perceptions of the team's motivational climate, *Psychology of Sport and Exercise*, 13, 484–90.

Steinbrecht, G. (1884) *Gymnasium des Pferdes*, Potsdam: Döring.

Ste-Marie, D. M. (1996) International bias in gymnastic judging: conscious or unconscious influences? *Perceptual and Motor Skill*, 83, 963–75.

Ste-Marie, D. M. (2003) Memory biases in gymnastic judging: differential effects of surface feature changes, *Applied Cognitive Psychology*, 17 (6), 733–51.

Ste-Marie, D. M. and Lee, T. D. (1991) Prior processing effects on gymnastic judging, *Journal of Experimental Psychology*, 17, (1), 126–36.

Ste-Marie, D. M. and Valiquette, S. M. (1996) Enduring memory-influenced biases in gymnastic judging, *Journal of Experimental Psychology: Learning, Memory, and Cognition*, 22, 1498–502.

Ste-Marie, D. M., Valiquette, S. M. and Taylor, G. (2001) Memory-influenced biases in gymnastic judging occur across different prior processing conditions, *Research Quarterly for Exercise and Sport*, 72, 420–6.

Sterba, J. A. (2007) Does horseback riding therapy or therapist-directed hippotherapy rehabilitate children with cerebral palsy? *Developmental Medicine and Child Neurology*, 49 (1), 68–73.

Sterba, J. A., Rogers, B. T., France, A. P. and Vokes, D. A. (2002) Horseback riding in children with cerebral palsy: effect on gross motor function, *Developmental Medicine and Child Neurology*, 44 (5), 301–8.

Stewart, M. J. (1989) Social support: diverse theoretical perspectives, *Social Science and Medicine*, 28 (12), 1275–82.

Symes, D. and Ellis, R. (2009) A preliminary study into rider asymmetry within equitation, *Veterinary Journal*, 181, 34–7.

Tabachnik, B. G. and Fidell, L. S. (2001) *Using Multivariate Statistics*, 4th edn. New York: Harper Collins.

Tajfel, H. and Turner, J. C. (1986) The social identity theory of intergroup behavior, in S. Worchel and W. Austin (eds), *Psychology Of Intergroup Relation*, Chicago: Nelson Hall, pp. 7–24.

Taylor, C. R., Heglund, N. C., McMahon, T. A. and Looney, T. R. (1980) The energetic cost of generating muscular force during running, *Journal of Experimental Biology*, 86, 9–18.

Taylor, R. R., Kielhofner, G., Smith, C., Butler, S., Cahill, S. M., Ciukaj, M. D. and Gehman, M. (2009) Volitional change in children with autism: a single-case study design of the impact of hippotherapy on motivation, *Occupational Therapy in Mental Health*, 25 (2), 192–200.

Telegin, D. Y. (1986) *Dereivka: A Settlement and Cemetery of Copper Age Horse Keepers on the Middle Dnieper*, BAR International Series 287, translated from Russian by V. K. Pyatkovskiy, edited by J. P. Mallory, Oxford: British Archaeological Reports.

Terada, K., Clayton, H. M. and Kato, K. (2006) Stabilization of wrist position during horseback riding at trot, *Equine and Comparative Exercise Physiology*, 3(4), 179–84.

Terada, K., Mullineaux, D., Lanovaz, J., Kato, K. and Clayton, H. (2004) Electromyographic analysis of the riders' muscles at trot, *Equine and Comparative Exercise Physiology*, 1, 193–8.

Terry, P. C. and Lane, A. M. (2000) Normative values for the profile of mood states for use with athletic samples, *Journal of Applied Sport Psychology*, 12, 93–109.

Tharp, R. G. and Gallimore, R. (1976) What a coach can teach a teacher, *Psychology Today*, 9, 75–8.

Thomas, O., Maynard, I. and Hanton, S. (2007) Intervening with athletes during the time leading up to competition: theory to practice II, *Journal of Applied Sport Psychology*, 19, 398–418.

Thornton, J., Pagan, J. and Persson S. (1987) The oxygen cost of weight loading and inclined treadmill exercise in the horse, in J. R. Gillespie and N. E. Robinson (eds), *Equine Exercise Physiology 2*, Davis, CA: ICEEP Publications, pp. 206–15.

Torres-McGehee, T. M., Monsma, E. V., Gay, J. L., Minton, D. M. and Mady-Foster, A. N. (2011) Prevalence of eating disorder risk and body image distortion among national collegiate athletic association division I varsity equestrian athletes, *Journal of Athletic Training*, 46 (4), 431–7.

Traeen, B. and Wang, C. E. (2006) Perceived gender attribution, self-esteem, and general self-efficacy in female horseback riders, *Journal of Equine Veterinary Science*, 25 (10), 439–44.

Treasure, D. and Roberts, G. (1998) Relationship between female adolescents' achievement goal orientations, perceptions of the motivational climate, belief about success and sources of satisfaction in basketball, *International Journal of Sport Psychology*, 29, 211–30.

Trotter, M. A. and Endler, N. S. (1999) An empirical test of the interaction model of anxiety in a competitive equestrian setting, *Personality and Individual Differences*, 27, 861–75.

Trowbridge, E. A., Cotterill, J. V. and Crofts, C. E. (1995) The physical demands of riding in National Hunt races, *European Journal of Applied Physiology*, 70, 66–9.

Tulloch, M. (1995) Gender differences in bullying experiences and attitudes to social relationships in high school students, *Australian Journal of Education*, 39 (3), 279–93.

Turner, M., McCrory, P. and Halley, W. (2002) Injuries in professional horse racing in Great Britain and the Republic of Ireland during 1992–2000, *British Journal of Sports Medicine*, 36, 403–9.

Uchiyama, H., Ohtani, N. and Ohta, M., (2011) Three–dimensional analysis of horse and human gaits in therapeutic riding, *Applied Animal Behavior Science*, 135 (4), 271–6.

Ulrich, R. S. (1993) Biophilia, biophobia, and natural landscapes, in S. R. Kellert and E. O. Wilson (eds), *The Biophilia Hypothesis*, Washington, DC: Island Press, pp. 73–137.

Umbarger, G. (2007) State of evidence regarding complimentary and alternative medical treatment for autism spectrum disorders, *Education and Training in Developmental Disabilities*, 42 (4), 437–47.

van Dierendonck, M. C. and Goodwin, D. (2005) Social contact in horses: implications for human–horse interactions, in F. de Jonge and R. van den Bos (eds), *The Human–Animal Relationship: Forever and a Day*, Assen: Royal Van Gorcum, pp. 65–81.

van Dierendonck, M. C., DeVries, H. and Schilder, M. B. H. (1995) An analysis of dominance, its behavioral parameters and possible determinants in a herd of Icelandic horses in captivity, *Netherland Journal of Zoology*, 45 (3–4), 362–85.

Vanden Auweele, Y., Boen, F., De Geest, A. and Feys, J. (2004) Judging bias in synchronized swimming: open feedback leads to non–performance-based conformity, *Journal of Sport and Exercise Psychology*, 26, 561–71.

Visser, E. K, Van Reenen, C. G., Van der Werf, J., Schilder, M., Knaap, J. H., Barneveld, A. and Blokhuis, H. (2002) Heart rate and heart rate variability during a novel object test and a handling test in young horses, *Physiology and Behavior*, 76, 289–96.

Visser, E. K., Van Reenen, C. G., Blokhuis, M. Z., Morgan, E. K., Hassmén, P., Rundgren, T. M. and Blokhuis, H. J. (2008) Does horse temperament influence horse–rider cooperation? *Journal of Applied Animal Welfare Science*, 11 (3), 267–84.

Visser, E. K., Van Reenen, C. G., Hopster, H., Schilder, M. B. H., Knaap, J. H., Barneveld, A. and Blokhuis, H. (2001) Quantifying aspects of young horses' temperament: consistency of behavioral variables, *Applied Animal Behavior Science*, 74, 241–58.

Von Borell, E., Langbein, J., Després, G., Hansen, S., Leterrier, C., Marchant-Forde, J., Marchant-Forde, R., Minero, M., Mohr, E., Prunier, A., Valance, D. and Veissier, I. (2007) Heart rate variability as a measure of autonomic regulation of cardiac activity for assessing stress and welfare in farm animals: a review, *Physiology and Behavior*, 92, 293–316.

Walberg Rankin, J. (2006) Making weight in sports, in L. Burke and V. Deakin (eds), *Clinical Sports Nutrition*, 3rd edn. Maidenhead: McGraw-Hill Professional, pp. 175–99.

Wall, M. and Côté, J. (2007) Developmental activities that lead to dropout and investment in sport, *Physical Education and Sport Pedagogy*, 12, 77–87.

Waller, A. E., Daniels, J. L., Weaver, N. L. and Robinson, P. (2000) Jockey injuries in the United States, *JAMA*, 283, 1326–8.

Walters, S. R., Schluter, P. J., Oldham, A. R. H., Thomson, R. W. and Payne, D. (2012) The sideline behavior of coaches at children's team sports games, *Psychology of Sport and Exercise*, 13, 208–15.

Wanderer, J. J. (1987) Social factors in judges rankings of competitors in figure skating championships, *Journal of Sport Behavior*, 10, 93–102.

Waran, N. (ed.) (2002) *The Welfare of Horses*, Dordrecht, The Netherlands: Kluwer.

Waran, N., McGreevy, P. and Casey, R. A. (2002) Training methods and horse welfare, in N. Waran (ed.) *The Welfare of Horses*, Dordrecht : Kluwer Academic Publishers, pp. 151–80.

Warren-Smith, A. K. and McGreevy, P. D. (2008) Equestrian coaches' understanding and application of learning theory in horse training, *Anthrozoös*, 21 (2), 153–62.

Warren-Smith, A. K., Curtis, R. A., Greetham, L. and McGreevy, P. D. (2007) Rein contact between horse and handler during specific equitation movements, *Applied Animal Behavior Science*, 108, 157–69.

Warrington, G. D., Dolan, E., McGoldrick, A., McEvoy, J., MacManus, C., Griffin, M. and Lyons, D. (2009) Chronic weight control impacts on physiological function and bone health in elite jockeys, *Journal of Sports Sciences*, 27, 543–50.

Wasserman, K., Whipp, B. J. and Castagna, J. (1974) Cardiodynamic hyperpnea: hyperpnea secondary to cardiac output increase, *Journal of Applied Physiology*, 36, 457–64.

Weinberg, R. S. and Gould, D. (2010) *Foundations of Sport and Exercise Psychology*, Leeds: Human Kinetics.

Weinberg, R. S., Seabourne, T. and Jackson, A. (1981) Effects of visuo-motor behavior rehearsal, relaxation, and imagery on karate performance, *Journal of Sport Psychology*, 3 (3), 228–38.

Weiss, M. and Gould, D. (1986) *Sport for Children and Youths*, Champaign, IL: Human Kinetics.

Wenger, H. A. and MacNab, R. B. J. (1975) Endurance training: the effects of intensity, total work, duration and initial fitness, *Journal of Sports Medicine and Physical Fitness*, 15 (3), 199–211.

Westerling, D. (1983) A study of physical demands in riding, *European Journal of Applied Physiology*, 70, 66–9.

Whaley, M. H., Brubaker, P. H. and Otto, R. (eds) (2007) *ACSM's Guidelines for Exercise Testing and Prescription,* 7th edn. Philadelphia: Lippincott Williams and Wilkins.

Whipp, B. J., Davis, J. A., Torres, F. and Wasserman, K. (1981) A test to determine parameters of aerobic function during exercise, *Journal of Applied Physiology*, 50, 217–21.

Whissell, R., Lyons, S., Wilkinson, D. and Whissell, C. (1993) National bias in judgments of Olympic skating, *Perceptual and Motor Skills*, 77, 355–8.

Whitaker, T., Hargreaves, A. and Wolframm, I. A. (2012) Differences in elite showjumping performance between male and female riders, *International Journal of Performance Analysis in Sport*, 12 (2), 425–35.

Whiting, H. T. A., Vogt, S. and Vereijken, B. (1992) Human skill and motor control: some aspects of the motor control–motor learning relation, in J. J. Summers (ed.), *Approaches to the Study of Motor Control and Learning*, Amsterdam: Elsevier Science, 81–111.

Whitlock, M. R. (1999) Injuries to riders in the cross-country phase of eventing: the importance of protective equipment, *British Journal of Sports Medicine*, 33, 212–16.

Whitlock, M. R., Whitlock, J. and Johnston, B. (1987) Equestrian injuries: a comparison of professional and amateur injuries in Berkshire, *British Journal of Sports Medicine*, 21, 25–6.

Wiersma, L. D. (2000) Risks and benefits of youth sport specialization: Perspectives and recommendations, *Pediatric Exercise Science*, 12, 13–22.

Williams, A. M., Davids, K. and Williams, J. G. (1999) *Visual Perception and Action in Sport*, London: Taylor and Francis.

Williams, J. and Perry, J. (1998) Relationship of intensity and direction of competitive trait anxiety to skill level and gender in tennis, *The Sport Psychologist*, 12, 169–79.

Williams, J. K. (1978) *A Behavioral Analysis of a Successful High School Basketball Coach*, Unpublished Masters thesis, Arizona State University, Tempe.

Williams, J. M. and Krane, V. (2001) Psychological characteristics of peak performance, in J. M. Williams (ed.), *Applied Sport Psychology: Personal Growth to Peak Performance*, 4th edn. Mountain View, CA: Mayfield, pp. 162–78.

Williams, M. (1999) *Understanding Nervousness in Horse and Rider*, 2nd edn. London: J. A. Allen.

Wilmore, J. H. and Costill, D. L. (1994) *Physiology of Sport and Exercise*, Leeds: Human Kinetics.

Wilson, E. O. (1984) *Biophilia*, Cambridge: Harvard University Press.

Wilson, E. O. (1993) Biophilia and the conservation ethic, in S. Kellert and E. O. Wilson (eds), *The Biophilia Hypothesis*, Washington, DC: Shearwater Books, pp. 31–40.

Winchester, P., Kendall, K., Peters, H., Sears, N. and Winklsy, T. (2002) The effect of therapeutic horseback riding on gross motor function and gait speed in children who are developmentally delayed, *Physical and Occupational Therapy in Pediatrics*, 22 (3), 37–50.

Winter, D. G., John, O. P., Stewart, A. J., Klohen E. C. and Duncan, L. E. (1998) Traits and motives: toward an integration of two traditions in personality research, *Psychological Review*, 105, 230–50.

Witt, J. K. and Dorsch, T. E. (2009) Kicking to bigger uprights: field goal kicking performance influences perceived size, *Perception*, 38, 1328–40.

Witt, J. K. and Proffitt, D. R. (2008) Action-specific influences on distance perception: a role for motor simulation, *Journal of Experimental Psychology: Human Perception and Performance*, 34, 1479–92.

Witt, J. K., Linkenauger, S. A., Bakdash, J. Z. and Proffitt, D. R. (2008) Putting to a bigger hole: golf performance relates to perceived size, *Psychonomic Bulletin and Review*, 15, 581–5.

Wolf, E. S. (1988) *Treating the Self*, New York, NY: The Guilford Press.

Wolf, E. S. (1994) Selfobject experiences: development, psychopathology, treatment. Presented to 24th Annual Margaret Mahler Symposium on Child Development. Philadelphia, May 1, 1993, in S. Kramer and S. Akhtar (eds), *Mahler and Kohut: Perspectives on Development, Psychopathology, and Technique*, Northvale, NJ: Jason Aronson, pp. 65–96.

Wolff, A., Hausberger, M. and LeScolan, N. (1997) Experimental tests to assess emotivity in horses, *Behavioral Processes*, 40 (2), 209–21.

Wolframm, I. A. (2011a) *Psychological Traits and States in Equestrian Sport: Influences on Horse–Rider Performance*, Unpublished doctoral dissertation, University of Essex, United Kingdom.

Wolframm, I. A. (2011b) *Personality Traits, Competitive Level, and Discipline in Equestrian Sport: An Investigation*, unpublished manuscript.

Wolframm, I. A. and Micklewright, D. (2009) Pre-competitive levels of arousal and self-confidence among elite and non-elite equestrian riders, *Comparative Exercise Physiology*, 5 (3–4), 153–9.

Wolframm, I. A. and Micklewright, D. (2010a) Pre-competitive arousal, perception of equine temperament and riding performance: do they interact? *Comparative Exercise Physiology*, 7 (1), 27–36.

Wolframm, I. A. and Micklewright, D. (2010b) A preliminary investigation into pre–competitive mood states of advanced and novice equestrian dressage riders, *Journal of Applied Sport Psychology*, 22 (3), 333–42.

Wolframm, I.A. and Micklewright, D. (2011a) Effects of trait anxiety and direction of pre-competitive arousal on performance in the equestrian disciplines of dressage, showjumping and eventing, *Comparative Exercise Physiology*, 7 (4), 185–91.

Wolframm, I. A. and Micklewright, D. (2011b) The effect of a mental training program on state anxiety and competitive dressage performance, *Journal of Veterinary Behavior: Clinical Applications and Research*, 6, 267–75.

Wolframm, I. A. and Meulenbroek, R. G. J. (2012) Co-variations between perceived personality traits and quality of the interaction between female riders and horses, *Applied Animal Behavior Science*, 139, 96–104.

Wolframm, I. A., Bosga, J. and Meulenbroek, R. G. J. (2013) Coordination dynamics in horse–rider dyads, *Human Movement Science*, (in press). Available online at http://dx.doi.org/10.1016/j.humov.2012.11.002.

Wolpert, D. M., Ghahramani, Z. and Flanagan, J. R. (2001) Perspectives and problems in motor learning, *Trends in Cognitive Sciences*, 5 (11), 487–94.

Woodman, T. and Hardy, L. (2003) The relative impact of cognitive anxiety and self-confidence upon sport performance: a meta-analysis, *Journal of Sports Sciences*, 21, 443–57.

Worley, G. H. (2010) Promoting the use of equestrian helmets: another opportunity for injury prevention, *Journal of Emergency Nursing*, 36 (3), 263–4.

Wright, R. and Peters, D. M. (2008) A heart rate analysis of the cardiovascular demands of elite level competitive polo, *International Journal of Performance Analysis in Sport*, 8, 76–81.

Wylleman, P. and Lavallee, D. (2004) A developmental perspective on transitions faced by athletes, in M. Weiss (ed.), *Developmental Sport and Exercise Psychology: A Lifespan Perspective*, Morgantown, WV: Fitness Information Technology, pp. 507–27.

Young, R. J. and Ismail, A. H. (1978) Ability of biochemical and personality variables in discriminating between high and low physical fitness levels, *Journal of Psychosomatic Research*, 22, 193–9.

Zetterqvist Blokhuis, M., Aronsson, A., Hartmann, E., Van Reenen, C. G. and Keeling, L. (2008) Assessing the rider's seat and horse's behavior: difficulties and perspectives, *Journal of Applied Animal Welfare Science*, 11 (3), 191–203.

Zimmerman, M., Dyson, S. and Murray, R. (2011) Close, impinging and overriding spinous processes in the thoracolumbar spine: the relationship between radiological and scintigraphic findings and clinical signs, *Equine Veterinary Journal*, 44, 178–84.

Zuckerman, M. (1983) Sensation seeking and sports, *Personality and Individual Differences*, 4, 285–93.

Index

achievement goal theory 88

advanced riders: coaching responsibilities 75, 79; emotional control and performance 53, 56, 60, 62; fine motor control 8; improved rider position 15; injury risk 111, 112

amateur riders: anxiety, effects of 56–7; definition of 158–9n; headgear, lack of 107; injury, equine-related 122–3; mental strategies 66, **67–8**; personality traits **54**; rider fitness 39; womens' dominance 42

anthropomorphism 112, 134, 135, 138, 140

anxiety: cognitive 59; meaning of 57; rider psychology, effect on 51–2, 56–7; somatic 59–60

arousal: debilitative effect 60–1; horse–rider interaction 143; self-confidence, facilitative role 61–3

artificial aids 116

athlete development models 93–5, **95–7**

biomechanics 6

biophilia hypothesis 135–6

breeding associations 141

canter 9, 14, 16–17, 37–8

children/youth: coaches' career path 83; coaching strategies 91, 93–5, **95–7**; injury, equine-related 106, 108, 109, 111–12; pets and emotional support 128, 137, 139; riding, therapeutic benefits 128, 129, 130, 131; riding school practices 92

Churchill, Winston 1

Clarke, Stephen 17

closed-loop theory 8–9

competition: coach behaviour 90–1;

emotional control and performance 53, 56, 59, 71; gender and participation factors 146–7; mindset issues 46; self-confidence, facilitative role 62; stress management 64

Cornelissen, Adelinde 17, 26–7

dressage: cognitive anxiety, effect of 59; elite rider standards 17; judging bias 100; performance physiology 38; psychological skills, application of 70; riders as athletes 26–7

Dujardin, Charlotte 17

dynamic systems theory 132

elite riders: competitive stress management 64, 146–7; dedicated practice, duration of 82; definition of 158n; emotional control and performance 62; excellence through practice 82; expected standards 17; horses as commodities 134; injury risk 111, 112; performance physiology 37–8, 40; psychological skills valued 66, **67–8**, 68–9; role models for safety 108; single-mindedness 51

equestrian coaches: allegiance debate 74; appropriate behaviour guidance 79–81; behaviour of, rider's perceptions 90; career development, paths to 82–4, **84, 85**; coaching responsibilities 75–6, 77; coach-rider relationship 92; competition pressure, reaction to 90–1; horse–rider interaction 99–100; information conveyance 77–8; knowledge/experienced based training 84–5; learning theory, application of 153; motivational strategies 87–9; negativity, detrimental effect 87, 88,

196   *Index*

26342793R00116

Printed in Great Britain
by Amazon